T0340221

AN ECONOMIC HISTORY OF INDIA 1707–1857

This new edition of *An Economic History of Early Modern India* extends the times-pan of the analysis to incorporate further research. This allows for a more detailed discussion of the rise of the British Empire in South Asia and gives a fuller context for the historiography.

In the years between the death of the emperor Aurangzeb (1707) and the great rebellion (1857), the Mughal Empire and the states that rose from its ashes declined in wealth and power, and a British Empire emerged in South Asia. This book asks three key questions about the transition. Why did it happen? What did it mean? How did it shape economic change? The book shows that during these years, a merchant-friendly regime among warlord-ruled states emerged and state structure transformed to allow taxes and military capacity to be held by one central power, the British East India Company. The author demonstrates that the fall of warlord-ruled states and the empowerment of the merchant, in consequence, shaped the course of Indian and world economic history.

Reconstructing South Asia's transition, starting with the Mughal Empire's collapse and ending with the great rebellion of 1857, this book is the first systematic account of the economic history of early modern India. It is an essential reference for students and scholars of Economics and South Asian History.

Tirthankar Roy is Professor of Economic History at the London School of Economics, UK. He has published extensively on South Asian history and development and has taught courses on South Asia and Global History. His recent books include *An Economic History of Colonialism* (with Leigh Gardner, 2020), *Crafts and Capitalism* (Routledge, 2019) and *A New Economic History of Colonial India* (co-edited with Latika Chaudhary, Bishnupriya Gupta, and Anand V. Swamy, Routledge, 2015).

AN ECONOMIC HISTORY OF INDIA 1707–1857

2nd Edition

Tirthankar Roy

Routledge
Taylor & Francis Group

LONDON AND NEW YORK

First published 2022
by Routledge
2 Park Square, Milton Park, Abingdon, Oxon OX14 4RN

and by Routledge
605 Third Avenue, New York, NY 10158

Routledge is an imprint of the Taylor & Francis Group, an informa business

British Library Cataloguing-in-Publication Data
A catalogue record for this book is available from the British Library

Library of Congress Cataloging-in-Publication Data
Names: Roy, Tirthankar, author.
Title: An economic history of India, 1707–1857 / Tirthankar Roy.
Other titles: Economic history of early modern India.
Description: 2nd Edition. | New York : Routledge, 2021. | Revised edition
of the author's An economic history of early modern India, 2013. |
Includes bibliographical references and index.
Identifiers: LCCN 2021012346 | ISBN 9780367770419 (paperback) | ISBN
9781032002927 (hardback) | ISBN 9781003173540 (ebook)
Subjects: LCSH: India--Economic conditions--18th century. | India--Economic
conditions--19th century.
Classification: LCC HC434 .R698 2021 | DDC 330.954/029--dc23
LC record available at https://lccn.loc.gov/2021012346

ISBN: 978-1-032-00292-7 (hbk)
ISBN: 978-0-367-77041-9 (pbk)
ISBN: 978-1-003-17354-0 (ebk)

Typeset in Bembo
by SPi Technologies India Pvt Ltd (Straive)

CONTENTS

FIGURES

TABLES

MAPS

PREFACE

This is a much revised and enlarged version of the book (*An Economic History of Early Modern India*), first published in 2013. Since then, the field has seen new research, which called for a new book and a different way of organizing it.

There is another difference. *Early Modern India* wanted to contribute to two debates that were popular in 2012. One of these was the great divergence debate, and the other one discussed whether there was more growth or more decline in the 1700s. Both these debates are obsolete now. The book is not about the origin of world inequality and needs to keep a distance from that debate. The growth versus decline topic is problematic because most contributors to that discussion offered conjectures. Recent statistical work has left it behind.

One proposition the book did make, but in an understated way. The period was significant in Indian economic history for the emergence of a merchant-friendly regime and for an innovation in state structure, from a decentred political system towards the consolidation of taxes and military capacity in one centre. This book builds on that proposition.

I have explored the thesis with evidence in several recent works. Among others, I have drawn on several versions of an essay eventually published in Anne Booth and Ewout Frankema, eds., *Fiscal Capacity and the Colonial State in Asia and Africa, c. 1850–1960* (Cambridge, 2019), and on 'The Mutiny and the Merchants,' published in *The Historical Journal*, 2016.

I wish to thank Mrinmoyee Roy who read and suggested improvements in Chapter 1.

Tirthankar Roy

1

INTRODUCTION

In the years between the death of the emperor Aurangzeb (1707) and the annexation of Maratha territories by the British East India Company (1818), the Mughal Empire and the states that rose from its ashes declined in wealth and power, and a British Empire emerged in India. By 1857–1858, when British rule in India faced a crisis and survived it, the empire had grown in scale, reformed institutions to make its power more secure, and sponsored an economic system that looked very different from economies in the past in this region.

The transition raises several questions. Among the contenders for power after the Mughal collapse, the Company was not the most obvious candidate to succeed. It was a business firm, not a military force. Why would it want to take over the government? Why now? Although always close to British politics and commanding arms, it was not militarily stronger than its rivals like Tipu Sultan of Mysore or the Marathas in western India. Why did it prevail in the contest for power that followed the Mughal collapse? What kind of a state did it create? How did political change shape economic change in the region in the long run? This book is an attempt to answer these questions. The answers help to understand the dual transition in politics and economics in India between 1707 and 1857 – a key process in the making of modern India.

While describing what happened, the book will also prove a thesis. The formation of the Company state stood for a strong form of political integration based on the concentration of military and taxation power. Political integration facilitated market integration. Therefore, a new type of state delivered a new economy, which gave stability to the state. Britain's empire in India did not arise from conquering or exploiting a weak power by a stronger one. It appeared instead by using the weaknesses and building on the strengths of the Indian political economy of the time. Taxation was a weakness of indigenous states; a robust business world was a strength. The Company solved the taxation problem and made the business world its ally.

These movements created a militarily stronger state, encouraged trade, expanded the variety of goods traded, helped the merchants, and harmed the warlords. The shift in wealth and power generated a fierce backlash in 1857, but the shift was also responsible for the rebellion's failure. Many warlords opposed the regime, and the merchants and bankers supported it. However, the transition did not profoundly transform the lives of ordinary people, especially those in the countryside. The colonial state had neither the will nor the money to make a significant difference to peasants and labourers. The growth of commodity trade may have helped some peasants in some places, but the effect was modest in scale.

The bare facts of the origin of the British Empire in India are well known. A quick recap may still be useful.

The emergence of British rule in India

Shortly after Aurangzeb's death, the Mughal Empire that had ruled over the Indo-Gangetic Basin since 1526 started breaking up.[1] In Bengal Hyderabad and Awadh former provincial governors established independent rules. In Deccan, eastern Rajasthan, and north-western India, landlords and warlords rebelled. Several new states emerged from this turmoil. Militarily the most powerful was the dominion of the Marathas ruled by several clans. Battles between rivals and alliances became common.

British rule in India began with the trading enterprise of the East India Company. The Company was established as a trading firm in 1600, with a licensed monopoly (charter) to trade in the Indian Ocean. Negotiating rights to trade in India and staving off rivals and private traders pushed the Company into playing a political role from time to time. Towards the end of the 1600s, the Company's local officers had set up three bases on the coast – Madras, Bombay and Calcutta – mainly to protect themselves from other Europeans.

Until 1740, the three ports were small settlements of traders and soldiers. But in the 1740s, many Indian traders and bankers fled the embattled inland states and moved into the safety of these three towns. In the backdrop of the Mughal Empire's collapse and conflicts among Indian states that came after the rule, the Company engaged more frequently with politics. Their naval stronghold came in handy some times. After 1800, the three cities enjoyed peace. The wealthiest people in these towns around 1820 were Indians, interested in shipbuilding, Indo-China trade, coastal trade, Arabian Sea trade, and overland trade. Their migration had made these spots centres of wealth. They were already centres of power. From these bases, the Company joined the military contest inland.

The origin of the British Empire in India can be described as a sequence of two stages. In the first phase, 1765–1784, the Company officers acquired territories, experimented with systems of rule, and faced charges of a conflict between private or commercial and the public interest. The Company acquired control over eastern and south-eastern India around 1770. The regime expanded towards north, west, and south India via strategic alliances and warfare. With the end of the third Anglo-Maratha war in 1818, the Company's empire was secure.

In 1784, the British Parliament began to oversee Indian administration. In the second stage that started in 1784, the private mercantile interest behind political decisions receded, and institutional and military reforms set out the plan for imperial rule. In 1813, the charter to trade in India as a monopoly ended. Until the mutiny-cum-rebellion of 1857, the state acquired more territories and spent more time and energy on infrastructure and institutions. Christopher Bayly called the rule between 1780 and 1830 British 'imperial meridian,' meaning that an opportunistic form of power transformed into a directly governing one in this time, in turn engaging the home government in foreign rule more deeply than before. A militaristic state started thinking beyond its survival and about public goods and institution-building. The end of conflicts and military threats was necessary to make that transition possible.[2]

Why did the East India Company succeed in the contest for power? In the late 1700s, the steps that led to a Company state in India did not follow a blueprint designed at the firm's head office but followed the instincts of those running the branches in India. These people did not leave enough testament for us to guess whether it was their scheming nature or a perception of threat that led them to join Indian politics. In one version of history, deceit and cunning do receive more emphasis.

Saviours or villains?

The emergence of a British Indian state is sometimes explained in terms of some exceptional qualities of India's early Company rulers. In imperialist history, the Company's officers were gifted and far-sighted people. They did a favour to the Indians who were suffering from the misrule of the indigenous kings by establishing a state. The scholars and publicists who justified England's conquest of India argued that colonialism had brought peace to a divided and violent society. James Mill's *History of British India*, and 60 years later, John Strachey's *India: Its Administration and Progress* are examples of this style of writing. Both writers believed that the early East India Company government was sometimes corrupt and cumbersome, partly because it relied too much on Indian partners and Indian tradition in its government. But both believed Robert Clive when he justified 'assuming the power that is in us of conducting … the affairs both civil and military of this settlement,' by saying that the alternative would be 'anarchy, confusion, and, what is worse, an almost general corruption.'[3] 'In place of constant anarchy, bloodshed, and rapine,' echoed John Strachey, 'we have given to [India] peace, order, and justice … it is the strong hand of England alone which maintains peace …'[4]

In recent studies, the emergence of a British Indian state is again explained in terms of the exceptional quality of the British adventurers who created that state. But now, that quality is the opposite of what Mill and Strachey celebrated. In this image, the Company succeeded because it was corrupt, opportunist, and manipulative. For the East India Company, 'honour was an irrelevant concern,' writes Shashi Tharoor.[5] Combining 'the license to loot everything' with 'perfidy, chicanery and cupidity,' the Company extracted wealth from the native princes, and by these means established a rule that was 'hardly a … contribution to good governance.' The 'conquest of India,' writes Deepak Lal, built upon 'perfidious deals.'[6] The Company, says William Dalrymple, 'remains today history's most ominous warning about the potential for the abuse of corporate power.'[7] The British 'conquest' of India, according to him, was the 'supreme act of corporate violence.'

These two images are identical; the only difference being that the Europeans and the Indians switch roles. Both stories flatten differences within each set. And both are unconvincing for the following reason. The idea that the emergence of a British Empire in India had owed to some unique quality of the British merchant adventurers of the late eighteenth century begs assumptions about their Indian rivals. To believe – as Mill or Strachey did – that the Company officers were peace-loving implies that all their Indian opponents were violent. Mill and Strachey had no evidence to prove this. To believe – as Tharoor and Dalrymple do – that the Company officers were venal implies that their Indian opponents were too honest for their own good. '[F]airly decent,' Tharoor airily calls the Indian forces of the time. That set included the Maratha mercenaries of central India, long-remembered in western Bengal for rape and pillage. Mill and Strachey were not sufficiently well informed to bat for the imperialists. Tharoor and Dalrymple are not sufficiently well informed to bat for the Indian warlords. Claims like theirs peddle sentiments – triumph or righteous outrage – but they are not correctly based on evidence and not reliable as history.

To say that the Company abused corporate power amounts to saying that the Indians were too stupid to see what was going on and adopt the same organizational models. Of course, the Company was a corporate firm, and landlords and warlords ruled the Indian states. That difference could explain their choice of allies and partners. Beyond that, corporate identity mattered little. The larger states, like the Peshwa territory based in Pune in 1760, commanded enormous revenues. Initially, these states could command land armies that were many times larger than the Company's forces. The London shareholders and directors did not want the branches to join military contests; the branches defied orders from above. The Company's empire happened not because of but despite the corporate form.

Popular history of this kind assumes that the empire in India was a violent conquest. Europeans, the myth goes, invaded Indians, who did not want to be subjugated and went down fighting. The sentiment of triumph in imperialist history and outrage in nationalistic history follow from this narrative. The only difference between the two is that the Indians appear in one story as villains and in another as a tragic hero. Turning the emergence of the empire in this way into a battle between good and evil creates melodrama; it invites the reader to take sides in a fake holy war. But if good soap opera, it is bad history. The empire was not an invasion. Many Indians, because they did not trust other Indians, wanted the British to secure power. They preferred British rule over indigenous alternatives and helped the Company form a state, as we see next.

The shifting alliance theory

The empire emerged mainly from alliances. It emerged from lands 'ceded' to the Company by Indian friends, rather than lands that it 'conquered.'[8] What had made the alliances possible, even likely? Since the early 1980s, when Christopher Bayly published path-breaking works on the East India Company rule, historians have known that the Company was nothing without its Indian allies. '[A]t every stage,' writes P.J. Marshall, 'accommodations between British and Indian interests were … crucial to the rise of British ascendancy.'[9] This accommodation was based on shared self-interest. To understand its political success, then, requires an understanding of the interests of those who allied with this force. The Company came to rule India because many Indians wanted it to rule India. '[T]he story of Britain's rise to global supremacy,' to cite Marshall again, 'needs to be more than an analysis of Britain's undoubted strengths. Whether these strengths could be used effectively or not ultimately depended on the dispositions of the peoples whom the British encountered …'[10]

The idea that the British Empire in India was the product of alliances found its fullest development in C.A. Bayly's classic *Rulers, Townsmen and Bazaars*.[11] In 1983, when the book was published, 'this insistence on the indigenous component in European expansion' was already 'pervasive, even cliché-ridden.' But the contact point between European expansion and indigenous society had remained indistinct. In Bayly's reading, 'the junction' formed of 'a range of intermediate entities [between the state and the peasants] with strong internal organisation from which were recruited, ultimately, the Indian middle class… The incoming colonial power and European traders succeeded when they were able to cajole, entice or manipulate these intermediate groups.'[12]

No single class shared more interest with the British than did the merchants. Collaborations with them were the basis on which European trade functioned. In most places, especially in Bengal, the Company found collaborators because there was already a rich and powerful set of capitalists in these regional economies. The post-Mughal states or successor states depended on the capitalists for their survival. The mutual dependence and shared interests between the ruling classes and the groups like these is indisputable. Merchants, therefore, figure in a large way in Bayly's narrative.

The book dealt with a part of the Indo-Gangetic Basin over which the Mughals had firm control once but was losing control from the early 1700s. A fertile and commercial zone, the landscape being dominated by the preeminent service-oriented town, Benares, the British Company wanted to control the region, and succeeded from the 1770s in doing so. In turn, the Benares bankers and merchants who feared state collapse more than British rule, declared unqualified support for the new regime on many occasions (see below). Further east in Bengal, the example of Jagatseth, the court banker who secretly helped Robert Clive, again supports the theory that an alliance between two sets of businesspeople could cause a transfer of power. A part of the argument applies to all successor states, the British in Bengal included. In peacetimes, the successor states encouraged commerce and trade. Nearly all region-bound economic histories show that they did.[13] As Tilottama Mukherjee suggests for Bengal under Nizamat rule, the wish to do so stemmed from the states' dependence on inland customs duties, which was significantly greater than often imagined.[14] Because they had gained, traders might be readier to make common cause with the Company if they expected instability and extortion by indigenous warlords to grow.

This account of a merchant–merchant alliance, however, is neither wholly persuasive nor generalizable to all of India. It is not totally persuasive for two reasons. First, the mutual dependence between the East India Company and the indigenous merchants was not risk free. Despite the overlap of economic interests, the Company did not trust the Indian merchants. The relationship was an unstable one and filled with mutual suspicion as long as the Indian actors remained close to the successor state courts. Only in the cities directly ruled by the Company, the relationship was more stable. Second, the account overstates the successor states' ability to sustain commercialization. The costs of internal trade remained high, possibly increased after Mughal disintegration (see below). The larger states had to spend more money than they could afford on wars. Warlords eager to fight with a formidable enemy would not be the best choice as debtors for any banker. During the Maratha raids in western Bengal, the collapse of authority in the Indo-Gangetic Basin, and interstate wars in west India, Bengali, Marwari, and Khatri merchants left homes to seek the greater safety of the Company's port cities. The Parsis similarly left Surat for Bombay. In other words, what we might think of as an 'alliance' was in fact no more than a flight of capital into the safety of the Company ports.

The narrative is not generalizable either. The intermediate group is essentially a Gangetic Basin construction. The idea of a capitalistic alliance, or what Bayly calls a 'middle class,' does not work well in central, southern, or western India, where the partnerships were more formal, more military, and formed among political actors. These drier geographical zones neither had large urban centres nor a significant intermediate group. In fact, the Indo-European alliances in most places came from another, mainly political, source. In the 1770s or the 1780s, the British in India were regarded as a force but not necessarily the future empire. Something else worked for them, the greater stability of the alliances they struck than those their rivals did. Mandar Oak and Anand Swamy consider what factors made these alliances stable or unstable. They show that after the Parliament inserted itself in the governance of Indian territories in 1784, the Company commanded more trust among some Indian political actors. That element of trust was missing or weak among Indian rivals. Alliances, in other words, worked asymmetrically among contending powers.[15]

The alliance theory shifts attention from the Company and its employees towards the elite prominent in the successor states, who may have had a reason to want a Company state. What about the states themselves? Surely, they were not equal in their capacity to build and sustain military projects? Where did that capacity come from?

The superior force theory

European trade in the Indian Ocean relied on an infrastructure consisting of ports, fast ships, gunships, employees trained in using arms, and occasionally the right to call in royal military help, which could be used to inflict damage on rivals and defend against rival attacks. Much of that infrastructure was directed at European competitors. The sponsorship of 'mercantilist' states took that warlike element to another level with the British East India Company.[16] The Company was also a political entity in its own right. 'The line between governmental and commercial enterprise,' writes Jay Geller, 'had always been uncertain' in eighteenth-century India.[17] Philip Stern says that the Company was 'a form of early modern government,' using the idea to question a conventional distinction between a 'trading era' and an 'imperial era' in the Company's history.[18]

It is necessary to be clear what such power can or cannot explain. It cannot explain why the Company was an extraordinarily profitable firm. It was profitable not because of the state's backing but because it was an efficient firm. A monopoly charter from the Crown might have helped to reduce competition from other British traders but did not help the firm deal with competition from other European or Indian enterprises in the Indian Ocean. It was profitable because it was a good firm, not because it was a state-like entity. It succeeded in trade because it could pool in a lot of capital, offer incentives to its employees, build stable collaborations with Indian agents and brokers, understand and study markets, and get goods manufactured to exact specifications.[19] For much of its career, the Company had little political power in India to bully its suppliers.

Power does not explain profits. But proximity to power might explain a readiness to take political risks, especially when profits came under threat. In this sense, the Company's political moves in India were consistent with its sense of itself as a firm close to the state. Too sharp a distinction between the commercial and the political profile of the Company suggests, wrongly, that the empire was an accident. It was not. However, that the Company was a state-like enterprise does not explain why it could prevail in the contest for dominance in the late eighteenth century. There were Indian states in the competition that were stronger.

A reference to its military power likewise would not explain why it could prevail on the battlefields. The Company controlled the seas with more force than any Indian coastal state of the time, and it had access to the Royal Navy when in trouble from rival Europeans. The decisive battles in the eighteenth century, however, happened on land. In land warfare, the Europeans brought into India some useful knowledge relating to infantry formation, command structure, professionalized officer corps, flintlock guns, cannons made of cast iron, and mobile artillery.[20] But these did not count as advantages because both battlefield strategy and military hardware had a ready market in the eighteenth century, and all contestants had access to that market. Indian states hired French and Portuguese advisers to close the gap if there was any. If the British were always militarily superior, they would not need the many alliances and partnerships they forged with the Indian powers.

Kaushik Roy shows that Western warfare methods were not superior to indigenous ones in the eighteenth century. They could not be distinguished since both the European and Indian forces attempted to construct hybrid methods, choosing elements that seemed to work best. In doing so, the Indian powers relied on European advisers and mercenaries when they needed to. The Company nevertheless prevailed in the game. 'The Westernization programme,' writes Roy, 'put a heavy strain on the economies of the Indian rulers. This was especially true for the Marathas. However, the principal problems were political and military.'[21] Whereas this interpretation places more weight on strategic differences (better use of the horse artillery by the Company forces, for example), I stress the fiscal aspects in this book. I stress the economic reforms that enabled the Company to raise more money and thus fund a bigger army and command it from a single centre.

The fiscal capacity theory

The successor states were a work-in-progress, and most could not finish reforming the finances to suit their military ambitions. Conflicts in the Deccan Plateau among states that lived on little money and had no time to consolidate their finances drained all of them of resources and sovereign authority, made them reliant on regional chiefs and warlords, and drove some to make alliances with the British.

Why the scramble for finance? Much of India consists of drylands where agriculture produces a small subsistence thanks to a low land yield. States that lived on land taxes were as poor as the peasants that they taxed. This was true of the Mughal Empire and of the successor states that followed the empire. Indeed, it was true for most Asian empires before the nineteenth century. Along a wide space running from West through South to East Asia, imperial states in the seventeenth century earned a very small revenue per head compared with contemporary states in Western Europe.[22] Resource-poverty made states fiscally and militarily weak and dependent on the loyalty of regional elites and warlords. Like the Mughal Empire earlier, these states had more control over and knowledge of an agriculturally well-endowed area and collected a tribute from a semi-arid periphery that was practically independent. Such dualism persisted into the eighteenth century in the affairs of the successor states.

The Mughal imperial state survived on the back of the military supplies that came from the regions and the landed magnates' loyalty. They collected taxes and supplied soldiers in battle. The imperial centre's hold upon the regions was never totally secure. The South Asian mainland had access to the sea, maritime trade, port cities, irrigable deltas, and river valleys, and these resources sustained industry, commerce, finance, and states. But the extra resources did not create rich imperial states because the seaboard itself was not an integral part of the inland empires. The centre's dependence on the local magnates did not diminish since a lot of the taxes came from the land.

When such an empire broke up, it unleashed a competition for limited revenues. The successor states could, in theory, try to centralize their taxes and, in the process, reduce the courts' dependence on the warlords and chiefs who collected the taxes. Very few rulers took this course. Tipu Sultan of Mysore contemplated it but did not get very far. Therefore, competition for taxes took the form of extortion of weaker states and led to frequent conflicts.

If conflicts and competition impoverished the successors, it affected the Company differently. Soon after it came in possession of Bengal, one task occupied it above all, drawing in more taxes to the centre. Control of the land was the source of military power and fiscal power in India. Over the 1770s and the 1780s and culminating in the Permanent Settlement of 1793, the Company's reforms in property rights removed any right to control land that did not derive from ownership. Many people who earlier had a right to tax the peasants, and therefore commanded arms, but did not own or cultivate land lost their power to tax. The long-term effect of that policy was the concentration of land taxes and military power at the top.

The Company formed the strongest state in India because it was a different rule from the post-Mughal successors. To a greater extent than any other South Asian state of the past, the British demilitarized the armed groups like jagirdars and zamindars, who earlier collected taxes and enjoyed local political power. Such people, if they rebelled together, could and did bring an empire down. To suppress them and secure its future, the British raised a standing army, combined it with a navy, funded the whole enterprise by a bureaucratic fiscal machine, and through that army, imposed political unity on a region where power had always been fragmented and decentralized. 'By the end of the nineteenth century,' wrote John Richards, 'North Indian rural society was disarmed as thoroughly as any similar social formation across Eurasia.'[23] The region that once supplied part-time soldiers to a whole variety of rival armies became the recruiting ground for a single military machine. Soldiers could earlier choose employers. Now, service demanded loyalty, traded against a round-the-year salary and a pension plan.

Besides the standing army that replaced the mercenaries bearing arms, the measures that contributed the most to the demilitarization plan included attacks upon weaker princely states, auctioning large estates in Bengal, and non-aggression pacts with states. The philosopher Edmund Burke, a fierce critic of the Company's administration in Bengal and a campaigner for a just empire in India, singled out one act of injustice and inequity above all, the recklessness with which the first Governor-General Warren Hastings supervised 'the ruin and expulsion of great and illustrious families, the breach of solemn public Treaties, the merciless pillage and total subversion of the first Houses of Asia.'[24] During Hastings' tenure, the Company officers also perfected a system of treaties with Indian kings. In its final shape, the terms of the treaty implied that the kings would maintain armies in their territories but would not command these independently. If this clause took away their independence on one vital point, it made them more secure from potential attacks by other kingdoms, for British India would then come to their assistance.

All this was not part of a plan. Being commercially minded and of part-European origin, the regime carried a suspicious attitude towards the indigenous aristocrats. It created a government less dependent on regional chiefs than its predecessors. It did not bring all the periphery under direct rule. Nor could it expand the tax base a lot more. But it could draw in a lot more money to the centre than its rivals and predecessors and use that money to build an army. That innovation made the core more robust than before.

Therefore, the British Empire represented a different type of state from its predecessors because it introduced an innovation in the state structure, consolidation of taxes, and armies in one centre. The most direct measure, if not the only meaningful measure of a state's strength, is the revenue that it can collect (see Chapter 3). By this benchmark, the Company was both more successful and a more distinctive kind of state. Most Indian rules did not function in this way, and some tried but failed to concentrate military-fiscal authority.

Seaboard access, the Royal Navy's backing, and a standing army that the Company raised built the foundation of a military despotism unprecedented in its strength in this region. Early British writings about Indian states loosely employed this term, military despotism, to refer to others. Bayly applied it to the Company.[25] I draw an economic implication from it. What difference did it make to long-term economic change? Concentrated power of that kind could be deployed for different purposes. This state's priority was to promote commerce, thus making for the emergence of a new economic system in colonial India. As its military might grew, the empire could create an integrated political space in South Asia, the like of which the region had not seen before. Political integration secured integration of markets for commodities, capital, and labour, and closer union between internal trade and maritime trade. Most of the princely states that retained their independence accepted the idea of an economic union without much resistance. Even the mutiny-cum-rebellion did not challenge the economic union, nor was it essentially a rejection of the union. Military despotism had already made agreement on an economic union an accomplished fact.

The new economy

Possibly from the second quarter of the nineteenth century or a little after, internal trade revived after a period of depression during fragmentation and collapse of state power. In the 1700s, wrote Dwijendra Tripathi, fragmented power meant 'a network of customs barriers… existence of innumerable systems of currencies … and frequently fluctuating exchange rates.'[26] The problem of transaction costs to internal trade had increased manifold with the collapse of the Mughal Empire. Sumit Guha has recently shown that at the height of its power, the Mughal state gathered half its gross revenue from inland trade duties and customs.[27] Like nearly all other tax types, the trade taxes did not all reach the central treasury but were retained by local officers for their upkeep. What would have happened after the Mughal collapse was that the taxes remained, but the authority and the right to tax disintegrated down to local warlords, potentially increasing uncertainty on the rates and the legitimacy of the right to collect. While these obstacles did not stop the growth of regional markets, they 'were detrimental to the growth of any large-scale commercial undertaking,' wrote Tripathi.[28]

That disorder receded somewhat with the consolidation of the Company as a territorial power. Inland transit duties were centralized and reduced, and abolished in 1838. In 1840, the Company collected 7–10% of its revenue from trade taxes, a massive decline from the 47% that the Mughals hoped to get by taxing trade. Among all the livelihood classes, the traders would have gained the most from the British Indian state's action.

A more long-term effect of the new state's rise was economic integration between the countryside and the port city. The Company emerged from the seaboard. Whereas most empires of the past had limited access to the seaboard, the British controlled the seaboard firmly and used that control to foster maritime trade. That control did not make them more powerful inland. But it did make the port city attractive for many Indian merchants. The other side of the shifting alliance was a growing synergy between the British Empire and the firms engaged in commodity trade.

The first formal example of the support of Indian businesses for the British Indian state was a pair of petitions prepared in 1787 by the residents of Benares, the leading hub of Indian banking and trade, in support of the government. The signatories in the second petition numbered several hundred, and many were bankers and traders. Several other similar testimonials followed in the next few years, 'signed or sealed by *amils*, zamindars, pandits, *ulema* and *muftis*,' which Warren Hastings used in his impeachment trial to show how popular he was in the civil society and the business world of India in his time. In 1792, after the conclusion of the third Anglo-Mysore war, another declaration of support followed; again, a third of the several hundred signatories were merchants and bankers.[29] More statements of support followed from Benares on every occasion the Company was engaged in a battle or won one. Again, businesspeople organized these collective shows of support.

Such shows of support lost their purpose after the empire consolidated. But the regime needed it badly in 1857. By 1857, the East India Company had left its commercial legacy far behind in the past. Trade was in Indian hands mainly. Indian merchants did not just declare support; they staked materiel and money to help the British military operation in northern and central India. With its enhanced power and commercial orientation, the Company had created an army of stakeholders in the emerging world of commerce; these people came to its aid.

That it was good for business there can be no doubt. Did the Company state make the ordinary Indians better-off?

Who gained?

The imperialist view discussed earlier suggests that the collapse of the Mughal Empire unleashed anarchy and economic decline. Some present-day historians agree that the Mughal Empire's collapse had a catastrophic effect, among other reasons, because the firms connected with imperial finance and trading in luxury manufacture in the towns suffered greatly.[30]

From the 1980s, an alternative narrative took shape, which said that the Mughal Empire's breakup saw the emergence of wealthy regional states and that the eighteenth century was, in fact, a time of economic growth rather than one of decline. This positive message has struck deep roots in popular history, much of which contends that the Company's rise squeezed the life out of indigenous capitalism and made Indian businesses serve Europe's interest. Some historians go much further than that. 'Ruled by Muslims [*Sic.*] before the British,' writes Jon Wilson in the *Guardian* newspaper, 'India was a prosperous, rapidly commercialising society... British rule pauperised India.'[31] Wilson does not say where the data to show this came from.[32]

Was India a rich place before the Company rule emerged? Did its emergence make the Indians poorer? Statistical studies now available dispute both claims. Research by Stephen Broadberry, Bishnupriya Gupta, Peter Lindert, and Robert Allen, among others, shows that India was already an impoverished region long before British rule began, poorer than Britain at the end of the seventeenth century.[33] These comparisons are open to question because of the doubtful methods they use.[34] What about trends? Estimating India's average real income, Broadberry, Custodis, and Gupta show that the income fell between 1600 and 1750 when the Mughals ruled India and did not change in the next 50 years when the Company was rising.[35] The best dataset on the levels of living of the poorer Indians (agricultural labourers) that we now have suggests that there was a small improvement in their conditions between 1801 and 1851.[36] It is safe to say that the company state's rise made *almost* no difference to the *average* Indian.

But there was no such thing as an average Indian. The banker Jagatseth had nothing in common with the farm servant in south India. It makes no sense to try to average these entities. These dissimilar individuals would not be affected in the same way by the kind of political transition taking place in the eighteenth century. In theory, the emergence of a new state or political power can change economies in three ways. It can enforce a deep integration of commodity, capital, and labour markets within the territory it has control over. It can change institutions, especially the institutions of capitalism. And it can spend on healthcare, defence, education, and infrastructure. The Company state performed all these roles with varying degrees of effectiveness. Its effect upon strengthening markets, however, was far greater than its impact on public welfare. Markets favour the capitalist and those with goods and services to sell; markets can be inequalizing. The Company's legacy was greater inequality between capitalists and skilled workers on the one side and unskilled or manual workers on the other. Merchants who replaced the Jagatseth gained; the south Indian farm servant did not gain much.

More than any pre-British state in India, this state aided market integration. Its capacity to change India more or less exhausted there. Despite the extra authority that enabled it to win battles, the Company state was still poor in tax take per head. For much of its career, it struggled to gather information on livelihoods, let alone taxing these. Its tax take was significantly bigger than its rivals' but not big enough to spend significant amounts of money on infrastructure and public welfare. Given the small size of the state, the military expenditure that it had to undertake crowded out spending on public goods, leading to its greatest failing, an inability to transform rural livelihoods. Throughout the timespan covered here, and for much beyond it, agriculture remained poor, trapped in low yield, and mainly rainfed. A change came only in a few areas where the government invested money in canal irrigation, and the geography permitted such constructions. The best defence of that dismal record is that the Mughals or the Marathas were no better at meeting that challenge.

Even as the interior did not change much, private capital based in the port cities faced exciting prospects. It looked to the interior, returned inland, and started taking firmer control over the agricultural commodity trade on a scale unprecedented in the region. In this integration of the two business worlds, one based in the land and the other in the seaboard, an operation funded largely by the seaboard capitalists, the significance of this time can be found. Neither of the two features – the integration and the leading role of seaboard capitalists in that process – was a part of Indian business history until the late 1700s.

When removed from India's formal rule, the East India Company had long ceased to be a trader. But it understood India's commercial importance, not least because private European traders were often former employees of the firm or their friends. After 1857, the British Crown carried on the commitment to protect overseas trade, increasingly driven by a belief that the Indian Ocean region was crucial to securing Britain's future. Many pre-British regimes in India may have entertained ambitions of fostering market integration on a large scale. But they did not have the means to do so. Mughal ports like Surat or Hooghly were almost certainly much smaller in scale than Bombay, Calcutta, or Madras in the nineteenth century, and more loosely tied to the imperial capital and intercontinental maritime trade than the port cities established by the Company.

None of this was planned. Still, by the end of the timespan covered in the book, the key processes – fiscal consolidation, political unification, and market integration – were visible. A new type of state had delivered a new political economy. These trends formed the foundation using which colonial rule could expand itself; nineteenth-century globalization could penetrate India; the surviving successor states ended up as economic satellites of British India; and Bombay and Calcutta's industrialization became possible.

In the nineteenth century, the transformation of these cities from small ports to Asia's leading business centres was an extraordinary fact of economic history. It was, not only because of the scale in which the transformation happened but also because every textbook prerequisite for a modern capital-intensive business to emerge was missing in India. Capital in the region was expensive, and the capital market was inaccessible to most entrepreneurs. And yet, a modern factory industry appeared and was the leading producer of textiles and engineering goods in the tropical world. Industry concentrated in the three port cities, Bombay, Calcutta, and Madras, which had seen rapid population expansion since the late eighteenth century when these were still centres of the Company's commercial activity. The growth continued into the nineteenth century.

Chapter outline

The rest of the book breaks up the subject matter into seven detailed themes: state formation, state consolidation, cultivation of land, business, the urban economy, levels of living, and the great rebellion. Chapters 2 and 3 deal with states; they describe the history of collapse and consolidation among regional states and the rise of the Company's power in the region. In the process, the chapters also look at state capacity, military-fiscal strategies, and institutional dimensions of state formation.

Chapter 4 describes the conditions of peasant agriculture. Chapters 5 and 6 deal with the non-agricultural economy. Chapter 5 surveys the large scholarship on maritime trade and the export industry, rethinks what we know about domestic and overland trade; and interprets the institutional change in commercial transactions and industrial production. Chapter 6 surveys patterns of urbanization, which were fundamentally reshaped by state formation. Chapter 7 takes stock of quantitative historical research to answer how deeply and in what direction the changes described in the book affected the welfare of ordinary people. Chapter 8 discusses the great mutiny or rebellion and shows that it failed because most indigenous merchants chose to support the British Indian state.

The last chapter (Chapter 9) concludes with a restatement of the main findings and discusses the implications of these findings.

Notes

1 Aurangzeb (1618–1707) reigned between 1658 and his death in 1707. The last of the so-called 'great Mughals,' his reign was distinguished by two things to which the rapid collapse of the empire after his death is sometimes attributed. These were rebellions on the fringes of the empire and a long and debilitating campaign to bring the Deccan uplands within the empire. The latter ended with the emergence of the Marathas as a military force, and as one of the post-Mughal successor states. On this transition and the related historiography, see Seema Alavi, ed., *The Eighteenth Century in India*, New Delhi: Oxford University Press, 2002, 1–56 (Introduction).

2 Christopher Bayly, *Imperial Meridian. The British Empire and the World 1780–1830*, London: Routledge, 1989.

3 Cited in James Mill, *The History of British India from 1805 to 1835* (edited by H.H. Wilson), 3 vols., London: James Madden, 1858 (originally published 1817), vol. 2, 235.

4 John Strachey, *India: Its Administration and progress*, London: Macmillan, 1902, 159, 392.

5 Shashi Tharoor, *Inglorious Empire: What the British did to India*, London: Hurst, 2017.

6 Deepak Lal, 'Asia and Western Dominance,' *Journal of the Asia Pacific Economy*, 8(3), 2003, 283–99.

7 William Dalrymple, *The Anarchy: The Relentless Rise of the East India Company*, London: Bloomsbury Publishing, 2019.

8 The terms conquest and cession formed parts of a discourse with which the Company justified its territorial acquisition in Britain. Conquest referred to land captured through

war, and cession to land inherited through gift from a friendly state or a parent state. The idea of a parent state is significant, for many among those making the justification believed that the East India Company was the just successor of the Mughal Empire. Until the early nineteenth century, the Company preserved this image of itself in official rituals. For more discussion on the subject, see Clara Kemme, 'The History of European International Law from a Global Perspective: Entanglements in Eighteenth and Nineteenth Century India,' in Thomas Duve, ed., *Entanglements in Legal History: Conceptual Approaches*, Frankfurt am Main: Max Planck Institute for European Legal History, 2014, 489–542.

9 P.J. Marshall, 'Presidential Address: Britain and the World in the Eighteenth Century: III, Britain and India,' *Transactions of the Royal Historical Society*, 10, 2000, 1–16.

10 Marshall, 'Presidential Address.'

11 *Rulers, Townsmen and Bazaars: North Indian Society in the Age of British Expansion 1770–1870*, Cambridge: Cambridge University Press, 1983.

12 Ibid., 5.

13 P.J. Marshall, ed., *Eighteenth Century in Indian History*, Delhi: Oxford University Press, 2003, discusses the scholarship.

14 Tilottama Mukherjee, 'The Co-Ordinating State and the Economy: The Nizamat in Eighteenth-Century Bengal,' *Modern Asian Studies*, 43(2), 2009, 389–436.

15 'Myopia or Strategic Behavior? Indian Regimes and the East India Company in Late Eighteenth Century India,' *Explorations in Economic History*, 49(3), 2012, 352–366.

16 Dietmar Rothermund explores the connection between the infrastructure of violence and mercantilist ideology in *Violent Traders: Europeans in Asia in the Age of Mercantilism*, Delhi: Manohar, 2014.

17 Jay Howard Geller, 'Towards a New Imperialism in Eighteenth-Century India: Dupleix, La Bourdonnais and the French Compagnie des Indes,' *Portuguese Studies*, 16, 2000, 240–255.

18 Philip J. Stern, *The Company-State: Corporate Sovereignty and the Early Modern Foundations of the British Empire in India*, Oxford: Oxford University Press, 2011.

19 On organizational strategy, see Santhi Hejeebu, 'Contract Enforcement in the English East India Company,' *Journal of Economic History*, 65(2), 2005, 496–523.

20 Geoffrey Parker, *The Military Revolution: Military Innovation and the Rise of the West 1500–1800*, Cambridge: Cambridge University Press, 1988, 136. Also G.J. Bryant, 'Asymmetric Warfare: The British Experience in Eighteenth-Century India,' *The Journal of Military History*, 68(2), 2004, 431–469; and the brief discussion in Jeremy Black, *War and the World*, New Haven: Yale University Press, 152.

21 Kaushik Roy, 'Military Synthesis in South Asia: Armies, Warfare, and Indian Society, c. 1740–1849,' *Journal of Military History*, 69(3), 2005, 651–690.

22 See discussion in Patrick Karl O'Brien, 'Fiscal and Financial Preconditions for the Formation of Developmental States in the West and the East from the Conquest of Ceuta (1415) to the Opium War (1839),' *Journal of World History*, 23(3), 2012, 513–553; and the dataset, https://ata.boun.edu.tr/sevketpamuk/JEH2010articledatabase, accessed 18 September 2020.

23 John F. Richards, 'Warriors and the State in Early Modern India,' *Journal of the Economic and Social History of the Orient*, 47(3), 2004, 390–400.

24 Daniel I. O'Neill, 'Rethinking Burke and India,' *History of Political Thought*, 30(3), 2009, 492–523.

25 C.A. Bayly, *Indian Society and the Making of the British Empire*, Cambridge: Cambridge University Press, 1988, 84.

26 Dwijendra Tripathi, 'Occupational Mobility and Industrial Entrepreneurship in India: A Historical Analysis,' *Developing Economies*, 19(1), 1981, 52–68.

27 Sumit Guha, 'Rethinking the Economy of Mughal India: Lateral Perspectives,' *Journal of the Economic and Social History of the Orient*, 58(4), 2015, 532–575.

28 Tripathi, 'Occupational Mobility.'

29 Kamala Prasad Mishra, 'The Role of the Banaras Bankers in the Economy of Eighteenth Century Upper India,' *Proceedings of the Indian History Congress*, 34(II), 1973, 63–76.

30 Irfan Habib, 'The Eighteenth Century in Indian Economic History,' in Marshall, ed., *The Eighteenth Century in Indian History*, 100–119; M. Athar Ali, 'Recent Theories of Eighteenth Century India,' in Marshall, ed., *The Eighteenth Century*, 90–99.

31 https://www.theguardian.com/education/2003/feb/08/highereducation.britishidentity (accessed 20 September 2020).

32 Tharoor does have 'evidence' for this: that India produced 25% of world output in 1800 and 2–4% of it in 1900 (cover of *Inglorious Empire*). This is a careless argument. Any measure of world and regional output in 1800 is little better than speculation, to begin with. And a percentage change does not say that India was once rich and became poor. It only says that industrial productivity in the West increased 4–600% during this period. To see why that happened, we need to delve into Western Europe's history. It may well be that the Europeans exploited the Asians, but no realistic story of exploitation can explain the extraordinary efficiency gains that lie behind these numbers.

33 Stephen Broadberry, Johann Custodis and Bishnupriya Gupta, 'India and the Great Divergence: An Anglo-Indian Comparison of GDP Per Capita, 1600–1871,' *Explorations in Economic History*, 55(1), 2015, 58–75; Robert C. Allen, Jean-Pascal Bassino, Debin Ma, Christine Mollmurata And Jan Luiten Van Zanden, 'Wages, Prices, and Living Standards in China, 1738–1925: In Comparison with Europe, Japan, and India,' *Economic History Review*, 64(S1), 2011, 8–38; Peter Lindert, 'European and Asian incomes in 1914: New take on the Great Divergence,' available at https://voxeu.org/article/european-and-asian-incomes-1914-new-take-great-divergence (accessed 15 December 2020).

34 Some works find evidence to the contrary based on small non-random samples of wages (discussed more fully in Chapter 7). The ones that show exceptionally high wages come from well-watered regions of south India and are not representative of the arid regions. Most of South Asia is arid for a long part or whole of the year. The validity of building comparative historical narrative on such lightweight data – 'unfounded guess work' as one critical paper commenting on the procedure calls it – is an open question. Citation from Kent Deng and Patrick O'Brien, 'Establishing Statistical Foundations of a Chronology for the Great Divergence: A Survey and Critique of the Primary Sources for the Construction of Relative Wage Levels for Ming-Qing China,' *Economic History Review*, 69(4), 2016, 1057–1082. Wages data, if useful at all, are useful to infer trend, not levels.

35 Broadberry, Custodis and Gupta, 'India and the Great Divergence,' Allen et al., 'Wages, Prices.'

36 P.B. Mayer, 'Trends of Real Income in Tiruchirapalli and the Upper Kaveri Delta, 1819–1980: A footnote in honour of Dharma Kumar,' *Indian Economic and Social History Review*, 43(3), 2006, 349–364.

2

STATE FORMATION

Within decades of the death of Aurangzeb (1707), the Mughal Empire began to disintegrate. As Delhi witnessed the phenomenon that James Tod called 'phantoms of royalty [flitting] across the scene,' major provincial rulers still loyal to Delhi, such as the Nizam-ul-mulk of Hyderabad (1671–1748, reign 1720–48), Murshid Quli Khan in Bengal (c. 1665–1727, reign in Bengal c. 1717–27), and Saadat Khan or Burhan-ul-Mulk (reign c. 1724–39) and his nephew Safdarjung (reign 1739–54) in Awadh consolidated their finances and armies, and in their capacity as advisers to the emperor grew more powerful than the emperor himself.[1] While formally owing allegiance, some of them also profited from the emperor's troubles trying to cope with rebellions and invasions. In the process, the territory from which Delhi drew its revenue rapidly shrunk, and its vassals in the east, west, and south, became independent states or colonies of the newly emerging powers.

The fragmentation of political power intensified conflict. Individually, many new states could not raise more taxes with their existing military and administrative means. Therefore, the drive to expand the revenue base employing extortion and conquest of weaker neighbours was always present. Even so, in the second half of the century some of the more stable political constituents had established institutions of government in the regions from where they originated, or which they had held long enough. In these zones, the regimes tried to recast the relationship between the state and the peasantry to encourage cultivation and tax collection and sustain the military enterprise. If the eighteenth century is taken as a whole, these two contradictory tendencies – predatory tactics and consolidation of governance – were always present. By the end of the eighteenth century, one of the regional rulers, the East India Company had emerged as the dominant political force. The Company employed a similar combination of predation and fiscal consolidation. But having had more success with the fiscal side of the enterprise, it could begin to dominate the game.

State formation is much discussed in the historical scholarship on eighteenth-century India. The subject matters for economic history for three reasons. First, wars increased inequality. Warfare benefited those who supplied money or material to the war effort but was stressful for most others because the latter lost access to markets and resources. Second, wars affected state capacity. The proportion of revenue spent on military heads was high in the eighteenth century. While this factor did stimulate the military labour market, it compromised the state's capacity to supply public goods necessary to expand economic activity. Third, to sustain the war effort, states had to make innovations in the fiscal system, which affected class relations and the production system. Throughout India, the relationship between the states and the court officers, landlords, tax farmers, mercenaries, and warlords, all who ran the fiscal system, was changing in the eighteenth century. The emergence of the Company as the dominant force depended on how it managed the game.

This chapter describes the process of emergence and collapse of states. What *was* the precolonial state?

The precolonial state

Although most states in India around 1700 earned a great deal of money by taxing trade, military power, and most of the revenue flowed from the control of agricultural land. The central state was that body with authority to give and withdraw land grants. By and large, medieval rulers maintained territorial control by assigning land revenue grants to military commanders, who in turn relied on the local landlord for collection of taxes from the peasants, for organizing extension or improvement in cultivation, for maintenance of law and order, and military supplies. In Mughal India, the command of cavalry was an honour the emperor bestowed upon deserving candidates for distinguished military service and was a mark of acquired nobility. But such command was also a potential threat to royal power. Therefore, the revenue assignment that the military elite were rewarded with (jagir) was in principle transferable. In its pure form, the jagir signified a notional share over a region's tax resources; the holder of that office had little actual contact with or even knowledge of the region concerned.

Underneath these groups were the gentry or the landlord (zamindar was the term commonly used in north India). They lived near the peasant and sometimes rose from the ranks of the latter. Technically a tax collector rather than proprietor of the land, the landlord in most cases enjoyed a practically hereditary right. Like the jagirdars, they almost always owned arms, but their status depended on control of cultivation rather than control of soldiers. The landlord class can be further divided into groups that were more militaristic and those more peasant-like (see Chapter 4). Some of these divisions crystallized through the eighteenth-century conflicts.

The situation in southern, western, and eastern India was similar to the northern one in having a tiered structure of rights based on the land-tax collection. One difference was that in peninsular India, local military authority was often vested in a tributary king. The tributary king lived on land tax, lived in a fort, and was in command of an army at the regional state's service, but this king was more of a regional chieftain than a member of the courtly aristocracy. In the Deccan sultan-ates and Gujarat, tributary kings were common. Furthermore, in the arid uplands of southern or western India, a gentry-landlord class was rare. The figures in authority in the countryside were not militaristic landlords but state officers who sustained themselves by a land grant.

Such states' capacity and stability depended on how many tiers there were and whether or not the interest of the king and the interest of the land grantees were aligned. If interests were compatible, there should not be any problem running the state. If there were too many types of land grantees, economies of scale in gover-nance could be lost and potential conflict of interest be more likely. The warlords and landlords would consider if they had a reasonable chance of escaping punish-ment if they refused to deliver their share of the taxes to the treasury because the king's attention was engaged on a number of fronts. The more the number of tiers that thought this way, the more likely the empire's collapse became. Eighteenth-century politics intensified this tendency because warfare led to giving away more land grants, increasing chances of rebellion.

A weaker king does not necessarily mean a more fragile economy. It could even be good for business if the merchants and bankers earlier functioned in a restrictive regime dominated by the warlords. Business communities could come up with or strengthen alternative forms of regulation. Consistent with that prospect, the period saw market expansion in some areas, notwithstanding conflicts on the political plane.

Historians attribute the Mughal Empire's breakup to various factors, mainly an expensive and, in the end, futile campaign to bring the Deccan into the folds of the empire.[2] The overextension of the military elite class was another factor.[3] As central authority became contestable, between 1690 and 1720, the equation between the four major constituents of states – the king, the commander, the landlord, and the peasant – began to change. The transferability of jagir rights became more chal-lenging to enforce. Armies were unwilling and unable to defend Mughal territorial claims outside the Gangetic plains. Landlords rebelled near Delhi, in Rajasthan, and the western and eastern Gangetic plains. There was a consolidation of local military power and a weakening of imperial power. Bankers and financiers, who might come to the state's aid, were more active in the newly emerging provincial centres of com-merce and manufacture rather than in the imperial cities. In this backdrop, a set of successor states emerged, following two pathways.

The first pathway was one wherein some of the richest of the imperial provinces, Bengal, Awadh, and Hyderabad, retained most of the taxes. New states formed with-out rebellious action. Imperial governors or Nawabs remained close to the court in Delhi, visited it often, sometimes at the behest of the emperor, and issued coins in the emperor's name. But they sent less money to Delhi than before. In some cases, they stopped all payments except for the occasional gift and appropriated the impe-rial privilege of granting jagirs and mansabs (rank of nobility) within their terri-tory. One common feature of these regimes was that they were militarily not very secure. All of them relied on conventional armies and battlefield strategies and were averse or unable to introduce innovations. Given that these regimes represented a continuity of the Mughal administration, the armies were not seriously tested, and building military strength was not a priority for these states.

Elsewhere, state formation followed a different trajectory. The west ruled by Rajput states, the western Deccan by the weak state of Bijapur, and in the south, the states left behind by Aurangzeb's unfinished conquests had never been administratively or politically integrated into the empire. Ambitious neighbours contested their authority. From the turmoil, four major territorial and military powers emerged in peninsular India – the Marathas based in Pune, Mysore under Haidar Ali, the British East India Company in Madras, and the French East India Company stationed in Pondicherry (Map 2.1). If the companies are excluded, then the pathway to state formation in these examples involved the assertion of independence by the two intermediate orders – warlords and landlords – at the nobility's expense. In the Deccan, Mysore, Punjab, and the lands populated by Rajput, Jat, and Rohilla Afghans, these agents claimed either kingship or vassal status in the empire.

The regional states' political history can be told in several ways – grouping them by east, west or south; or by type of state (former Mughal provinces, or

MAP 2.1 Geographical zones and political formations, 1800.

independent states); or by chronology. There are advantages and problems involved in adopting any one of these modes. I follow a roughly region-based narrative but will take up the major nineteenth-century British annexations, Punjab, Sind, and Assam, at the end.

Awadh and Rohilkhand

Awadh was the richest and geographically the most homogeneous province of the Mughal Empire. In the late eighteenth century, tax collection per square mile was among the highest in this area. It was also politically and culturally close to Delhi. The Awadh Nawabs were powerful in the Mughal court. The court treated them with respect that allowed the governors to take much liberty with the finances and make political alliances. This indirect authority increased after 1707 to such an extent that Awadh rulers were only nominally vassals of the Mughal state.

Despite its commercial and cultural wealth, Awadh was a militarily weak state and survived by avoiding battles. Having suffered by opposing and then making peace with Nadir Shah, the Persian invader of Delhi (1739), Awadh rulers frequently joined hands with the empire's tormentors, from the Afghan king, Ahmad Shah Abdali, to the Marathas, to secure their survival.[4] But such alliances did not save them from rebellions within. In the early eighteenth century, Zamindari rebellions had already troubled them, making for an excuse to retain more revenue within the province rather than releasing it for Delhi.

Muzaffar Alam has shown that the success of Awadh in continuing as a relatively peaceful successor state to the Mughals owed to the economic prosperity of the region and the long period of tranquility that it had enjoyed under the Mughals. In this zone, the zamindars became more assertive because of their growing economic power; that is, they had gained from rising rents. Merchants and long-distance trading networks operated throughout the Gangetic plains from the eastern coastal regions to the western trans-Himalayan trading zones.[5] Strong peasant lineages, who also controlled trade routes and small towns, such as the Baiswara Rajputs or the Bhumihars of Benares region, revolted against provincial authority. The Awadh Nawabs successfully contained the revolt in the west but were less successful in the east, where groups commanded more resources and military strength.

One significant loss was Benares. Bernard Cohn discusses the origins of the Benares raj in the early eighteenth century, calling it 'a typical eighteenth century story.' About 1710, Mansa Ram was a substantial Rajput peasant landlord in charge of collecting taxes on behalf of the amil, the Mughal revenue officer. Having gained enough confidence in the provincial court, Mansa Ram cut out the amil from the scene and appropriated that office. When the ruler of Awadh died, he secured for his son Balwant (Figure 2.1), the title of a king and the zamindari of three large and populous districts by making lavish presents and promising to remain a loyal revenue payer.[6] Thus began the Benares raj.

In the late eighteenth century, the Awadh state grew weaker because of rebellions and territorial losses. Military capacity had been neglected. When the Awadh state

FIGURE 2.1 Balwant Singh (1711–1770) of Benares. Caught up in conflicts between the northern powers and the Company, the Benares economy under Singh expanded, and stimulated trade and banking. © Granger Historical Picture Archive / Alamy Stock Photo.

joined the deposed Nawab of Bengal in 1764, the East India Company defeated his army. In the next few years, since the Company was not sure of its might against a possible combination of the Maratha and northern forces, Awadh survived by ceding much of its eastern territories. However, when from the early nineteenth century, the military balance had changed in favour of the Company, Awadh increasingly appeared to the strategists at the Fort William in Calcutta as a convenient extortion target.

After the Battle of Buxar, and especially after the death of Shuja ud-Daula (1732–75, Nawab 1754–1775), the kingdom of Awadh turned into a satellite of the Company. The latter extracted an enormous tribute partly as reparations, imposed a free-trade agreement, forced the ruler to reduce ties with the French, demilitarized the region, and coerced the ruler to hand over a part of the territory in 1801. All that was done to meet 'the need for a large army having to be maintained by His Majesty King George III to confront the excessively large force of Bonaparte.'[7] Taking over the entire state, then near-bankrupt, in 1856 was a formality (see below). Although the size of the payment was large, the Awadh economy derived considerable advantage from its association with the East India Company and the European traders. Awadh was easily connected with Bengal and overseas trade via rivers and roads. Awadh state and residents purchased securities floated by the Company. The textile trade and production in the eastern parts of the state revived after the restoration of peace.[8]

In the west and centre of the Indo-Gangetic Basin, Awadh shared a border with Rohilkhand or Katehr, an agriculturally prosperous region ruled by Rajput princes. Their rebellious tendencies induced Aurangzeb to grant Rohilla Afghans military tenures in the region. In the late seventeenth and early eighteenth century, more of their brethren migrated to become mercenaries, landlords, and peasants. Taking advantage of strife among the Rajputs, the Rohilla chiefs established an independent rule in the region between 1710 and 1750 and secured it with an efficient revenue administration. The success meant the end of old Rajput landlords and village officers' proprietary rights and the handover of the revenue collection system to contractors. The region saw a series of conflicts in the third quarter of the eighteenth century, first with the Marathas whom the Rohillas had fought in the third battle of Panipat, then with the Awadh state, technically their overlords, and finally with the friend of the Awadh state, the East India Company, which annexed Rohilkhand in 1774.

Bengal

Bengal was annexed to the Mughal Empire in the last decade of the sixteenth century. It was never an easy province to rule. In large areas near the southern and eastern seaboard or the submontane north, Mughal authority was notional. The imperial governors did not have the means to impose their lordship on the chiefs in the forested uplands of Chotanagpur. Token tributes were all that they could collect. As Philip Calkins points out, seventeenth-century Bengal experienced only a slight increase in the region's revenue burden, suggesting that the local administration and its representatives commanded enough power to resist imperial demands made upon them.[9]

When Aurangzeb was pressed for funds, he sent a Deccan noble, Murshid Quli Khan, as the Diwan or fiscal administrator of Bengal (in power $c.$ 1700–27). Satisfied with Murshid Quli's performance, his successors allowed the two key imperial offices, Governor (subahdar) and Finance Minister (dewan), to merge in the position held by Murshid Quli. The usual practice was to reserve the subahdar office for kin of the emperor. Murshid Quli raised money via a transfer of old jagirs, confiscation of estates of defaulting landlords and their consolidation into larger and more efficient units, conversion of some of the more fertile lands into state-owned estates, and unleashing selective coercion upon recalcitrant zamindars. This reshuffling created a small number of large and loyal zamindari estates, including the premier zamindari in British Bengal, the Burdwan raj. The reshuffling also, indirectly, stimulated the business of bankers willing to lend to the defaulting zamindars.

At the time of Murshid Quli's death in 1727, Bengal had turned into an independent state. For example, the succession remained within the family of Murshid Quli with no more than the symbolic involvement of the emperor. The tribute still being paid to Delhi continued for the time being, but in many other ways, Bengal was effectively independent. The policy of coercing the landlords had reached its limit, however. The new Nawab had to loosen the hold of the king upon the zamindars. Geography and difficulty of access to the outlying regions placed limits upon how much exaction the state could impose on the landlords.

The zamindar-Nawab relationship changed between Murshid Quli's death (1727) and the Company takeover (1765) somewhat. Some of the larger zamindaries, like the Burdwan Raj, prospered in the eighteenth century.[10] Others faced serious problems. A big source of problems was Maratha raids into western Bengal in the 1740s. The Nawab Alivardi Khan (reign 1740–56, Figure 2.2) needed to press many western zamindars into direct or indirect military service, which would have been a drain on their resources. Further, continued low-intensity conflict between the Nawab and the Company added to the revenue pressure. Such pressure reached a peak during Mir Kasim's brief reign (1763–64).

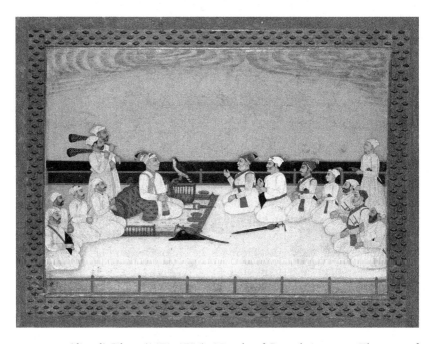

FIGURE 2.2 Alivardi Khan (1671–1756), Nawab of Bengal, in court. The son of a Mughal state officer, Alivardi Khan took over Bengal around 1740 and spent most of his reign fighting the Maratha forces of central India. An astute general, he left a state in bad financial shape for his grandson Siraj ud-Daula (c. 1729–38 to 1757); and left a disgruntled brother-in-law Mir Zafar Ali Khan (1691– 1765) whose capacity as a general he had a low opinion of. A year after his death, the British plotted the downfall of Siraj ud-Daula with Mir Zafar's help. ©V&A Images / Alamy Stock Photo.

At this time, the western part of Bengal had several European settlements (see Map 2.2.) Until about 1740, the Company, while it zealously guarded its control of the sea routes and fortified its coastal and inland settlements, was a neutral spectator in the battle for supremacy on land. In Bengal, trading inland involved constant diplomatic engagement, mainly to extract favourable licensing terms and to keep important merchant-banker partners of the state happy. The most important functionaries were the ministers and the firm of the Jagatseth, who had control of the mint. Gifts and bribes could reasonably well serve the diplomatic mission, and applying force was still only a last resort. And yet, that possibility became more real as state authority weakened due to palace intrigues, assertive zamindars, Maratha raids, and Anglo-French wars. A constant bone of contention with the Nawabs was the private European merchants. The government gained little income from their right to trade because they used the license granted to the Company to trade free of tax. A dispute over this issue with the Nawab Siraj-ud-Daula, who had been

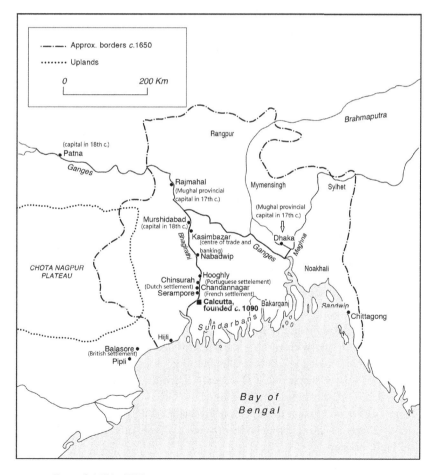

MAP 2.2 Bengal 1650–1700.

forsaken by many of his merchant allies and family elders, turned the conflict into a military engagement. In the Battle of Plassey or Palashi (1757), the Company defeated the Nawab's army and installed a puppet king on the throne on the promise of a share in the Bengal revenues as a reward.

The Company now became the kingmaker in Bengal, though still in possession of a small military force. The new Nawab proved incompetent in fulfilling the financial obligations and powerless militarily, so the agreement broke down. Mir Kasim, a rival noble, was installed on the throne in 1763. Mir Kasim was an able administrator and military general. Within a year, he raised the quantity of Bengal revenues by coercing the zamindars.

By the beginning of 1763, relations between Mir Kasim and the Company officers had soured over failed taxation agreements. Meanwhile, Mir Kasim had built a formidable army, a large part of which had been trained and headed by European mercenaries. The army was anywhere between 30,000 and 40,000 strong, about four times the size of the army under the Company's command. The Company's head stationed in Murshidabad (the former capital of the province), William Ellis, decided to teach Mir Kasim a lesson. Mir Kasim's generals, Makrar and Samru, easily won the encounter in Patna, inflicting heavy losses on the enemy. The Company declared that Mir Kasim was deposed as the ruler of Bengal.

In June, a much-depleted force under Major Thomas Adams moved north from Calcutta and captured Katwa and Murshidabad. In response, Mir Kasim had some European prisoners, including someone the Company had designated as an emissary, Peter Amyatt, killed. Adams' troops now advanced towards Mir Kasim's capital Monghyr, fighting three battles on the way in Suti, Giria, and Udhuanala. Adams scored success in each case, despite being vastly outnumbered. He had luck on his side, especially in Udhuanala where a European deserter from Mir Kasim's army told Adams a secret passage that he could use to skirt the enemy's defences and launch a surprise flank attack. In 1763, Monghyr and Patna fell, and Mir Kasim fled to the Awadh territory. His health broken, Adams returned to Calcutta and died in January 1764.

Mir Kasim then allied with the Nawab of Awadh and the Mughal Emperor Shah Alam II. Early in 1764, the combined army reached the border between Awadh and Bihar. In May, Mir Jafar and John Carnac's army defeated the allied army at the battle of Patna. The Company's army then almost disintegrated due to a mutiny, the cause of which was the knowledge that Mir Jafar had rewarded the European soldiers more generously than the Indians. Hector Munro, the new head of the army, suppressed the mutiny with ruthless measures, drilled the troops rigorously in the next few months, and led a slightly smaller but more disciplined body of troops into the decisive battle of Buxar on 22 October.[11] When the allied army lost the battle of Buxar in 1764, the Mughal Emperor gifted the Diwani (the right to collect taxes) of Bengal, Bihar, and Orissa to the Company against the payment of a tribute. The Governor, Warren Hastings, stopped that tribute ten years later. British rule in India began with this step.

In every one of these battles, from Palashi to Buxar, the enemy was many times larger in numbers and firepower. There was little difference between the two sides in the quality of tactical leadership. However, the divided command of the allied or Nawab's armies proved a weakness in every case. These armies were put together by joining several forces, each operating under the command of a warlord. Information did not pass easily between the divisions, with the result that minor reversals in the frontline could cause a panicked retreat at the back. By contrast, the smaller armies of the Company worked under a single chain of command.

Initially, governance remained divided between the Company's council at Fort William in Calcutta and the Nawab's ministers. The civil administration, for example, remained a duty of the Nawab. Even fiscal matters were entrusted to a local officer, Muhammad Reza Khan. As the need for finances increased, the division seemed more of a burden than help and ended in 1772. The battle of Buxar also induced the Company and private traders to venture further inland in search of commercial opportunities. By then, Awadh was effectively a British ally, and the move northwards opened up both a political and an economic frontier for the British merchants. Historians recognize the far-reaching consequences of this move inland both for British expansion in India and for the political economy of Awadh.[12]

The landlord–state relationship was recast on a market principle. After the Company took control of Bengal, much land revenue collection was farmed out because the fiscal administration could not possibly take over the job. Auctions of such rights became more frequent, more open, and the terms of the lease shorter. Auctions for default on revenue payments also became the general principle. The highest prices at the auction were frequently too high relative to the area's ability to pay, especially after the Great Bengal Famine of 1770. In that case, the right-holders either defaulted or tried to collect exorbitant rents from their tenants, who in turn fled from their land.

Following this experience, the Company settled upon a permanent contract directly with the zamindars. The Permanent Settlement (1793), which granted the zamindars saleable proprietary rights against the regular payment of a fixed sum of money to the government, was the culmination of this process. The settlement made zamindari property a marketable proprietary right, and the state made that right stronger by designing judicial procedures and a system of courts. The other side of the reform was that anybody could become a landlord now and not just someone commanding arms. Indeed, the old warlord class often found it hard to meet the new revenue obligations and sold or mortgaged their estates.

By contrast with these three regimes, new states almost everywhere else involved greater military and landlord elements. The most consequential example of this pathway was the Maratha dominion in the second half of the seventeenth century.

The Maratha dominion

In the second half of the seventeenth century, the individuals and families who later formed a Maratha dominion of political control were engaged by the Deccan sultans as military commanders and irregular army members. Their service under first the Bahmani sultans (1347–1527), and later Bijapur and Ahmadnagar states (c. 1500–1690) made them strong in the region. During these rules, '[t]he hillforts seem generally to have been garrisoned by Mahrattas.'[13] Rallying under Shivaji (1630–80), they first resisted the Deccan sultans, and later Mughal ambitions in the Deccan. Here, as Satish Chandra shows, the Deccan states' disintegration and the spread of Mughal power offered Maratha military families an opportunity to attempt to expand their political authority.[14] Shivaji's success in carving out a state in this region is owed to both military strategy in dealing with the Mughal and Bijapur commanders, governors, and jagirdars, and political strategy subduing internal rivalries.

In this second mission, the structure of the society from which soldiers were recruited played a favourable role. Maratha soldiery came from the peasant stock. Unlike in north India, the social distance between the military families and peasant cultivators in the western Maharashtra region was considerably narrower, which gave Shivaji's appropriation of kingship an image of popular legitimacy, and facilitated recruitment of loyal soldiers and commanders into the Maratha army. The sheer scale of Shivaji's military enterprise, especially after his final fallout with the Mughals c. 1670, was larger than any challenge the empire had to deal with in the north. By the end of the century, the Marathas exercised effective control over most parts of present-day Maharashtra.

Although Shivaji created an apparatus of the state and made some proclamations on good governance, his real legacy was not institutional but military. The army, consisting of an infantry and a mobile light cavalry, proved effective against the Mughal army, the core of which was formed of a heavily armed cavalry and moved slowly, followed by hundreds of thousands of camp-followers. By contrast, the Maratha forces were smaller, lighter, and speedier bodies. Instead of relying on revenue assignees for the supply of forces, Shivaji's army was a centralized force paid wages by the regimes that commanded it.

Succession disputes that followed soon after Shivaji's death continued until 1719, when the Peshwa, the prime minister, emerged as the strongest power. Mughal authority had by then grown too weak to enforce its writ over major provinces bordering northern and central India. The Marathas filled the vacuum. Their army moved north and scored a series of outstanding military successes. These successes are owed mainly to Peshwa Bajirao I (c. 1700–40) as a cavalry leader and strategist. Beginning with Malwa and Dhar in the first half of the 1720s, the army defeated the Nizam of Hyderabad in 1728, thus settling a conflict over Deccan revenues, captured Gujarat, and made Mewar (Udaipur) tributary in the early 1730s. The Maratha army fought and won several battles with the Mughal forces in 1737 and 1738. Though unable to subdue Delhi completely, they took Bundelkhand and extracted a revenue-sharing arrangement from the emperor, Muhammad Shah (1702–48, reign 1719–48).

The armies divided into bands that formed around chieftains. At the beginning of the eighteenth century, the troops were individually not large enough to pose a threat to an imperial army. Still, they were sufficiently large and mobile to make imperial armies ineffective.[15] Outright conquest, in other words, was not always a feasible strategy to raise taxable wealth. But sharp and frequent raids could paralyze the enemy enough to force a negotiation on tax sharing. In regions technically still allegiant to the Mughal Empire, Maratha demand for a share in the taxes led to a low-intensity but sustained conflict, which generated enough disruption to economic life to worry the local landlords. After Bajirao I's death in 1740, the strategy was successfully used in eastern India, yielding poorly defended, but also resource-poor regions such as Berar and Orissa to Maratha direct rule, and in extracting from Bengal shares of the state revenues.

In 1751, when an informal truce between the Mughals and the Marathas was drawn, Maratha command had splintered into five regional groups: Sindhia located in Gwalior and controlling Bundelkhand; the Peshwa in Pune controlling western Maharashtra; Holkar controlling Malwa; Bhosale in command of Berar and Orissa; and Gaekwad in Gujarat. The Peshwa still commanded symbolic authority over the whole dominion. While on the Rajputana borders, sharp raids continued to be used, the main Maratha army had moved away from guerilla tactics into forces equipped to conduct conventional warfare. In every major battle, all constituents contributed soldiers. They had also developed a few allies among the military tribes of Deccan and the Jats of north India. All of them had reason to resist the more established regional states. In this way, the army consisted of a core force and a large irregular one contributed by allies, jagirdars, and chieftains of various hues. These latter were not usually salaried soldiers. Many joined campaigns as fortune hunters.

By mid-century, the Marathas had established a complex network of revenue distribution that British writers variously called an empire, republic, or confederacy, and I will call dominion. Institutions of the state had consolidated in the core region, western Maharashtra. In western Maharashtra, military command and revenue assignments had begun to converge in the early eighteenth century, leading to increasing power and authority of local lords and local armies. Commanders were settled with land grants. As the landlords underneath them became more powerful, the ruling elite depended more and more upon tribute flowing in from the territories where the Marathas formed a thin layer of control.

The reliance on raid brought the Marathas of northern, western, and central India in direct conflict with Awadh and Bengal. The Awadh elite was worried at the ease with which the army marched into Delhi. The Nizam was not only an ally of the Mughals, but had long been fighting on their behalf against the Marathas. The outcome of these engagements had been neither positive nor decisive for the Nizam. Another nominal Mughal ally, Bengal under Alivardi Khan, suffered serious revenue and territorial losses because of Maratha raids on the western border areas.[16] In the 1750s, the Mughal Empire's north-western tributaries became a target of the Afghan rulers for tribute payment. The Marathas had also been making moves towards the north-west, escalating a contest with the Afghans.

The Durrani Afghan chief, Ahmad Shah Abdali, had made several invasions into northern India in the second half of the 1750s and left Delhi alone only on the latter's recognition of Afghan claims upon Punjab, Sind, and Kashmir. His hold on these territories, however, had been intermittent. When in 1760, Abdali returned to India with a large force to contain the Marathas, he was welcomed and supplied with resources and intelligence by the Awadh Nawabs and other allies of the Mughal court. In a series of short, bloody battles, Abdali defeated Sindhia and Holkar. Reinforcement now came from the Peshwa, in the shape of a large army under the generalship of Sadashiv Bhau (1730–61), the nephew of Bajirao I. He was joined by Ibrahim Khan Gardi, general of a mercenary musketeer army of the Deccan, the Jats of the north, what remained of Sindhia and Holkar forces, and the Gaekwads of Gujarat. A showdown between the two strongest contenders for supremacy in Punjab had become inevitable (Figure 2.3).

FIGURE 2.3 Sadashivrao Bhau with Ibrahim Khan Gardi. Generals on the Maratha side in the Third Battle of Panipat (1761), Sadashivrao died in battle, and Ibrahim Khan was killed by the enemy general after the battle. Their partnership was a rare attempt to form a pan-Deccan military front. © Matteo Omied / Alamy Stock Photo.

In the third battle of Panipat (1761), Afghan, Awadh, and Rohilla forces defeated the Maratha army.[17] By far the biggest battle fought in India in recorded memory, Panipat illustrated the many weaknesses that the Maratha military enterprise had acquired over time. Although a state army, it came to fight a battle with an indifference towards the budget, intelligence, and supplies. A long-standing practice of collecting tribute from local potentates while on the march was relied on. But the ensuing battle was far too big, and the run-up to the battle too long for such means to be sufficient.

The army and the camp-followers consumed available grain in Delhi in the monsoon months of 1760. Cash-strapped Bhau stripped the imperial palaces of any gold that he could find, displeasing friends. There were also leadership issues. This was a coalition army, even if the Peshwa was technically in charge of overall command. 'The spirit of military enthusiasm, so dangerous in a general without experience, completely took possession of his [Bhau's] mind.'[18] His arrogance distanced him from his allies. Military strategy was compromised. The transition from mobile light cavalry into a large state army confused the command. There was overreliance on a massive artillery unit that played no role in the battle. There were too many ill-assorted and cumbersome cannons the French had given the Bhau, which he was determined to carry to the front against his Jat and Deccan allies' advice. Intelligence gathering was poor. Immediately before the battle, a party bringing in treasure from Delhi lost its way into an enemy camp and was massacred. On the eve of the battle, disagreements were rife in the Maratha camp over strategy, intelligence, and supplies. Most soldiers in the coalition were poorly commanded irregulars and camp-followers. Almost all the soldiers were starving and angry over unpaid wages when on the morning of 14 January 1761, a series of violent skirmishes turned into a full-blown battle.

The Maratha-led army was larger in number than Abdali's. The Persian cavalry and the Rohilla Afghan infantry on the right flank of Abdali's army were unable to withstand the assault of the Maratha and Deccan forces' main constituents. Seeing his army facing reverse, Abdali sent in the reserves. In close combat, these heavily armoured soldiers prevailed over the enemy. What followed after that must remain one of the great mysteries in Indian military history. All accounts agree that the end of the battle came with a very sudden drain of morale. If one relies on the more dramatic reports, Bhau descended from his elephant and went into action while those following him thought he was lost. Some of the other generals were brought down from their horses by musket shots, and the Gaekwad and Holkar quietly left the battlefield. Sensing the end to be near, the Maratha army turned back and took flight.

In the next few hours, an appalling massacre followed. By conservative account, several hundred thousand were butchered by the pursuing troops. Many were trampled to death while trying to cross a moat dug up for defence, and hundreds of fugitives, who took shelter in the village of Panipat, were surrounded and murdered the next morning. For days, even months, stragglers were murdered by zamindars loyal to the northern alliance. Only a few managed to reach the Jat territory where safe haven was available. Almost all the generals and chieftains of distinction died in the battle. The enemy captured 50,000 horses.[19]

Although a debacle on an unimaginable scale, Panipat did not change political equations in northern India in any particular direction. Abdali had to hurriedly leave India, facing a possible mutiny in his forces over unpaid wages. Yet, the long-term consequences of the battle were important enough. One set of effects concerned the internal constitution of the Maratha dominion. Soon after Panipat, the ruling Peshwa died, reportedly of shock. The Peshwa overlord status within the dominion ended. Although losing the capacity to carry out further conquests, Maratha forces of Bundelkhand and Malwa regrouped and raided both the western Gangetic plains and eastern Rajasthan, but the military leadership had passed on to Sindhia and Holkar. The violent succession disputes that followed stripped the Peshwa of any moral claim to supreme leader status. There was little peace within the Maratha dominion. If one of the five constituents 'professed a deceitful submission to the commands of the Peshva, the other openly maintained his claim to superiority.'[20] Any attempt at cohesion was undermined by the distrust in which the constituents held each other.

With the Peshwa growing weaker, the flow of tribute to the political centre fell too. By the 1770s, the Peshwa territory was heavily indebted to bankers and losing the fiscal capacity to sustain a large-scale military enterprise. Even its survival as a state was in doubt. Michihiro Ogawa's research on fiscal reforms in the Peshwa's domain in the last decades of the rule in Pune shows that the state handed over tax rights to military commanders on a large scale.[21] Of the land revenue that the jagirdars or military tenure-holders collected, only a small percentage went to the centre. The centre had other incomes. But the small percentage still suggests that the centre delivered the right to rule to local chiefs along with military and fiscal powers. This was a story of desperation and losing control.

In the last quarter of the eighteenth century, Mahadji Sindhia (1730–94) raised a powerful north Indian army under the French mercenary Benoit de Boigne. So successful and formidable was the new army that, for a brief moment at the turn of the century, it seemed that the northern Marathas had outstripped the British and the French East India Companies in military capability by using a combination of indigenous and European elements.[22] The British East India Company had a stronghold in Bombay dangerously near Maratha territories and now began taking a close interest in Maratha affairs. The Company took sides in succession disputes of the Peshwas. A series of short battles ensued between Sindhia and Holkar and the Company troops in the second half of the 1770s. Mahadji Sindhia registered initial successes in 1777 but reverses in the next three years. Eventually, peace was declared between the Marathas and the Company and maintained for 20 years.

The Company joined as an ally of the Peshwa in succession disputes in 1802. A war between the other constituents and the Company became inevitable. The second Anglo-Maratha war was fought in two theatres, north India, where Sindhia's French commanders fought Gerard Lake's army, and central India (mainly the village of Assaye near Buldana in Maharashtra state), where Holkar fought against

Arthur Wellesley's army. The death of Mahadji in 1794 and the exit of de Boigne a year after had weakened and divided military command in the Sindhia camp. The new general, Pierre Cuillier-Perron, was not trusted by the king, Daulatrao Sindhia (1779–1827), or by many of the officers, Indian or European.[23] Dependence on a demoralized European command gave Lake's army near Delhi the chance to bribe the officers. Perron resisted the temptation for some time before giving in to the offer and reportedly crossed over with a large personal fortune earned from his previous service.

Assaye, by contrast, was fought without deception, and the heavily outnumbered Company troops fought a fierce battle before overpowering the Maratha cavalry and French gunners. The war led to substantial territorial losses, including well-cultivated Bundelkhand in north India and Orissa in the east. But the Marathas were left alone in central India, and Sindhia continued to claim tribute from the Rajputana states. Still, the dominion was growing steadily weaker. The revenue loss could only be dealt with through revenue farming, which consolidated the power of intermediate groups unconnected with cultivation.

Along with the financial crisis, and because of it, the army's dependence on irregular soldiers increased. The Delhi setback gave a lasting shock to what had so far been a successful collaboration between European soldiers and Maratha kings. The brief experiment in raising a well-equipped and efficient standing army, in place of the small raiding parties of old, came to an end with the second Anglo-Maratha war. Following these setbacks, the Marathas regrouped and returned to the old strategy of swift raids conducted by light cavalry, with the additional aid of mobile artillery units and newly recruited mercenaries from Awadh and Rohilkhand.

These Indian mercenaries were called Pindari in the British documents. In reality, these soldiers, mainly Pathans, may have formed a disbanded northern army regiment.[24] In any case, the Holkar used their services to coerce Rajput states to part with a share of their revenues. A fiscally devastated state armed with bandit soldiers moved towards a final reckoning with the Company, which had steadily increased in financial, military and organizational capacity. While the Pindari problem was a Maratha–Rajput affair, the Company had stayed aloof. Briefly, it entered a peace treaty with Amir Khan, the commander. However, the relationship was filled with distrust. Khan did not represent a territorial power and did not offer scope for standard forms of negotiation. There were rumours that parts of the court in Kabul could join Khan's army.

In 1813, hostilities broke out over raids by the Pindaries inside British territories. As the Company army set off against the Marathas, the Peshwa in Pune began to coordinate a campaign. The regular army much reduced, the campaign relied heavily on the Pindaries rallying under their general Amir Khan. The Company neutralized the Sindhia in 1817, and in three quick battles, routed the Peshwa, Bhosale, and Holkar in 1817 and 1818. The territories under their control were annexed to British India, with the symbolic exception of Satara, home of Shivaji's direct descendants.

Why did the dominion fall? One of the leading early histories of the Marathas called the dominion 'a huge building raised on a narrow base.'[25] The reference was to the fiscal administration of the empire. From Shivaji's kingship onwards, two strategies of revenue increase combined: extraction of tribute from zones of conquest and more efficient collection of taxes in zones of origin. In zones of origin, the western Maharashtra territories where the Peshwa ruled, numerous land grants were made to military chiefs ostensibly to provide sustenance for the troops under their pay, thereby creating a modified jagirdari system. The jagirdars, as well as the state, relied on Brahmin and other state officers to manage accounts. Some of these officers emerged into the mainstream and became kingmakers and jagirdars in turn. Unlike the Mughal jagir grants, all Maratha land grants were hereditary and held in perpetuity, subject to the receiver's loyalty.

On the other hand, in the conquest zones, the landlords who had served the Mughal provincial state continued to function under the Marathas. The revenues of the state depended on tribute rather than an improved system of collection. The Maratha presence in these zones was not deep enough to govern or colonize the regions. Instead, what was possible was to apply selective coercion and intimidation upon the chieftains and landlords so that a substantial number of them agreed to pay some form of tribute. A good example of this transformation was Malwa in the 1730s and 1740s. The Marathas had the military means to create obstacles for the imperial revenue system here, but did not have the administrative resources or even sufficient military force to erect a whole new revenue system. They could obstruct roads and trades and disrupt and divert supplies, which eventually led the zamindars to accept Maratha claims upon taxation.[26] There was, however, little change in the pattern of land control and peasant property. If the state gifted away access to taxable surplus to its constituents and partners in the zones of origin, it never gained access in zones of conquest.

With limited capacity to run a fiscal system, the only way state income could increase was by keeping the conquest machine on overdrive, which meant making a periodic demand on weak regimes, backed up by a credible threat of a raid. The money that came in as tribute in this way was an unpredictable income. In the first half of the eighteenth century, much of the gains went into the commanders and mercenaries' pockets, who depended on such chance earnings. The operation's logic bogged the chiefs down in a never-ending commitment to extortion and led them to neglect the task of improving civilian administration. In Bengal, the division of the loot led to bickering between the Peshwa and the Bhosale, of which the Nawab took full advantage.

In the Peshwa's domain, by contrast, an elaborate fiscal administration did take roots. The tenet of Peshwa fiscal administration was to erect a multi-layered tax collection office. Although James Grant Duff explained the state officers as representing long-established 'Hindu' tradition, it is more likely that the practice followed Deccan precedence. In the mid-seventeenth century Deccan, state officers (amils) were in charge of collecting the revenue. The amils would perform tasks that concerned the village's well-being, such as policing or dispute settlement. In western Maharashtra, the fiscal administration followed these established practices. In Malwa and Bundelkhand, the former Mughal domains were reassessed according to soil fertility, but the revenue administration did not change in essential respects. In western Maharashtra, by contrast, the revenue administration was strengthened and refined. There was much better record-keeping. Village officers and district officers increased in number, roles, power, and penetration.

The warlords were largely non-literate and without prior administrative experience. So from Shivaji's administration onwards, the agency of the Brahmin scribe, and the role of record-keeping more generally, had increased. Such agency made more information available to the state about potential revenues from land and added to the efficiency of revenue collection. The primary duty of the Patel, his assistant, the Chowgule, and the accountant, the Kulkarni, was to look after land and maintain accounts, but frequently they were also engaged in civil administrative duties. Between the village officers and the state were officers with jurisdiction over clusters of villages, variously called Desai, Deshmukh, and Deshpande.

After Panipat, and with increasing succession disputes, the fiscal apparatus began to weaken. The Maratha states never earned enough money to sustain a large standing army. Nor did they try to build one. While money flowed in from zones of conquest to subsidize the zones of origin, the dominion could sustain its military enterprise, despite giving away control of state revenues to privileged tenure holders in the zones of origin. However, 1761 put a check upon conquest, and 1803 saw a loss of the zones of conquest. By then, fiscal administration in the zones of origin had deteriorated so much that these areas could not sustain military effort on their own anymore. In the last years of the dominion, revenue farming increased and there were more claimants to tax income. Tax rates may well have increased in some areas, but in the main, the system failed to deliver enough of the taxable surplus to the state.

Increasingly, the Maratha states became dependent on bankers and lenders, who promised to supply money when needed and procure consumption articles for the military during campaigns by using their reputation to raise credit. Individually many of these bankers represented firms of small resources. Their move into state lending may have been involuntary and, in some cases, attracted by the prospect of advantageous trade licenses. The conditions offered extraordinary opportunities to groups, such as Chitpavan Brahmin families, for making money in unconventional businesses. V.D. Divekar says that this example of an unconventional business community calls into question older views of the risk-averse and tradition-loving attitude of Indian communities.[27] His work also demonstrates the exceptional character of the commercial efflorescence in Pune city under the Peshwas. This was not a normal trading world; it thrived on the growing poverty of the state.

Hyderabad

The Hyderabad state's origin can be traced to 1687 when the Qutb Shahi reign in Golconda came to an end due to a Mughal invasion. The kingdom was bifurcated into two parts: the northern being the territory of the later state of Hyderabad, and the southern, the Carnatic, later an ally of the British. The imperial state relied on zamindars for tax collection and sardars, namely commanders of cavalry forces, for military support. The two classes overlapped to some extent. However, peace eluded the southern province as the contest for control of the territory between the Mughals and the Marathas was intense and carried out at a huge cost to the provincial government.[28]

During the Mughal campaign, the group I called tributary kings became tributaries of the Mughal Empire. Called Nayakas locally and poligars by the British, they had evolved out of a layer of local commanders in charge of the defence of groups of villages. As the kings' authority weakened in the eighteenth century, they rose to the position of warlords, often in charge of hill forts, and diverted a part of the tax income formerly going to the courts towards themselves. The shift of loyalty made little difference to the fiscal administration of these territories.

The Nizams of Hyderabad were Mughal governors who established a virtually independent rule by the 1720s. Having suffered Maratha raids and entered a series of inconclusive engagements with the Marathas, the Nizam allied with the French. When the French became friendly with the two rival powers, Mysore and Maratha, the ruler Nizam Ali Khan allied with the British (1766), handing over the 'Northern Circars,' a large chunk of coastal Coromandel. In 1803, districts in the west and south of the state, including the fertile Raichur Doab, were also handed over. These gifts secured military stability for Hyderabad. And they also secured Hyderabad neutrality in the Anglo-Mysore and the Anglo-Maratha wars during Nizam Ali Khan's lifetime.

Going cautiously on the Deccan rivalries and benefiting from its position as a buffer between the Marathas and Mysore, the Hyderabad state had time to build stable governance institutions in the second half of the eighteenth century. These institutions followed the Mughal principle of awarding jagirs and awarding the right to award jagirs to nobles loyal to the king. But breaking away from the Mughal practice, jagirs were treated as heritable property rather than a transferable state office. The nobility earlier included old landlords and tributary kings, Muslim and Hindu, as well as new members such as vakils or negotiators. In the late eighteenth and early nineteenth century, as military service was no longer of critical importance, patronage politics benefited individuals holding administrative offices.[29]

South of Hyderabad, state formation was less tied to Mughal collapse and more to regional factors. One of these factors was the presence of local kingdoms ruled over by the Nayaka chieftains. In the seventeenth century, the Maratha conquest, including that of Tanjore, had threatened their already disputed and unstable authority. In the middle of this contest, one semi-independent province of Hyderabad, Arcot, or Carnatic emerged. The British and the French East India Companies maintained diplomatic relations with these polities because their safety in south India depended on it. Therefore, when Anglo-French rivalries broke out in the wake of the war of the Austrian succession (1740–48) and the Seven Years' War (1756–63), these states were engaged too. The Europeans joined succession disputes in Tanjore and Arcot as allies of opposing sides. A series of encounters followed. Eventually, the British defeated the French. Arcot became a dependent state, if not a colony.

Mysore and Tanjore

In the middle of peninsular India, the breakup of the Vijayanagar Empire (c. 1336-c. 1640) had led to the formation of several powerful kingdoms in south India, of which the Wodeyar clan, who came to rule Mysore, was one. The end of the seventeenth century, also the end of the long reign of Chikkadevaraja (1672–1704), was a turning point in different ways. The south Indian campaign of Bijapur state, which led Shivaji's half-brother Vyamkoji or Venkoji to become the ruler of Tanjore, happened in 1675. In the 1690s, the Mughals invaded south India. When they left the region, they left behind them several loyal tributary states in the southern Deccan. Surrounded by these potential troublemakers, Mysore, under Chikkadevaraja and his successor Kanthirava initiated moves to streamline the fiscal system to release more money for the army. The precise nature of these steps and the extent of success attained in raising more money remain unknown. The state began recruiting administrators from the Maratha territories to achieve this purpose.

Beyond that indirect and symbolic measure and attempts at monetary reforms, little is known about statecraft in early eighteenth century Mysore. We do know that the military build-up enabled the state to capture territories in the west and the south. However, these gains could not be sustained by the 1730s when the Nawab of Carnatic's western conquests imposed financial and territorial losses on Mysore. Accounting for this mixed record, Sanjay Subrahmanyam says that the Wodeyar kings' anxiety about administrative reforms stemmed from 'structural contradictions' in the fiscal system.[30]

In 1761, a military general, Hyder Ali (1720–82), became the de facto ruler of Mysore. With his military build-up, Mysore's relations with the Marathas, the Nizam, the Carnatic, Tanjore, and Travancore to the south-west worsened. The British and the French were soon drawn into these conflicts. The Anglo-Mysore wars of 1766–69 took place when the Nizam of Hyderabad, worried about the Marathas and Mysore's dual threat, called in the Company to assist him. The wars saw Hyder Ali lose his access to the western coast, but the scores were even on land.

The peace treaty signed in 1769 carried a promise of mutual military aid, which the British did not respect when the Marathas attacked Mysore in 1769. Hyder lost these battles and decided to ally with the French to beat the British. The alliance started a proxy war between the British and the French Company for control over the eastern coast. In the second Anglo-Mysore war, Mysore scored significant successes in 1782–84. Hyder Ali, however, died in the middle of the conflict, leaving the kingdom and the unfinished business of dealing with the

British and the Marathas to his son Tipu Sultan (1750–99). At the end of this conflict, the British were forced to sign a peace agreement with Tipu, and Tipu exacted his revenge on the Marathas by sacking Tanjore. In 1789–92, Tipu lost the third Anglo-Mysore war over control of another British ally, Travancore. He finally lost the kingdom and his life in 1799, in a joint attack by the Nizam, the Marathas, and the British.

Thus came to an end a regime that was militarily the most formidable in south India between 1761 and 1799. With its fall, Travancore escaped a persistent threat. However, Tanjore survived as an independent rule on promise to pay a tribute, which bankrupted the already weak state. Tanjore was finally taken over in 1855 under the 'doctrine of lapse' (see below).

The brief emergence of Mysore as a force in south India offers several lessons. The strengths of the regime derived both from military innovations that Hyder Ali and Tipu Sultan's reigns witnessed and from fiscal successes. Hyder Ali's 12-year reign was distinguished by efforts to overhaul military capacity. He incorporated European ideas into the infantry and European technology into the artillery. He pursued this goal by hiring European commanders and mercenaries and trying to bring trade in military equipment under the control of the state. This was a novel step and presaged a model of centralization and market regulation that Tipu Sultan took further forward.

A great part of Hyder Ali's extraordinary energies was taken up in matters of revenue. Between 1770 and 1790, the revenues flowing to the state increased fourfold. Almost all of it came from territorial expansion, and much of it was lost in the 1790s with loss of territory. On the point of increasing the capacity of the fiscal system to raise more resources, Hyder Ali's measures were somewhat ad hoc. They included the liberal use of coercion and extortion, especially of the wealthy merchants and bankers. In the end, he needed to maintain the flow of money from the tributary kings and landlords in the newly conquered territories. Several of the military expeditions he organized were aimed at subduing the poligars or rescuing loyal poligars from French coercion. In Coorg, he had to suppress a bloody rebellion organized by landlords. Thus, the regime's fiscal success was predicated on conquest rather than administrative efficiency and generated much resistance.

Tipu Sultan was aware of this dangerous dependence of revenue upon conquest and attempted to reform the administration to increase revenue collection efficiency. To this end, he issued detailed regulations that revealed an attempt to nationalize trades and streamline the land-tax system. One careful research work on the fiscal enterprise has interpreted Tipu's extensive regulatory orders as measures of actual success in governance.[31] How successful Tipu was in implementing these orders, however, is open to doubt. A close reading of the regulations would not suggest that he possessed sufficient means to effect a real transformation.

Tipu's regulations for the revenue officers set out to create a direct contract ('a promise of engagement from a superior to an inferior') between the state and the cultivator. In writing the contract, the main agent of the state was the amil, who would visit villages at the beginning of the cultivation year, record the number of ploughs of individual families, ensure that the corresponding area was manured and sown, and encourage an extension of ploughs and areas. The contract's actual implementation was left to the village officer, which was a hereditary office attached to the village and paid for with rent-free land. The regulations make it clear that neither this officer nor the amil, mutsuddy (clerk), and kelladar (fort in-charge) commanded the state's trust. The village officers had sufficient power to induce the peasants to work on the officers' lands, at the expense of the state's time. The regulations are filled with orders that start with the words, 'it has been the practice in the districts,' and warning that such practices could invite the 'severest displeasure' of the huzoor (government). These included revenue farming in which clerks, accountants, and other officers indulged. 'Falsehood is an offence of the highest nature... and God has declared the lyar to be a companion of Satan,' the regulations remind the amil. An appeal to divine justice was necessary because direct administrative checks on these officers were liable to fail.[32] In any case, the regulations did not provide for checks and balances.

It is possible that had Tipu lived on in peace, adequate implementation mechanisms could have been devised. However, the regulations themselves leave one with the impression that these were desperate attempts to mend a flawed system, flawed in that they were injunctions addressed to administrative officers who worked for self-interest, against the interests of the state, and got away with it.

Malabar and Travancore

The eighteenth-century emergence of the Travancore state is usually attributed to king Marthanda Varma's (1706–1758, reign 1729–1758) reorganization of the army. European and local merchants dealt in various highly profitable export goods, preeminent of which was pepper. The king's use of a monopoly right on the pepper trade and playing off the European merchant companies against each other secured him profits and established his authority.

Towards the end of his reign, conflicts broke out among the smaller states north of Travancore, and the conflicts drew in the regional superpower Mysore under Hyder Ali. Mysore's immediate target was the Malabar kingdoms, which it successfully converted into vassals, but 'Travancore had loomed large in the political settlement of the area as she had given shelter to the dispossessed chieftains of Malabar.'[33]

Meanwhile, the Anglo-French military contest spilled over from the interior to the western coast. Marthanda Varma's nephew and successor Rama Varma (1724–1798, reign 1758–1798) invited the British to counter Mysore, which was friendly to the French, and helped the British in the second Anglo-Mysore war (1780–84). In the next five years, Rama Varma, on his own initiative, engaged in a military build-up, a part of the policy being the purchase of disued Dutch forts. This Tipu Sultan considered an excessive provocation and a prelude to an invasion of Malabar and attacked Travancore (1790). However, Mysore's ambitions were cut short by the third Anglo-Mysore war and the treaty of 1792, in which Mysore effectively withdrew from the western coast. Travancore, therefore, continued as a princely state friendly to the Company. Much of Malabar, Coimbatore, and South and North Canara came into British possessions with the end of the fourth Anglo-Mysore war in 1799.

Gujarat and Rajputana

At the end of the seventeenth century, hundreds of independent kingdoms ruled over Gujarat and Rajputana. Only some in eastern Rajasthan were tributary to the Mughal Empire. In Gujarat, the Mughal authority was real only on the coasts and the eastern Gujarat cities, whereas in Saurashtra, the empire had little effective presence. At the peak of its power, the empire possessed the valuable port of Surat. The empire also derived some benefit from the flourishing textile industry and the presence of strong agricultural communities in the coastal areas.

Maratha forces conquered the Mughal province of Gujarat in 1709. A century later, the Company had acquired much of this territory. In the intervening time, Maratha Gujarat had kept a low profile in the battles in the north. Our knowledge of Maratha rule in Gujarat derives from reports prepared shortly after British takeover. In these regions, as in Malwa, the Maratha state had left the chieftains alone, only marginally reshaping the tax collection bureaucracy on the western Maharashtra model.[34] Two distinct policies were used to raise money. From the potentially troublesome chieftains, a token tribute was taken. The officers of the state, on the other hand, dealt with the so-called 'peaceful' villages. Upon taking over control in these regions, the British, therefore, found on one side armed Rajput landlords who refused to accept any overlord rights of the British, and, on the other, a hierarchy of officers whose rights and privileges had congealed into hereditary property rights. The first political challenge for the Company was to subdue and remove these layers of independent authority.[35] In Saurashtra and Cutch (Kachchh), the Rajput chieftains were left more or less alone since the taxable resources of these extremely arid regions were not worth a conquest, nor were the chieftains a threat to Company power.

The eastern Rajasthan regions directly governed by the Mughals witnessed a consolidation of landlord power at the end of the seventeenth century. R. Rana shows that it was feasible in eastern Rajasthan in the second half of the seventeenth century for some zamindars to appropriate jagirdari rights and convert non-zamindari villages into zamindari ones. As this process continued without significant resistance from above, and as the zamindars overcame such resistance as there was, the traditional partnership between the commercial and financial interests with the ruling class weakened, and the former began to ally with the zamindars.[36] In this way emerged a significant northern ally of the Marathas in the mid-eighteenth century, the Jats of Bharatpur.

The other principal eastern states of Rajasthan, Mewar, and Amber had been vassals of the Mughals at the beginning of the eighteenth century and became tributary to the Marathas after the fall of Malwa. Both states were racked by succession disputes, in which the Marathas inserted themselves. In turn, those occupying the throne made payments to the Marathas. James Tod, who referred to the northern Marathas as 'associations of vampires,' gave an account of the immense quantity of money that in this way changed hands between 1736 and 1777, and of the territories first mortgaged and later lost to Sindhia and Holkar by the Mewar state.[37] These regions contained well-cultivated districts and important trade routes, furnishing the state much income, though how stable that income was remains open to doubt. Conceivably, the tribute might not have to be paid at all if the major Rajput states could combine their military might. However, the Rajput clans were unable to resist such demands partly because they were in a constant state of civil war. Too often, claimants to the throne invited the Marathas to force their way to power or protect them from rivals. In effect, Mewar turned into a colony alternately of Sindhia and Holkar until 1803.

With internal and external forces joining hands in a spiral of decline and misrule, the states' fiscal systems collapsed. 'It is always a task of difficulty,' Tod wrote, 'to obtain any correct account of the revenues of these States, which are ever fluctuating.'[38] The state revenues came in partly from khalsa (demesne) lands but largely from jagirs. These jagirs were of variable size. Each one, being hereditary, was identified with a clan or a family lineage. Their position in the locality was, therefore, entrenched. Mewar and Amber's political difficulty further derived from the increasing power of the groups that mediated between landed estates and the state. Some of them rose from the older nobility of jagirdars, but many new groups were inducted into either military or fiscal service and rewarded with revenue share. Revenue farming increased in Jaipur through the eighteenth century.[39] And there was 'the growing inability of the state to check its officials from making illegal demands … [on] the peasants, artisans and menials.'[40] Dilbagh Singh's history of Bikaner in the second half of the eighteenth century again depicts 'a grim story of growing anarchy.'[41] As a consequence of the fragmentation of political authority, the nobles had more say in succession matters. As external forces and armed mercenaries joined in to support rival claims, the uncertainty increased further.

The major states of western Rajasthan, namely Marwar, Sirohi, and Jaisalmer, did not face a direct threat of invasion from Delhi or the east. And yet, the political situation in eastern Rajasthan destabilized them as well. With short interludes when some of the states were occupied by invading forces, the ruling Rajput clans continued on the throne undisturbed. Still, succession disputes were more frequent than before and became increasingly violent in almost all the states. So did festering clan hostilities and territorial conflicts that affected relations between states. In Marwar, the nobles became kingmakers. Long targeted by Marwar for tribute, Sirohi escaped a serious invasion but experienced sustained hostility with its neighbour in the eighteenth century. The clans of Jaisalmer too suffered predatory raids from eastern neighbours in the wake of internal disputes.

The exception to this seemingly universal cycle of disputed kingship, predation, and fiscal collapse was Kota and Bundi in the south-west, under Zalim Singh's rule.

Succession disputes were kept at bay in this zone, even though at the cost of an expensive treaty with the Marathas against Kota's traditionally hostile neighbours. Still, Zalim Singh managed to overhaul the revenue system sufficiently to increase state income.

In Rajasthan and Saurashtra, British paramountcy was accepted without serious discord. One reason for the relatively peaceful transition was the distrust the western Rajputs entertained for the Marathas. The sentiment was shared equally by the British, who, in their aversion to both the Mughals and the Marathas, warmed up to the Rajputs. Tod's three-volume history of Rajasthan displays this sentiment well. Their distance from the major rivals for power in north India made them less of a threat for the Company, and the low tax base of these arid territories made them less attractive as a prize. Nevertheless, the British officers became interested in Rajput affairs, frequently meddling in succession disputes.

Punjab

Further to the west, Punjab was a Mughal province until the 1710s, when conflicts between a discordant group of Sikh military chiefs and the Mughals became intense. Bordering Central Asia and Afghanistan, this region contained important overland trade routes and yielded much income for the state. Mughal domination in this region, however, had never been entirely secure. The provincial administration was populated by an elite of Central Asian (Turani) descent. Like the Awadh ruling class, they were close to the imperial court and strategically a crucial ally. But the landlords contested their authority.

Unlike in Awadh, the provincial administration failed to contain these revolts or arrive at a negotiated settlement, trying instead to intensify its revenue squeeze on the landlords and privileged jagirdars, thus worsening the conflict.[42] Khushwant Singh suggested that the conflict between the Mughal nobility and the Sikh peasants and military chiefs was also a conflict between group identities.[43] Shades of cultural assertion can be found in the Maratha–Mughal strife as well, wherein the Marathas often claimed to be fighting on behalf of the Hindu religion. But the Hinduist claims in the Maratha case were more tentative and strategic. In contrast, in the Sikh case, group identity was owed to the formation of a religious community through master and disciple succession and other institutions. Thus, integration of the Sikhs into the Mughal state, and integration of Muslims in the Sikh state created by Ranjit Singh, remained both unfinished and uneasy.

Ranjit Singh (1780–1839) came to power in 1799, when Mughal authority over Punjab had all but disappeared. His success as a ruler was shaped by two achievements, both of which involved farsightedness and diplomacy. Like Shivaji, he succeeded in uniting the majority of the clans and their chiefs into a viable alliance and kept that alliance intact in his lifetime. The resultant improvement in central finances enabled him to strengthen and modernize the army. Ranjit Singh was much impressed by the infantry's performance in the Company's troops during the second Anglo-Maratha war in the north, and hired two French commanders in

1822, Jean-Francois Allard and Jean-Baptiste Ventura, to create an infantry regiment. He handed over the royal iron foundry to the European gunners, who produced first-rate cannons in these factories.

The Sikh alliance became vulnerable within a year of Ranjit Singh's death in 1839. The army was divided up into factions ruled by their clan leaders. The resultant chaos, and what appeared to the Company as the promise of an easy victory, paved the way for the Anglo-Sikh wars. In the battlefield, the two sides were almost equally placed, and the Company's troops could well have lost the battle but for some opportune treachery in the other camp.

Following the takeover in 1846, the Company needed first to neutralize the clans and jagirdars, partly by coercion and partly by co-opting.[44] The co-opting strategies included recruitment of Punjabi soldiers in the Company's troops. How farsighted this move was became evident during the Indian mutiny of 1857 when prominent chiefs, who had suffered for being on the wrong side in the 1846 Anglo-Sikh wars, now sided with the British and the soldiers remained loyal. Punjab under Crown rule was rewarded for this vital support with an extensive network of irrigation canals.

Assam

Under the long rule of the Ahom kings, Assam remained independent until 1826. Militarily, its rule was never secure over all of modern Assam, and the territorial extent of the state was not fixed. Spread along the Brahmaputra floodplains, the territory shifted due to Mughal imperial campaigns and rebellions by tributary kings at different times. With the rise of Company power in Bengal, private traders and Bengal administration showed interest in joining trade between Bengal and Assam. The growing British interest in the region coincided with decades of intermittent rebellion and civil war in the Ahom kingdom. The Company regime entered the north-eastern region of India to offer protection to the royalists in Assam and serve commercial interest at the same time. Disputed claims to the court pitted the British against the Burmese king. After the third Anglo-Burmese war in 1826, the British annexed Assam.

Resorting to various strategies, including the doctrine of lapse, areas on the north-eastern frontiers of the Ahom kingdom were included in the Company's empire. Control over the Khasis came about after their defeat in the Anglo-Khasi War of 1829–1833. Cachar and the Jaintia kingdoms were annexed between 1832 and 1835. Upper Assam was briefly restored to the Ahom king before being taken back in 1838.

Sind

Sind was technically a province of the Mughal Empire, annexed by Akbar, but in practice, a region left to the authority of substantial landlords whose rights were hereditary. Between 1690 and 1740, the Kalhoro family managed to unify Sind under one rule by defying Mughal authority, making compromises with it and fighting with other landlords. The invasion of Nadir Shah (1739–47) and Ahmad Shah Abdali (1747–61) in quick succession, and demands for a share of the revenue, placed the Kalhoro regime under severe stress. These threats also had a salutary effect. The rulers invited Baloch nomads to dig canals off the Indus and its tributaries and settled them on concessionary terms in the new cultivation zones to raise taxes. The Baloch family of Talpur supplied soldiers to the state. In 1783, power had transferred to the Talpurs. Nothing substantially changed in the way Sind was governed, though the British who came later complained that the Talpurs had neglected the canals. An agriculturally well-endowed area, Sind was ruled by local landlords who supplied arms, paid taxes, and owned land and water. Most peasants were tenants without occupancy rights. Political and military power was distributed among 18 families.[45]

British interest in the region stemmed from the commercial possibilities of the Indus river. However, it was a remote and modest sort of interest until the First Anglo-Afghan Wars (1839–42), which made the task of securing a tranquil border with Afghanistan a priority. Already, the nervous landlords or amirs of Sind had entered peace and trade treaties with the British. In this scenario joined Charles Napier, commander of the army in Sind, and a firm believer in extending British military power over the region. Offering the new draft of a treaty, Napier did not wait for negotiations but advanced on the amirs and forced a confrontation. In a series of battles and fielding forces much smaller than the enemies' armies, the British Indian army defeated one amir after another in 1843. Napier was no imperialist, as he has sometimes been portrayed. He held a generally low opinion of the British Indian government and its rulers. But he did believe that he was capable of governing Sind better than the amirs. He had that chance, but poor health cut his reign short. One significant legacy he left behind was the proposal to develop Karachi as a port city in the style of Bombay.[46]

The last round of annexations

After the Maratha wars ended, British India's rulers followed 'the general principle of avoiding annexation if it could be avoided.'[47] It is generally believed that the Scottish statesman James Andrew Broun-Ramsay or Lord Dalhousie (1812–1860, Governor-General of India 1848–1856) reversed that principle to annex territories wherever he could, avoiding only those territories that would not be profitable to annexe or easy to rule. This, however, is a simplistic view of the moves he made.

Dalhousie was apparently reacting to a steady stream of complaints that some princely states erected informal barriers to trade with British India. At least some of the major expansions that happened during his tenure – Berar, lower Burma, and Awadh – did reflect an economic logic of seeking resources and markets. Berar was a cotton-rich region long troubled by demobilized soldiers; the Hyderabad state handed it over to the British. Awadh was a lucrative market for traded goods. Lower Burma promised mass settlement of peasants. On the other hand, in the absence of prospects of direct economic gains, Dalhousie turned against expansion in the Indo-Burmese and Indo-Chinese frontier areas, advocating coexistence via peace treaties.[48]

The majority of the states had shown no military ambitions or helped the British or were a protectorate like Mysore, and were left alone. Punjab was a more complicated affair. Ranjit Singh's state was always seen as a potential threat to British India, but not worth risking an expensive battle as long as Singh was alive. The British extended protection to the so-called Phulkian states outside Ranjit Singh's domain, Patiala, Nabha, and Jind, against a promise to supply grains and material when needed. The states kept that promise during a war with Nepal in 1830, and again, more crucially, during the mutiny.

To Dalhousie is attributed the 'doctrine of lapse,' – a principle that British India could rightfully annex kingdoms without a male heir. The doctrine had originated before Dalhousie's governorship began, but it was applied extensively by him to acquire Satara, Jhansi, and a few smaller states. None of the larger annexations, including Awadh, Berar and Punjab, was an example of the doctrine of lapse.

The doctrine was a strange mixture of Indian precedence and new conditions. The Indian precedence was a supposedly Mughal rule that all estates were technically jagirs assigned by the king as a one-off privilege rather than as a gift that would be hereditary and proprietary, and the king retained the right to withdraw the assignment.[49] The new condition was the disregard of the adoption of a male heir as a succession principle. Although only selectively applied to territories of minor importance, the gesture had great symbolic significance. That the British could claim to be inheritors of a Mughal heritage (even a fictional one) appeared as a violation, and underlined, for many warlords and soldiers in north India, the illegitimacy of British rule.

Conclusion

The eighteenth century was contentious in Indian history because wealth and power did not usually go together in post-Mughal India. Militarily-strong yet resource-poor regimes could claim a share in the revenues of the former imperial provinces. Some of the territories targeted were virtually stateless, whereas the others were rich states. Even if the prize was not always worth winning, the intense competition in a market for protection among the militarily weaker states made joining the contest lucrative. In the 1750s, the leading contenders in northern India were the Afghans and the Marathas. In the second half of the century, the Marathas lost a vital encounter, the Afghan factor receded, and the Company joined the contest.

The emergence of new militarily strong regimes in the backdrop of a market for protection gave rise to two parallel modes of governance. I would call these statism or attempts to control and improve the land revenue administration, and militarism, or the superimposition of a military outpost over a decentralized land revenue administration.[50] Until the end of the century, major Indian powers combined both strategies. The Maratha dominion combined statism in Maharashtra with militarism in northern India; the Company combined statism in Bengal with militarism in

Awadh; and Mysore, while targeting Travancore for militarism, tried to erect a statist setup in the core domain.

By 1800 there was a divergence between the Company and the Indian states. Increasingly, there was only one model of successful statism in eighteenth-century India, and the Company represented it. This was so because the Company's rise as a political power set off significant changes in administration. Chapter 3 discusses these changes.

Notes

1 The quotation from James Tod, *Annals and Antiquities of Rajasthan*, London: Humphrey Milford, 1920, vol. 1 of 3, 475. For further biographical details on the rulers of these states, see H.G. Keene, *An Oriental Biographical Dictionary founded on materials collected by the late Thomas William Beale*, London: W.H. Allen, 1894, 188, 336, 341.

2 J.F. Richards, 'Mughal State Finance and the Premodern World Economy,' *Comparative Studies in Society and History*, 23(2), 1981, 285–308. Muzaffar Alam and Sanjay Subrahmanyam, eds., *The Mughal State 1526–1750*, Delhi: Oxford University Press, 1998, 55–68.

3 J.F. Richards wrote, 'in the end the Mughal empire failed to convert the armed, warrior aristocracies of the countryside into quasi-officials in the major structural change that was needed for truly centralized rule,' John F. Richards, 'Early Modern India and World History,' *Journal of World History*, 8(2), 1997, 197–209.

4 Richard Barnett, *North India between Empires: Awadh, the Mughals, and the British, 1720–1801*, Berkeley: University of California Press, 1980.

5 *The Crisis of Empire in Mughal North India: Awadh and the Punjab, 1707–48*, New York: Oxford University Press, 1986.

6 'Political Systems in Eighteenth Century India: The Banaras Region,' *Journal of the American Oriental Society*, 82(3), 1962, 312–320.

7 Sayyid Ghulam Ali Khan, cited in Irfan Habib and Faiz Habib, 'Mapping the Dismemberment of Awadh 1775–1801,' *Proceedings of the Indian History Congress*, 75, 2014, 455–460. See also Sabina Kazmi, 'Colonial Intervention in Awadh: Indigenous Political Structures and Indirect Rule in Eighteenth Century,' *Proceedings of the Indian History Congress*, 74, 2013, 447–457.

8 Shalin Jain, 'East India Company's Trading Interests in Awadh, 1764–1787,' *Proceedings of the Indian History Congress*, 62, 2001, 390–399.

9 'The Formation of a Regionally Oriented Ruling Group in Bengal, 1700–1740,' *Journal of Asian Studies*, 29(4), 1970, 799–806.

10 John McLane, *Land and Local Kingship in Eighteenth-Century Bengal*, Cambridge: Cambridge University Press, 1993.

11 On the battles, see G.J. Bryant, 'Munro, Sir Hector (1725/6–1805/6)' and 'Adams, Thomas (1730?–1764),' both in Oxford Dictionary of National Biography, https://doi.org/10.1093/ref:odnb/19546 (accessed on 3 December 2020), and https://doi.org/10.1093/ref:odnb/134 (accessed on 3 December 2020); D.L. Prior, 'Carnac, John (1721–1800),' in Oxford Dictionary of National Biography, https://doi.org/10.1093/ref:odnb/4711 (accessed 3 December 2020).

12 P.J. Marshall, 'Economic and Political Expansion: The Case of Oudh,' *Modern Asian Studies*, 9(4), 1975, 465–482; Rudrangshu Mukherjee, 'Trade and Empire in Awadh 1765–1804,' *Past and Present*, 94, 1982, 85–102.

13 James Grant Duff, *A History of the Mahrattas*, London: Longman, Rees, Orme, Brown and Green, 1826, vol. I, 60.

14 Satish Chandra, 'Social Background to the Rise of the Maratha Movement during the 17ᵗʰ Century in India,' *Indian Economic and Social History Review*, 10(3), 1973, 209–217.

15 Stewart Gordon, 'The Slow Conquest: Administrative Integration of Malwa into the Maratha Empire, 1720–1760,' *Modern Asian Studies*, 11(1), 1977, 1–40.

16 After 1757, the dominant partner of the Bengal Nawabs, the East India Company, while not directly involved, improved the defences of Calcutta by digging what was then known as the Maratha Ditch, and later renamed Circular Road.

17 On the Maratha-Afghan military contest, see Jos Gommans, 'Indian Warfare and Afghan Innovation during the Eighteenth Century,' *Studies in History*, 11(3), 1995, 261–280.

18 Grant Duff, *History of the Mahrattas*, vol. 2, 138

19 Standard sources on the battle should include 'An Account of the Battle of Panipat,' *Asiatic Researches*, 3, 1799, 91–140, translation of the Persian manuscript by Casi Raja (Kashiraj) Pandit, *vakil* of Awadh and an eyewitness; and Ghulam Husain Khan, *The Siyar-ul-Mutakherin* (trans. John Briggs), London: John Murray, 1832.

20 E.S. Waring, *A History of the Mahrattas*, London: J.F. Richardson, 1810, 164.

21 Michihiro Ogawa, 'Socio-economic Study of Indapur Pargana (1761–1828),' PhD Dissertation of Pune University, 2012.

22 See, for example, the account in John Pemble, 'Resources and Techniques in the Second Maratha War,' *The Historical Journal*, 19(2), 1976, 375–404.

23 J. Thomson, 'An Autobiographical Memoir of Louis Bourquien,' *Journal of the Punjab Historical Society*, 9(1), 1923, 36–71. Bourquien was a French mercenary and possibly second in command after Perron in Sindhia's army. He was one of those officers who refused to join the enemy camp but was expelled by Daulatrao Sindhia anyway. Although his presence has been noted by military historians from other sources, his own autobiography and diary of events form an important resource that have not yet been fully utilized.

24 Nida Arshi, 'The East India Company, Rajput Chieftaincies and Pindaris: Changing Dynamics of a Triangular Relationship,' *Proceedings of the Indian History Congress*, 72(I), 2011, 650–662.

25 Waring, *History of the Mahrattas*, 164.

26 Stewart Gordon, *The Marathas 1600–1818*, Cambridge: Cambridge University Press, 1993, 126–7.

27 'The Emergence of an Indigenous Business Class in Maharashtra in the Eighteenth Century,' *Modern Asian Studies*, 16(3), 1982, 427–443.

28 J.F. Richards, 'The Hyderabad Karnatik, 1687–1707,' *Modern Asian Studies*, 9(2), 1975, 241–260.

29 Karen Leonard, 'The Hyderabad Political System and its Participants,' *Journal of Asian Studies*, 30(3), 1971, 569–582.

30 Sanjay Subrahmanyam, 'Warfare and State Finance in Wodeyar Mysore, 1724–25: A Missionary Perspective,' *Indian Economic and Social History Review*, 26(2), 1989, 203–233.

31 Nikhiles Guha, *Pre-British State System in South India: Mysore 1761–1799*, Calcutta: Ratna Prakashan, 1985.

32 *British India Analyzed: The Provincial and Revenue Establishments of Tipu Sultan*, London: E. Jeffrey, 1793, vol. 1, 90.

33 A. Ibrahim Kunju, 'Relations between Travancore and Mysore in the 18th Century,' *Proceedings of the Indian History Congress*, 23 (II), 1960, 56–61.

34 R. D. Choksey, *Economic Life in the Bombay Gujarat (1800–1939)*, London: Asia Publishing House, 1969.

35 Crispin N. Bates, 'The Nature of Social Change in Rural Gujarat: The Kheda District, 1818–1918,' *Modern Asian Studies*, 15(4), 1981, 771–821.

36 R. Rana, 'Agrarian Revolts in Northern India during the Late 17th and Early 18th Century,' *Indian Economic and Social History Review*, 18(3–4), 1981, 287–325.

37 Tod, *Annals and Antiquities*, vol. 1, 510

38 Tod, *Annals and Antiquities*, vol. 3, 1432.

39 Madhavi Bajekal, 'The State and the Rural Grain Market in Eighteenth Century Eastern Rajasthan,' *Indian Economic and Social History Review*, 25(4), 1988, 443–473.

40 Harbans Mukhia, 'Illegal Extortions from Peasants, Artisans and Menials in Eighteenth Century Eastern Rajasthan,' *Indian Economic and Social History Review*, 14(2), 1977, 231–45.

41 *The State, Landlords and Peasants: Rajasthan in the 18th Century*, Delhi: Manohar, 1990.

42 Alam, *The Crisis of Empire in Mughal North India: Awadh and the Punjab, 1707–48*.

43 Khushwant Singh, *A History of the Sikhs. Volume I. 1469–1839*, Princeton: Princeton University Press, 1963.

44 Andrew Major, *Return to Empire: Punjab under the Sikhs and British in the Mid-Nineteenth Century*, New Delhi: Sterling, 1996.

45 Feroz Ahmed, 'Agrarian Change and Class Formation in Sindh,' *Economic and Political Weekly*, 19(39), 1984, A149–A164.

46 Ainslie T. Embree, 'Napier, Sir Charles James (1782–1853),' *Oxford Dictionary of National Biography*, available at https://doi.org/10.1093/ref:odnb/19748 (accessed on 16 December 2020).

47 A.D. Innes, *A Short History of British in India*, London: Macmillan, 1919, 279.

48 J.B. Bhattacharjee, 'Lord Dalhousie on Naga And Garo Policy: The Non-Interventionist Face of an Expansionist Governor General,' *Proceedings of the Indian History Congress*, 61(I), 2000–2001, 612–616.

49 F.W. Buckler, 'The Political Theory of the Indian Mutiny,' *Transactions of the Royal Historical Society*, 5, 1922, 71–100.

50 These were not exclusive alternatives; in fact, statism would be impossible to attain without the capacity to perform militarism. Therefore, a militarily weak regime would have no choice at all.

3

STATE CONSOLIDATION

The shift in the military power balance described in Chapter 2 shaped Indian economic history in three ways. First, it led to the rise of European rule, a rule by a merchant company intent on integrating the business worlds of Europe and Asia, India and China, and overland and overseas trades. No regime quite like this one Indians had experienced before. Coastal-deltaic states were often outward-looking and friendly towards maritime traders. But no coastal-deltaic state had ever extended its power deep into the fertile Gangetic plains. Second, warfare had deprived large parts of the region of roads, famine and flood relief, safety and security. The third effect followed the East India Company's transformation from a trading body to governing power. In the process, the Company changed from a trader to a facilitator of trade; and an opportunistic political actor to a government. The transformation occurred through Parliamentary regulation on governance and lobbying by its competitors to end the monopoly charter (see also Chapter 5). As a government, the Company state went further than any contemporary regime in specific fields. For example, it redefined property right as an ownership right and was readier than most Indian states to intervene in commercial law.

This chapter is about the three types of change that followed from the political shift – the start of a new form of commercialization, attrition of certain types of public goods, and the remaking of public goods.

The decline of the East India Company as a business

The Company was still a business when it acquired a share of the revenues of Bengal in 1757. For some time, it was trying to change its business practice by moving away from procurement of goods via merchants-cum-brokers to direct purchase of goods through salaried employees. The change began in Bengal in 1753, and the Company Directors noted that it was a better system for coordination. Artisans, on the other hand, complained that the new system was oppressive. Whether it was more oppressive because the salaried agents sometimes used force or bilateral contracts bound the artisans securely to the Company, it is not known.

The immediate effect of the victories over the French (the battles around 1760) and the Dutch (a smaller engagement in 1759) was a disruption of the French trade and growing dependence of the Dutch upon the British for their trade. This situation left the British Company in a dominant-buyer position and consequently increased the salaried agents' coercive power.

Another significant change that followed British victory in 1757 was an immediate stoppage of the import of bullion. The Company could expect to use a part of the territorial revenues for the purchase of export articles. The Directors approved of that practice. It amounted to asking the peasant to pay the artisan, while the Company pocketed the trading profits. This was a scam. But it had neither much significance nor much impact. The Company trade formed a tiny proportion of the economy, even Bengal's economy. The use of territorial revenues for the trade would have occurred on a tiny scale too. It could not continue beyond a few years because the revenue was needed to conduct warfare in India. As early as the 1760s, possibly half to two-thirds of the Bengal revenues went into the fortification of Calcutta, Madras, and other settlements inland.[1]

In the absence of good accounts or budgets, the stoppage of silver imports can be confused to mean the use of tax to finance trade. '[T]he end and purpose' of British conquest of Bengal, Irfan Habib asserts, was 'to enable Britain to obtain Indian goods without any export of treasure in return.'[2] The truth is, all European companies, including the French and the Dutch, stopped importing silver from the 1750s. They had greater access to credit in India and relied on drafts and remittance instruments more.[3] European companies and private traders were emerging as the biggest clients of the bankers of Kasimbazar (see Map 2.2). Further, the Company's imports (especially metals and arms) were beginning to succeed as conflicts spread in India. And finally, the Company's political victory encouraged private trade, which did not fund trade with taxpayers' money. All of these effects steadily reduced the firm's commercial importance.

From the late 1760s, the Company's reputation as a business took a severe hit from the corruption scandals. A few individuals, including Robert Clive, profited lavishly from the conquest of Bengal. The Company's gain was a temporary one and soon lost due to a cycle of warfare. Its share prices fell continuously. Critics of the firm lobbied the Parliament for greater state control of the governance of the Indian territories. There was a limited attempt in 1772, followed by a more significant move in the shape of the 1784 India Act. The Act set up a body, the Board of Control, to rule British India. The Board had representation from the Company and the Parliament. The Company ruled as an agent of the British state. An implicit state guarantee saw its shares rise again, though its business continued to fall.

A fundamental break in statecraft took place in the last quarter of the eighteenth century. This break occurred in two senses: the Company fought using its army and relied less on landlords for the purpose than did the other regimes, and the new state raised the efficiency and taxable power of the land, thanks to this reduced dependence on landlords. What made this break possible?

Building the fiscal foundations of the state

Even after adjusting for changes in the territorial extent, there was a big rise in revenue in the British territories. In Bengal, revenue per square mile increased from Rs. 236 in 1763, to 520 in 1817, and 724 in 1853. This was a considerable rise in real terms. In the last quarter of the eighteenth century, as the revenue flows to the principal Indian states tended to fall even without territorial losses, Bengal's revenues increased from Rs. 26 million in 1763 to a little over 30 million on average in the 1770s, to accelerate rapidly after that.

What was all that money used for? It was used for military build-up first and foremost. The proportion of military expenditure in total expenditure was exceptionally high for all major states in India in the second half of the eighteenth century – between half and three-quarters. Several of the prominent Indian states, as they fought more battles, shrunk in revenue earnings and the army's size (Tables 3.1 and 3.2 on comparative data on state capacity). The Company managed to raise its revenue and the military's size while continuing the war effort over many decades (Map 3.1).

The divergence shows up in the emerging pattern of control over regional resources. With its strategic base in the seas, the Company had secured itself in the littoral and deltaic zones. The land was the chief tax source because the Company decided to rely little on inland customs and removed these altogether. The productivity of land varied enormously between the Indo-Gangetic Basin and the dry interior. Regions with higher land yield generated more revenue per square mile. The Company was fortunate in taking control of Bengal, a rich area of India.

TABLE 3.1 State income, 1667–1853 (million £)

	c. 1667	*1707–09*	*1764*	*1800*	*1818*	*1853*
Revenues of all states in India	26	38	–	22–29	–	34
British India	–	–	3	8	13	21
Indian states	26	38	–	14–21	–	13
Major Indian states (before annexation)						
Awadh	0.8	0.9	–	0.8	–	1.4
Hyderabad	–	2.8	–	–	–	1.5
Bengal, Bihar, Orissa	3.6	2.8	2.6	–	–	–
Peshwa	–	–	4.0	4.0	1.6	–

Sources and methods: Construction of the table and the dataset it draws on are explained more fully in Tirthankar Roy, 'Rethinking the Origins of British India: State Formation and Military-fiscal Undertakings in an Eighteenth Century World Region,' *Modern Asian Studies*, 47(4), 2013, 1125-56.

TABLE 3.2 Revenue in four British Indian territories and two princely states, 1850

	Revenue per square mile	Revenue per person
Bengal Presidency	510	2.5
North Western Provinces	563	1.3
Madras Presidency	375	2.3
Bombay Presidency	372	4.0
Hyderabad	174	1.4
Mysore	224	N.A.

Source: Edward Thornton, *A Gazetteer of the Territories under the Government of East India Company and the Native States on the Continent of India*, London: W.H. Allen, 1854.

MAP 3.1 Political divisions, 1930 (shaded areas belong to princely states or autonomously governed territories).

Awadh, a late acquisition, was also tax-rich. On the other hand, Mysore, Berar, Bundelkhand, Punjab, or Hyderabad yielded per head tax that was half or a fourth of the levels in Awadh and Bengal.

Access to larger revenues did not mean that the Company could finance wars from its income, but it did mean that it was more creditworthy. Credit was also critical to the Maratha state finance and any of the other states of the time. There was, however, a difference between British territories and their Indian rivals in the manageability of their debt burden. The debt service ratio to the net income of the Indian states was high, reaching a third in the Peshwa's territory in the 1760s. In British India in the 1810s, debt service as a proportion of revenue was much smaller than this and fell steadily to a manageable level. Access to more extensive and more stable revenues, and a favourable debt–income ratio, enabled it to expand the regular army between the Mysore and the Sikh wars. In contrast, among its rivals, there was a trend towards increasing dependence on mercenaries.

Just pointing at the Company's convenient access to the tax resources of Bengal and Awadh begs the question: why did the Bengal and the Awadh Nawabs not set up the next empire in India? The Company had no obligation to defend an indigenous military heritage. The fact that it came from a (European) world that had been adapting to constant wars through the centralization of finances and conscriptions made it readier than any Indian state of the time to try to concentrate power rather than distribute it away among warlords. Most Indian states knew of no other model to carry on warfare except to give away sovereignty and taxation rights to regional chieftains. The resource-poor among them did not have a choice in the matter.

Thus, while all states relied on territorial expansion to raise their incomes, the process could have different outcomes on the internal politics of states. In most indigenous states, conquest empowered the military aristocracy who shared the fruits of the new acquisitions and thus weakened the centre. In Company-ruled Bengal, conquest strengthened the centre, supported by a standing army. The Indian states had a heritage to live with, namely, shared sovereignty with communities and individuals who supplied useful services. Conflicts, therefore, led them to give away more powers. The Company set out to neutralize the intermediaries, whereas the Indian regimes depended ever more on them. The Company needed the landlords' loyalty less than did the others and subdued them by a capitalistic weapon, the land market. Simultaneously, persistence with shared sovereignty weakened the Indian states in the face of sustained conflict. This difference showed up in the statistics on how much money the state could wrest from the local tax collectors, such as zamindars.

Comparisons between Mughal state finances and the East India Company's finances as a state would illustrate the rupture well. Mughal practice was the model for almost all states in India until the rise of British power, and for some time for the latter as well. It is a well-known fact that only a fraction of the revenues the Mughal state claimed to be its due reached the central treasury, the rest retained as salary assignments. These assignments were like a contractual lease of state offices, rather than bureaucratic employment; to that extent, they represented a sharing of sovereign authority. The degree of control was variable. According to John Richards, 24–33% of the total revenue ('effective jama' in his words) in 1595 came from crownlands, which the imperial establishments lived on. 'All remaining revenues were shunted directly to the holders of salary assignments.'[4] The collection-to-assignment ratio above also suggests the distribution of military and government power between the central state and the provinces and regions. It would measure the extent of concentration or decentralization of power. Around 1600, the ratio was between 1:3 and 1:4.

In the logic of things, in times of wars and rebellion, the central state's reliance on assignees increased, and the centre could, in principle, lose control over the allocation of offices altogether. Something like this transpired in the mid-1700s in most states that succeeded the Mughal Empire. A recent measure of revenue collected over time shows that in money as well as in real terms, this figure fell in the eighteenth century. According to Broadberry et al., real revenue collection in all of India in 1766 was as low as 6% of what it was in 1600, suggesting attrition of state capacity to an extraordinary degree. After 1766, there was a sharp recovery, and in 1871, the real collection was above the 1600 level.[5] In other words, whereas both the Mughal and the British Empires succeeded by wresting state capacity from the regional warlords, the period intervening saw a regression. The recovery happened on the back of greater centralization of the state finances. The Company abolished the salary assignments, retaining very few merit-based ones. It raised the ratio of federal to provincial revenue to 1:1.

Securitization was another element in the story. Mughals obtained their revenues from 'plunder, tribute, and taxation.'[6] Their budgets had only a current account. Revenues grew by territorial expansion. 'Plunder from victory swelled the imperial reserves.'[7] Military conquest 'repaid the costs.'[8] When there was peace, 'additional taxes levied' raised extra money. This was essentially a redistributive fiscal system; it had no inherent flexibility to grow without wars and conquest of territory. The Mughal cities had big banking firms, bankers financed trade, and sometimes funded office-holders' temporary deficits. But public debt and bankers' capital did not play a systematic role in public finances. Karen Leonard suggests that the withdrawal of credit by 'great' banking firms hastened Mughal collapse. Richards criticized the thesis for the lack of evidence, either on banking firms or on balance sheets.[9] It may be that the bankers' main clients were the local salary assignment holders rather than the imperial state, in which case, evidence would be difficult to find. In any case, securitization of debt existed neither in Mughal India nor among the successor states.

For much of the eighteenth century, the Company ran a similar setup in India; that is, deals between bankers and the state were localized, individualized, and sporadic rather than being mediated by the budget. The eighteenth century saw so many conflicts in India that wars needed to be financed by territorial conquest, engendering more wars. A merchant firm, the Company was readier to borrow and was a more credible debtor than most warlords and landlords.

From 1800, debts started being securitized. Public debt was a legacy of the Anglo-French wars at the turn of the nineteenth century. Debt volume began to rise. During the Burma wars (1824–26), the Company floated a large loan.[10] This was a new development because a loan of such size was taken by the public rather than by bankers. Expatriates and wealthy Indians purchased the government securities. During the mutiny, 90% of the debt stock was held within India in this way. After the mutiny, as British capital started flowing into the railways, the government found it easier to raise money in London. After that, London's share rose rapidly. Throughout, Indian stocks carried a lower interest rate in London than in India, which justified the shift.

Military build-up

The Company's effort to raise revenue enabled it to form a standing army. Its rivals' armies formed of smaller standing armies and many more irregulars, mercenaries, and soldiers contributed by chieftains and warlords. In 1765, the Company's military expenditure was £1.5 million; in 1793, £3 million, in 1834 £7 million, and 1846, £12 million. It is hard to be exact, but it is likely that the army's share in expenditure was as high as 70–75% in 1765 and fell to around 35 in 1856. The scale still increased. It increased so much that the British Indian state could insist upon practically a freeze upon the military capacity of all Indian states of the time, effectively standing guarantee to their defences.

The standing army originated in the troops raised and maintained in Bengal, Bombay, and Madras. They were known as the Presidency Armies. From the mid-eighteenth century, British regiments went to fight in India. Until 1784, the expense of British regiments in India was paid from the British budget; after that, the Board of Control could hire British regiments and pay the cost with Indian revenue. Limits were set on the numbers to be hired from Britain. From the early nineteenth century, the army's cost was paid mainly from the Indian revenues. When the mutiny began, about 350,000 military personnel received pay from the Company. They consisted of British and European infantry, cavalry, artillery, and 'native infantry' regiments and battalions numbering over 200,000. The mutiny broke out among the native infantry.[11]

The Indian soldiers mainly came from a recruiting pool of peasants in the Indo-Gangetic Basin. From that pool, other north Indian powers too recruited soldiers. In the years before Buxar (1764), there was not much difference between the British and their rivals in the character of these forces, except (as mentioned) that the Company army fought under one command. In contrast, the larger troops of the Nawabs fought under divided command. As a small mutiny in 1764 showed, the Indian army was still a work in progress. During the eighteenth century, the Company relied on its small standing army and recruited soldiers from a range of local mercenary groups, as in Mysore.[12] However, the character of the Company's army changed very rapidly and moved away from the mercenary roots. For an idea of how much and how fast the scale of the military enterprise increased in the late eighteenth century, the army in the Battle of Udhuanala (1763) was a few thousand strong; that in the Third Anglo-Mysore war (1790–2) was over a hundred thousand strong.

After around 1800, military service was a fully paid job and not a part-time occupation as in earlier times. Invalid and retired soldiers were sent back to their villages with a land grant; the land served as a pension. The promise of a pension encouraged further recruitment from the same area. And increasingly, the military labour market turned monopsonist. Older forms of recruitment died away – 'with only one employer left, the role for brokerage, for labour agents and jobber-commanders (jamadars) dwindled to almost nil.'[13]

More than fighting with rivals, the army was crucial for the more difficult task of demilitarizing the population at large. It is tempting to think that South Asia's population, with its history of famines, migration, and the reliance of states upon part-time peasants and mercenaries, always had a significant number of people who were not formally soldiers but who carried arms. Like the north Indian ascetics Dasnami Sannyasis, the groups were farmers or bankers for part of the time and soldiers when needed. Ananda Bhattacharya calls them a 'transient and peripatetic political force.'[14] In the last decades of the eighteenth century, famines and demobilization of soldiers pushed a large number of armed people towards organizations like these, who tried to bargain with the rural magnates and state officers. The Sannyasis in Bengal were also moneylenders, and certain regulations upon moneylending had hurt their business interests. This context led to a series of what is often called the Sannyasi rebellion in Bengal. The nineteenth century and the end of the Maratha wars added fresh challenges as bands of former mercenaries like the Pindari regrouped and raided trade routes.

Reform of property right

The Company state was capitalistic. That is, not only did it believe, in common with other Indian regimes of its time, that private property like that on land deserved to be protected, but it also believed, unlike the Indian regimes, that making land easily marketable was necessary to encourage improvements in the productivity of land. It acted on that belief distinctly, recognizing only one kind of right on land – ownership – effectively derecognizing all other rights like the zamindar's right to collect a tax or the tenant's right to use land.

What was the Indian tradition that the new state wanted to change? Whereas private property in agricultural land was recognized, and land sale was in theory possible, in practice, such sale was not common at all (see also Chapter 4). Instances of sale can be found, but these were exceptions to the norm. The practical obstacle to land sale was the convergence of multiple interests on land represented by the warlords, the landlords, and the peasants. No one actor, not including the occasional revenue farmer, had an unencumbered right. If sales were at all possible, it was a sale of the specific right to the service of the land, not of the plot of land as such. A poorly defined property right did not mean that property was insecure. All of these agents needed to keep the peasant settled on the land. Arbitrary eviction was rare, as far as we can tell.

Evidence of recorded sale laws, courts, judges, and case judgements remains rare. Courts of law sponsored by the regional states had a sectarian character and were minimal in reach. Nawabi courts practised Islamic law and had almost no presence beyond the major towns. The engagement of these courts in the day-to-day affairs of the peasants, artisans, and merchants was rare. The peasant communities may have settled some disputes through community courts or panchayats that followed their own procedures. But nothing much is known about how solid these institutions were and what process they followed. No state actor needed to care about these bodies' constitution, and therefore, there is hardly any documentation on how they functioned and what kind of cases they settled.

Not entirely by design, the Company made changes on all fronts. It decoupled ownership of land from taxation rights and duties, secured ownership with a legal document, introduced judicial procedures, and set up a hierarchical system of law courts. If earlier both law and legal procedures had been decentralized into communities, now there was a divorce of procedures from laws. The judges in British Indian courts settled community disputes employing a new set of procedures that applied to all. Because the procedures had made the British Indian court the highest court of law, many disputes related to land and business began to come into the Company courts. State law penetrated society deeper than ever.

In the Bengal land market, these changes resulted in an immediate spike in the sale of large landed estates shortly after the Permanent Settlement of 1793. There was a rapid subdivision of such property. The peasant property or ryotwari institution in southern and western India (Chapter 4) made many administrators anxious that land would change hands rapidly as the peasants sometimes mortgaged land to borrow. Beyond the initial burst of sales, land sales in both zamindari and ryotwari regions were more restrained than the administrators had expected would be the case. Land served several functions in the countryside, insurance, security, prestige, and a provider of subsistence. The mere fact of a clear ownership title did not necessarily make land more saleable. In the ryotwari areas, the government intervened in the late nineteenth century with special laws to prevent land transfers between the indebted peasant and their creditors. This development happened beyond the book's timespan.

There was another reason why land was not easy to sell. There was a clear ownership title no doubt, but it was often held jointly by an extended family. The problem had owed to the particular conception of Indian common law that the Company officers and legal experts wanted to conserve. In the 1770s, when a discussion began about the principles by which India's newly acquired territories should be governed, Warren Hastings (Governor-General 1773–85) represented a lobby that believed that India should be governed by Indian law. The foundation of property and succession law was seen to be religious because Hindu and Islamic codebooks were full of injunctions about such subjects. Therefore, the Hastings project led to an attempt to register indigenous religious codes, gave employment to scores of legal scholars (pandits and ulemas), and saw the start of schools of Hindu and Islamic traditions in Benares and Calcutta. The project led to the compilation of some excellent code-books of law but failed in the courtroom and was effectively abandoned from the mid-nineteenth century. One reason for the failure was that the codebooks seemed to empower the family's rights to property and with the Hindus the rights of the agnate lines in the family, over individual rights and women's rights. That provision made sales difficult while increasing the potential for disputation among family members. In practice, the judges often departed from these norms.

So far, I have discussed the political transition in eighteenth-century India as a move from a failed to successful militarism. The states failed or succeeded by other benchmarks too. Conflicts had left a countryside bereft of the essential services that the precolonial states would normally supply to local communities and private enterprise. The rise of a British Indian state did not dramatically improve public goods' quality in the countryside. But it did succeed in reviving internal trade due to enhanced safety on the roads.

Internal trade: Decline and revival

As we have seen in Table 3.1, most states were over-committed on financing the military enterprise. The proportion of their earnings spent on the military was high by any benchmark and stayed high throughout. Therefore, the formation of a new state in the backdrop of warfare and extortion reduced all states' capacity to spend on non-military goods and services even if it stimulated the military demand for labour and food. While there was urban growth in the towns directly or indirectly connected to Indo-European business enterprise, these new towns did not have access to the overland trade routes that had earlier converged in the empire's core domains (see also Chapter 6).

Accounts of northern India's major towns contain many references to closing access to the former highways of traffic (see Chapter 6). Maratha raids in western Bengal, insurrections in Bihar, landlord revolt, Magh raids in eastern Bengal, and Ahmad Shah Abdali's campaigns in northern India severely disturbed the internal trade of Bengal, greatly reducing the scale of one of the most lucrative commodities in internal trade, raw silk, and reducing the wealth and organization of Kasimbazar merchants and bankers who lived on the trade.[15]

During the famines of 1770 and 1783, relief operations were rudimentary, possibly occurred on a worse scale than before (see also discussion in Chapter 4). Around 1800, archival documents on public works and travelogues report discoveries of abandoned large-scale river embankments near Patna on the Ganges, Cuttack on the Mahanadi, Sylhet on the Surma, Murshidabad on the Ganges, and disused four-teenth-century canals in the western Gangetic plains.[16] East India Company officers observed decaying tanks (manmade lakes) in the early nineteenth century, both large and small constructions everywhere in the Tamil countryside. An estimated 30,000 such tanks had once been in operation.[17] They presumed that the decline was the result of a decline in state power. North Indian canals had been unused for decades, even a century. Roads in the central uplands were unsafe, not least because of the local chiefs' constant demands for tolls. No one was in charge of the river and seafront embankments in Bengal. And the urban infrastructure of the major cities was in a state of collapse (see also Chapter 6).

The findings of a recent study on market integration are broadly compatible with this picture. The study finds that the extent of regional market integration was relatively small in the late eighteenth and early nineteenth centuries.[18] We do have accounts of overland trade. But the common examples available, such as food supplies by caravans for the armies, or cotton supplies for weavers serving foreign markets, relate to special markets and war-induced markets. The bullock caravan system's capacity towards the end of the eighteenth century was tiny compared with the estimated grain output of peninsular India (see Chapter 5).

In areas under British control, trade revived. Well-watered regions of the Indo-Gangetic Basin saw expansion in cultivation after the British takeover. Some of that expansion might have been due to high revenue pressures.[19] A little over fifty years after Buxar, the eastern part of the Indo-Gangetic Basin, a buffer between the Awadh state and British Bengal, saw a significant trade growth. The growth had owed to the opium and cotton trades, which attracted European and Indian investment. Two trading towns, Mirzapur and Ghazipur, rose to prominence, even as the towns located further west lost trade and people. In Mirzapur, trading profits flowed into artisanal industries and indigo processing. The small town on the Ganges emerged as an important place of settlement for European merchants and companies.[20]

A growth in cotton export trade from Bombay port to China from the end of the eighteenth century encouraged the migration of Parsi, Bhatia, and Marwari business families to the city. They brought with them experience in Asian trade and overland trade. The Marwaris were mainly bankers but moved into trade. British victory over the Marathas in 1818 brought a vast tract of cotton-growing region into direct link with the city and export market.[21]

Public goods in British India

Cutting out intermediaries in tax collection, I have shown, helped the British Indian state to raise more revenue. Although inland duties were reduced, salt and opium taxes were beginning to pay more. Much of that money went to the army. The other areas of intervention received considerably less finances, but some had an impact disproportionate to the amount of money spent. These areas included currency, canals, law and justice, education, and embankment construction. By 1857, a beginning was made in setting up a postal system, a railway network directly funded by private investment and indirectly funded by the budget, and the telegraphs. But most of these developed in the second half of the nineteenth century.

Around 1799, three major currencies were in circulation, and numerous minor ones. The three were Bengal silver rupee, the Arcot silver rupee, and the Madras gold pagoda.[22] Smaller local exchanges used copper coins or cowries (a type of seashell). The Company's attempt to make the Bengal rupee the only legal tender did not find favour because the gold–silver price ratio varied between Madras and Bengal. In 1835, a silver rupee of uniform weight came into circulation throughout the region. The announced exchange rate between the rupee and the pound sterling was 10:1.

Canals were another area where the state became active. It was apparent to any ruler of this tropical-monsoon region where famines were a common occurrence that the only way to prevent famines was to store water for the dry months and recycle water from the perennial rivers to regions of scarcity. Engineers in the British Indian army wrote about disused canals in the southern deltas and the Indo-Gangetic Basin and proposed plans to revive and develop more of these. The restored works appeared on the Jumna (Yamuna, 1817–1840s), the deltas of the Cauvery (1830s and 1840s), Godavari and Krishna (1840s and 1850s). An accent on large riparian projects may have led to a neglect of local storage systems like tanks in the Tamil Nadu region.[23]

As mentioned before, in legal matters, the state persisted with indigenous law, mainly because the officers believed they had found in Sanskrit and Persian-Arabic codebooks a hint of common law.[24] The state stuck with tradition only in property law, especially land ownership, succession, and inheritance. Commercial law, such as a contract or negotiable instruments or company law, was less burdened by respect for tradition. In this sphere, a state keen to develop trade was also keen to achieve uniformity between British law and Indian law, and legislators freely imported British and Western models. This drive, however, took off after 1858.

Until then, disputes between European traders and Indian merchants and producers were quite frequent. At times, the Company officers and private European merchants felt powerless to enforce contracts in the absence of a judiciary and laws that could admit commercial disputes of such nature.[25] Indian businesses settled some of their disputes informally by resorting to community courts. But many new business groups, such as the Europeans, were not part of these communities. Therefore, in Indo-European trade, attempts to protect capitalist interests usually involved striking deals with the Indian headmen and brokers and leaving the contract's enforcement to whatever authority these agents commanded over the producers. That hands-off approach led to abuses by the intermediaries and strengthened the demand for commercial laws. The outcome was a series of commercial laws instituted soon after Crown rule began in 1858.

In property law, respect for Indian tradition created new problems. The precolonial system of courts did not leave many documents to show how traditional law worked in practice. The British rulers only followed codebooks. But these religious codes did not agree on most matters. Further, religious law was often iniquitous and unfair because it upheld the privilege of caste, community, joint family, and the family's male members as property owners.

While these anomalies raised the legal system's disputatious potential, more disputants were encouraged to come to court because of judicial reform. The Royal Charter of 1726 sanctioned the principle that anyone living in the territories under the Company's control and seeking redress under English law could do so. In the port cities, Mayor's Courts tried cases involving European residents. The Royal Charters became more detailed from then on. The 1774 one allowed a Supreme Court to be established in Calcutta. At that time, the Nawab Nazim courts, or the Nizamat courts, administered criminal law. The Company established civil courts, which decided cases according to the personal laws of the Muslims and the Hindus. From the late eighteenth century, the criminal and civil courts tended to merge, and by 1860 a hierarchical system of courts had emerged. At the top was a Supreme Court, where the judges were Crown appointees and recruited from Britain. In the provinces, mainly Indian judges decided cases according to religious law. The language of the local courts was Persian rather than English. By the 1840s, there was much less support than before for Persian language courts and traditional religious law. The judges often departed from religious codebooks to settle cases between Indian parties.

The accent on Persian and Sanskrit codes as the basis for laws had led to state sponsorship of classical Indian education since Warren Hastings' times (the 1770s). The general population, especially the literate or business-oriented peoples of the port cities, did not care about classical Persian and Sanskrit education. They thought it was too literary and remote from the needs of the time. Indigenous schools did exist but were never open to all castes and rarely educated girls. As traditional education was devalued in the early nineteenth century, these schools suffered a serious decline. Where they could, the richer Indians sponsored English education or home-schooled their sons. Although the orthodox Hindus like Radhakanta Deb and reformist Hindus like Rammohun Roy debated publicly on social conduct matters, the elite Hindus, without exception, 'ranging from wealthy merchants to the Rajaguru from Nadia, was in favour of English education.' Their only worry was missionary interference in the spread of education.[26] The Company, too, broadly speaking, was wary of the missionaries.

This elite set warmly welcomed a manifesto about state sponsorship of mass education that the English scholar–writer Thomas Macaulay drafted in 1835. Macaulay said in the manifesto (known as 'minute') that the state should sponsor only secular and scientific knowledge in schools. He also dismissed Indian learning as worthless despite being ignorant of the subject. Wealthy and influential Indians forgave him for that lapse and supported the ideological stance that Macaulay advocated. Government spending on education increased. Most leading institutions set up in the cities received significant private sponsorship too.

Princely states

A scholarship exists on the larger princely states' political history – Mysore, Hyderabad, Travancore, and Baroda. Mysore was a semi-independent state from 1799 until 1831, when following a peasant revolt, British India administered it. Hyderabad, Travancore, and Baroda had an undisturbed princely rule until the mutiny. None of these major states joined the mutiny, making for a degree of continuity in the rule.

Their survival as independent states in the nineteenth century depended on a one-sided treaty with the British and the British-appointed Resident's watchful eye in the capitals of the states. From the very small number of studies available on their institutional history, one would think that the continuity of princely rule secured by a defence treaty with British India made for institutional inertia. This is a misreading. What happened was that the Resident's authority in policy-making increased significantly, and it was not in the interest of the Resident to make a radical institutional change. Almost everywhere, the British took a hard and close look at the kingdoms' armies, and where necessary, changed its composition to remove anything perceived as a threat. In Baroda, the military reforms weakened some of the traditional mercenary groups and weakened the bankers who financed the state.[27]

Despite this bias against reform, the states did do continuous experiments with their land revenue systems. Revenue farming was widespread in Hyderabad, Mysore, and Baroda. But the participants in the process changed often. Hyderabad, which drew most of its income from agriculture, designed a modified ryotwari system. Some of these experiments with the landed property will figure in Chapter 4. Not much systematic knowledge exists in other fields of reform – law, education, irrigation, roads, monetary system, and internal security. Some of these states forged ahead in overseas and overland trade and banking, but much of that development happened from the turn of the twentieth century.

Conclusion

There is sufficient statistical data to suggest that a deep economic decline occurred in the eighteenth century. We cannot be sure of where and when it was at its worst. We can be sure of the causes. Warfare eroded state capacity to spend on non-military heads. The universal condition at the end of the 1700s was disused canals, embankments in disrepair, unsafe roads, overland trade in disarray, and urban decay. The rise of Company rule in one corner of this world made little difference. But it did initiate an institutional change and encouraged trade. The emergence of the Company as a state rested upon building an enormous and highly efficient military machine that the state had full control over – a departure from tradition in this region. The other side of that development was a change in property rights. As legal reforms divorced property ownership from obligations to collect taxes or supply arms, the landlords and peasants gained saleable assets but lost military power.

Did the process of state formation affect peasant property rights? Did these effects have any bearing on agricultural production? Chapter 4 considers these questions.

Notes

1 Soumitra Sreemani, 'Problems of Writing a History of Calcutta of the Late 18th Century,' *Proceedings of the Indian History Congress*, 59, 1998, 579–586.
2 'Studying a Colonial Economy – Without Perceiving Colonialism,' *Modern Asian Studies*, 19(3), 1985, 355–81, cited text on p. 358.

3 K.K. Datta, 'India's Trade with Europe and America in the Eighteenth Century,' *Journal of the Economic and Social History of the Orient*, 2(3), 1959, 313–323.
4 J.F. Richards, *The Mughal Empire*, Cambridge: Cambridge University Press, 1995, 77.
5 Stephen Broadberry, Johann Custodis and Bishnupriya Gupta, 'India and the Great Divergence: An Anglo-Indian Comparison of GDP Per Capita, 1600–1871,' *Explorations in Economic History*, 55(1), 2015, 58–75.
6 Richards, *Mughal Empire*, 68.
7 Ibid.
8 Ibid.
9 Karen Leonard, 'The 'Great Firm' Theory of the Decline of the Mughal Empire,' *Comparative Studies in Society and History*, 21(2), 1979, 151–167; J.F. Richards, 'Mughal State Finance and the Premodern World Economy,' *Comparative Studies in Society and History*, 23(2), 1981, 285–308.
10 Douglas M. Peers, 'War and Public Finance in Early Nineteenth-Century British India: The First Burma War,' *International History Review*, 11(4), 1989, 628–47.
11 T.A. Heathcote, *The Military in British India: The Development of British Land Forces in South Asia, 1600–1947*, Manchester: Manchester University Press, 1995.
12 Mesrob Vartavarian, 'An Open Military Economy: The British Conquest of South India Reconsidered, 1780–1799,' *Journal of the Economic and Social History of the Orient*, 57(4), 2014, 486–510.
13 Dirk H.A. Kolff, 'Peasants Fighting for a Living in Early Modern North India,' in Erik-Jan Zürcher, ed., *Fighting for a Living: A Comparative Study of Military Labour 1500–2000*, Amsterdam: Amsterdam University Press, 2013, 243–265.
14 Ananda Bhattacharya, 'Reconsidering the Sannyasi Rebellion,' *Social Scientist*, 40(3/4), 2012, 81–100.
15 Rila Mukherjee, 'The Story of Kasimbazar: Silk Merchants and Commerce in Eighteenth-Century India,' *Review*, 17(4), 1994, 499–554.
16 For discussion and some of the citations, see Tirthankar Roy, *Natural Disasters and Indian History*, New Delhi: Oxford University Press, 2012, Chapter 3.
17 David Mosse, 'Colonial and Contemporary Ideologies of "Community Management": The Case of Tank Irrigation Development in South India,' *Modern Asian Studies*, 33(2), 1999, 303–38.
18 Roman Studer, 'India and the Great Divergence: Assessing the Efficiency of Grain Markets in Eighteenth- and Nineteenth-Century India,' *Journal of Economic History*, 68(4), 2008, 393–437.
19 Anita Prakash, 'Indigenous Knowledge System and Colonial Intervention in Central Doab in Early Nineteenth Century - Some Observations,' *Proceedings of the Indian History Congress*, 70, 2009 2010, 113 120.
20 Neha Lal, 'Mirzapur: Did the Railways Change its Commercial Narrative?,' *Proceedings of the Indian History Congress*, 76, 2015, 408–425.
21 Archana Calangutcar, 'Marwaris in the Cotton Trade of Mumbai: Collaboration and Conflict (Circa: 1850–1950),' *Proceedings of the Indian History Congress*, 73, 2012, 658–667.
22 Amiya Kumar Bagchi, 'Transition from Indian to British Indian Systems of Money and Banking 1800–1850,' *Modern Asian Studies*, 19(3), 1985, 501–19.
23 Prasannan Parthasarathi, 'Water and Agriculture in Nineteenth-century Tamilnad,' *Modern Asian Studies*, 51(2), 2017, 485–510.
24 Tirthankar Roy and Anand V. Swamy, *Law and the Economy in Colonial India*, Chicago: University of Chicago Press, 2016.

25 R.E. Kranton and A.V. Swamy, 'Contracts, Hold-up, and Exports: Textiles and Opium in Colonial India,' *American Economic Review*, 98(3), 2008, 967–89; Bishnupriya Gupta, 'Competition and Control in the Market for Textiles: Indian Weavers and the English East India Company in the Eighteenth Century,' in Giorgio Riello and Tirthankar Roy, eds., *How India Clothed the World: The World of South Asian Textiles, 1500–1850*, Leiden: Brill, 2009, 281–308.

26 Rajesh Kochhar, 'Hindoo College Calcutta Revisited: Its Pre-History and the Role of Rammohun Roy,' *Proceedings of the Indian History Congress*, 72 (I), 2011, 841–862.

27 M.A. Patel, 'Indigenous Banking into the Baroda State during the Closing years of the 18th Century and the Beginning of the 19th Century,' *Proceedings of the Indian History Congress*, 40, 1979, 768–773.

4
THE AGRARIAN ORDER

Control over land was the source of military and state power. The new state needed to act on that knowledge and strengthen its own position. What did it do? On the other hand, agricultural production and farmland productivity exerted the deepest influence on ordinary people's levels of living. Any change at the top, if it had an impact on cultivation, would affect peasant livelihood and well-being. What was the effect?

The key interventions by the new state had two overriding aims: demilitarization of the countryside and increasing the saleability of land. Any land-controlling magnate who maintained soldiers was potentially a threat. Where a substantial number of such people threw their weight around, the state needed to either repress them or offer them something in exchange of lasting peace. In the early acquisitions in Bengal and the south-eastern coast, the state offered them secure sole ownership right to land. In southern, western, and northern India acquired later, land fertility was not such as to accommodate many land-controlling magnates, and the state offered ownership rights to the peasants. All rights to land other than ownership were disallowed. Ownership, the expectation was, would make land more saleable and invite investment in land.

Not all of these expected outcomes realized. Overall, the demilitarization aim was successful. Warlord-type landholders retreated relatively speaking. Land became technically more saleable, but little investment followed. However, by suppressing the power of local chiefs, the new state did create conditions for smoother market integration in the territories it controlled. Agricultural trade in the eastern Gangetic plains recovered, as Chapter 3 has shown.

Despite changes in trading conditions, two structural features changed little, the geography and the agricultural village. The tropical monsoon conditions made water an expensive resource and offered limited scope for human interventions to raise yield. With the physical conditions of production unchanged, the collapse of states or the emergence of colonial rule made an insignificant difference in the situation of the village landlords, peasants, and peasant collective bodies. Neither demilitarization nor ownership represented a radical shift in the conditions of the peasants.

It is appropriate to begin the chapter by discussing the geographical and institutional setup and how it changed.

Geography

Tropical heat and the high evaporation of surface water made agriculture heavily dependent on monsoon rains. That dependence would make for one short season of cultivation, idleness in the rest of the year, and leave the peasant, landlord, or the state poor. Seasonality varied regionally. In the Indo-Gangetic Basin, fertile alluvial soil, the availability of rivers and channels that received Himalayan snowmelt and had water throughout the year, and easy access to groundwater made for intensive cultivation in many areas. In the peninsular, surface water was scarcer because snowmelt did not exist, and hard rock formations made accessing groundwater expensive. Still, in all regions, peasants faced many days of idleness in an average year.

The high seasonality of agriculture imparted two effects that might combine to add to political instability. First, many peasants in the region were available to join local armies as soldiers. The greater the dependence of agriculture upon the rains, the greater was the potential supply of part-time soldiers. Much of the Deccan Plateau was rainfed, where the Mysore and the Maratha armies recruited, drawing on this resource. And second, whereas in the Indo-Gangetic Basin, river floodplains, and deltas, easily accessible groundwater made intensive agriculture feasible, in the rest of India, arid conditions prevailed.

Mughal power concentrated in the Indo-Gangetic Basin. As the empire weakened, the combination of these two conditions increased the chances of attacks upon areas under intensive agriculture to coerce the political elite into tax-sharing arrangements. The solution to such a perennial threat would be to combine under a grand military alliance. The Mughals had designed one type of alliance – the British another. In between, predation and negotiation continued.

What difference did the instability make to the village?

The institutional setup before colonial rule: Landlords

In most regions at the end of the seventeenth century, the state was not a set of salaried individuals running a bureaucracy. Instead, it was a collection of the military elite, who hired individuals to keep accounts, collect taxes, carry out policing duties, and operate some of the courts of justice (see also Chapter 3). The elite's primary duty was the command of soldiers. Among those they depended on were the landlords, people with smaller military resources, and settled in or near the agricultural village. Landlords came in different forms. A useful distinction (after Eric Stokes) is that between secondary landlords, who commanded many villages and were more like military officers, and primary landlords, who were more like a substantial

FIGURE 4.1 'Zamindars and Rajas, of the Northern provinces of Hindustan.' A nineteenth-century sketch of a group of landlords, provenance uncertain. ©

cultivator. In north India, where there were more intensive cultivation and more surplus to support the elite, both types existed (Figure 4.1). Below these people, there were the actual tillers, sometimes functioning from within collective bodies that controlled common property such as grazing land or small irrigation works.

The right to individual plots of land was shaped by the state's share of the taxes, the secondary landlord's claim to repay the cost of running the revenue system, the primary landlord's share to repay the cost of looking after cultivation and collection of the taxes, and the peasants' share to repay the labour expended. Carrying out a sale of land entailed substantial transaction costs for any one party. It would be impossible to secure an agreement between all parties and achieve perfect compatibility of interest. Although the right was not readily saleable, property right was not necessarily insecure. Each type of interest wanted cultivation to continue normally and to expand when the state needed cash.

In the eighteenth century, two external forces upon the rural economy began to intensify; the first was the pressure of wars upon the state's fiscal needs. The second one was population growth. The demographic impact varied by region, and not enough is known about it; but there is data to show the effect when famines made a sharp difference in the balance between land and people. As the need for taxes increased, pressures from the top to the bottom layers increased. However, the top layer had little means to coerce the bottom layers. In most cases, the Maratha state system in Pune is a good example, the state negotiated with the local warlords, offered them incentives to encourage more cultivation, giving them more power instead of taking away their control.

The village or primary landlord was a more familiar figure in northern India than in south India. The military aristocracy was more extensive in scale, more complex and divided, and more distant from the countryside in the North. Further, large provinces of the Mughal Empire located in the Indo-Gangetic Basin like Awadh, Bihar, and Bengal felt the fiscal pressure less intensely than did the arid-zone states, Marathas or Mysore, leaving landlord power intact too.

In fact, as the central state's authority weakened either because it was preoccupied with warfare or because it was under attack, the landlord's position became somewhat more secure – a process called gentrification. Fiscal pressures at the top led to extensive revenue farming and dependence on anyone with the political means to collect taxes on behalf of the state. The zamindars in north India were such a set in the eighteenth century, which class now had some merchants and bankers who had joined auctions for tax contract. The primary or village landlords, too, may have gained from this process of empowerment.

Another side to the gentrification process was that the village-based landlord took more part in civil administration. The police and justice systems were effectively managed by the people whose authority bridged the village with the state. We may think that the community, or panchayat, ran the administration. It may have done so, but the likely scenario is that landlords controlled these bodies, and entry into the community was not open. As the elite's position became well defined, wealth inequality came to be expressed in terms of caste and other social status markers. Over much of the Gangetic plains, this tendency was observed and attributed to a similar set of causes. In northern and eastern India, the zamindars, in eastern Rajasthan, the bhomias, in deltaic southern India, the mirasdars, all had a superior form of right to land, commanded a relatively larger land area than that controlled by the ordinary peasant, and took some part in civil administration.

In parts of southern India, individuals who were somewhat more like officers appointed by the state called the shots in the village. For example, accountants possessed sufficient political resources to access the best lands or the peasants' free labour. If gentrification means empowerment of the village landlord, this process represents a form of 'de-gentrification' or empowerment of the state's officers.[1] These variations depended on the fertility of the land and the capacity to sustain a local landlord group. Landlords were rarer in arid zones, and village officers more common.

Revenue farming – or auctioning off estates to the highest bidder, was an extensive practice among all states from the late 1700s. The practice reflected the states' incapacity to erect a viable fiscal administration at the local level and their dependence on the banker and merchant for war finance. The Company administration in Bengal, in its early days, fell into this pattern of indirect engagement with the land, and much of the data that it collected in the third quarter of the eighteenth century dealt with the revenue grants. Ordinarily, tax farming need not make a great deal of difference to the peasants. But in Bengal, there was a difference. While it relied on the tax farmers, the Company did not trust them and wanted to avoid dealing with them. To verify if the intermediaries were doing their best or not, it collected more data on the land's productive capacity, setting out a mode of engagement with the peasant economy that was unprecedented in its reliance on local information.

The Maratha state in western Maharashtra also collected much information on land. It was a relatively young state headed by Brahmin scribes who liked paperwork. Under pressure, the state created a large number of new military-fiscal tenures. Documentation on these new land grants carried information on the peasantry but only in the second half of the century. This is also true for the Northern Circars, and increasingly the western Gangetic plains. That does not alter the fact that the overwhelming concern in administrative records throughout the late eighteenth century was negotiations between landlords and administrators rather than between peasants and administrators. While these negotiations continued, the administration tried to understand and control the production system (Bengal) or lost touch with it and lost control (western Maharashtra).

The landlords, warlords, and officers did not have much scope to drive the peasants harder.

The institutional setup before colonialism: Peasants

Nineteenth-century historians like James Tod believed that the struggle over revenue occurred at the expense of the cultivator. Most historians would now think that coercion upon the peasant played little systematic role in pursuing revenue. Many old agricultural areas were already taxed to the limits and could not yield more without reducing subsistence. The states did not have enough administrative control over the village to police individual cultivators. There was enough surplus land, and replacing one farmer with another would not be easy. New agricultural areas were short in hands. Peasants controlled production instruments such as ploughs, livestock, pastures, and water bodies and understood their use better than the warlords. If oppressed, they could relocate to another region that had available land. Such moves happened at a cost. But they were also costly for the oppressors. That such moves were relatively common in some regions is evident from the land rights structure that explicitly defined and accommodated a temporary migrant right. The migrant who developed land enjoyed privileged rights as opposed to migrants who came to the already cultivated land.

A 'fine web of checks and counterchecks,' one authority on eighteenth-century Deccan writes, ensured that the 'village level land revenue functionaries… could not push farmers beyond a point that was determined by bargaining strengths.'[2] The village escaped being turned upside down despite the frequent change of regime, warfare, and famines. The states pursued their revenue objective mainly via readjustments of their relationships with the landlords and warlords.

One element in this picture of relative solidity was the cooperative community, 'the internal domain' that was relatively impervious to external shocks.[3] Within the village, market exchange tended to be limited. Producers tended to cooperate, especially in such matters as maintaining irrigation works and bargaining with the moneylender, who was usually an outsider to the peasant society. The bonds of the community would have increased with the need for collective labour and collective bargaining. Cooperation did not mean equality. The community was never an egalitarian or a democratic unit. Usually, these formed of families bound by kinship relations so that systems of collective control of land, labour, and capital excluded the labourers and usually excluded the women.

Peasants were not immune to change. As mentioned before, incentives were offered to induce peasants to develop new cultivation settlements. Migrations were frequent, and sometimes a sign of distress. The peasant property right over land strengthened in the aftermath of famines that temporarily depopulated land. But famine and war could also weaken the migrants because of loss of working relationships, knowledge of the market, capital assets, and a variety of rights enjoyed by the settlers and denied migrants. Some distress-driven migrants came to developed and settled areas where not enough land was available. Losses also included lives and days of work sacrificed in the act of moving. We have no way of knowing what these costs were and how many migrants did not make it compared with those who could peacefully resettle into a livable new home. Still, a cultivable land frontier was available in the forests and steppes, which was a potential resource both for the state and the farmer.

Whereas many types of farmer migrations occurred in northern India, the movements took a specific character in southern India. Social historians of south India have made use of a distinction between rainfed dry regions and irrigated wet regions, associating the former with less hierarchy and inequality and the latter with more inequality.[4] The former zones were more likely to send people to the latter, mostly where the two zones were contiguous. Outside south India, in Rajasthan, arid tracts and relatively well-watered tracts were often next to one another, giving rise to emigration from the former and different patterns of inequality.[5]

From the end of the eighteenth century, the British Indian regime began to recast the landlord–peasant–state relationship under a new principle. What was the direction?

How institutions changed

The basic facts of these reforms are so well known that the subject does not need a lengthy restatement.[6] The reforms created a marketable property right by defining land ownership and disengaging property rights from tax-collection duties. Tax collection became a state office managed with salaried officers. By implication, the topmost layer in the old regime – the state – changed from a group of military nobles rewarded with land grants to an administration supported by the local police. Property as ownership right was recognized by new laws of ownership and inheritance and protected by the new law courts.

This broad movement took two forms. In Bengal, the Permanent Settlement or zamindari settlement (1793) delivered ownership rights to the secondary landlords, or zamindars, who were then prominent. Some were a potential threat to the

Company state. The delivery of ownership right carried a fixed tax obligation in money. Everywhere else, property rights went to one of the three claimants below the secondary landlord, the primary or village-based landlord, the peasant, or the peasant collective. These later land settlements came about after new territories in northern, southern, and western India went into the Company's hands in the wake of the Mysore and Maratha wars. The broad rubric was 'ryotwari' or temporary settlement with the peasants, and meant giving over ownership right to cultivators. In practice, the owner was an actual peasant, in the true spirit of ryotwari, or a prominent peasant (mirasdar in south India, bhomia in Rajasthan), a primary landlord more akin to the peasant than the zamindar of north India (malguzar in central India, talukdar in Gujarat), or a peasant kinship group (mahalwari or bhaiachara in parts of north India). The Company, thus, chose in one case the secondary landlord (the Permanent Settlement, 1793), and in another, the peasant, the primary landlord, mirasdar, officers, and tenant-cultivator (the Ryotwari Settlement, c. 1820) as the future holder of ownership right. It adapted to the initial conditions in the region.

Did institutional reform change production conditions? The best way to answer the question is to depart from generalizations and move into the regions.

Eastern India

Although the Ganges-Brahmaputra delta dominated its landscape, eastern India was a much more diverse territory than historians usually realize. The central axis of overseas commerce formed along the western river Bhagirathi, where the textile export business concentrated. Along the river Ganges, and to a smaller extent the other rivers, much grain also moved around. But beyond these riparian arteries of trade, in the forests or sub-Himalayan regions such as Assam, the eastern uplands, and vast tracts of forested lands in the interfluvial zones, little long-distance trade existed. Within the larger region, the better-connected lower Bengal delta and areas accessible by river transportation took part in commercialization that benefited from an interdependence between overseas and overland trades. In contrast, interior Orissa and Assam regions were cut off due to political instability.

In the Ganges delta, in the four decades after the Battle of Palashi or Plassey (1760–1800), grain trade expanded, credit relations penetrated deep, and zamindars provided incentives to induce expansion in the area of cultivation.[7] This commercialization gained from the early colonial rule, which, anxious to impose its authority on the landlord order, succeeded in weakening, if not removing altogether, some transit duties. Landlords founded new markets to earn income by taxing fixed markets rather than goods in transit.[8] Grain prices were rising.[9]

In this backdrop came the Permanent Settlement. We may think that the new system weakened the peasant cultivator. But that would be an exaggeration. The zamindars were squeezed by high tax demands made on them, and their distance from cultivation did not help them take control of cultivation either. Ratnalekha Ray suggested that some members of the emerging cultivating groups in possession of superior tenancy rights, called jotedars, were locally powerful enough to resist the zamindars' attempts to collect more rent and threaten eviction. The zamindars needed these groups. The argument led Ray to conclude that the new property rights in land 'long regarded as the propelling force behind a revolution in Bengali rural society, would appear to have effected a less fundamental change than is usually supposed.'[10] Such local power came from the fact that the land frontier expanded in some parts of Bengal, at times compelled by the state's demand for more money or arms to deal with the Maratha threat in western Bengal. A slow process of an eastward expansion was an even earlier trend, connected with the shift of the active river delta towards the east.[11]

In another reading, more market exchange had made the peasants more vulnerable.[12] They became dependent on creditors when they began buying and selling in volatile markets. This dependence increased the market power of merchants and bankers. How plausible these pictures are depends somewhat on how we read the long-term effects unleashed by the 1770 famine. The peasant empowerment story is not inconsistent with merchant empowerment. It is possible that the peasants gained in political power while losing market power; that some of them could claim and extract more privileged tenure in negotiating with the landlord, whereas they paid more in interest; or even that some peasants turned into merchants.

The 1770 famine owed to a combination of harvest failures and the diversion of food for the troops.[13] Western Bengal and drier regions suffered more. Recovery was quicker in the more water-rich eastern Bengal delta. In the winter of 1768, rains were scantier than usual in Bengal. The monsoon of 1769 started well but stopped abruptly and so thoroughly that the main autumn rice crop was scorched. The winter rains failed again. In the Bihar countryside, the repeated passage of armies through villages already short of food worsened the effects of harvest failure. Towards the end of 1769, rice prices had doubled over the previous year, and in 1770, prices were on average six times what they had been in 1768. Through the summer months of 1770, death was everywhere. The rains were heavy in the monsoon of 1770, but that brought little cheer among survivors. Emaciated and without shelter from the rains, roving groups and families fell victim to the infections common during and after the rains. Large areas depopulated due to death, disease, and desertion. For several years after the famine, deserted villages, and villages engulfed in forests, were a common sight, and piracy and robbery in the Hooghly river delta became more frequent.

The state mishandled the famine. No state in these times had the infrastructure or the access to information needed to deal with a natural disaster on such a scale. On top of that problem, this was not a normal state. The Company was in charge of taxation, whereas the Nawab looked after governance. The two partners did not trust one another. The situation meant that those who had the money did not have local intelligence. The standard custom was a tax holiday for the secondary landlord, expecting the benefit would be passed on to the primary landlord and onwards to the affected peasants. However, the Company neither knew nor commanded the secondary landlords' loyalty and distrusted the Nawab's officers' information on what was going on. Consequently, there was resistance to using this option, yet no other instruments were available to the Company to deal with the famine.

The famine shook up the balance of power between the cultivator and the landlord.[14] William Hunter cited contemporary accounts to describe a persistent and acute shortage of labourers, a sharp recovery in agricultural conditions despite a third of the lands remaining as waste, and a weakening of revenue farming. If valid, the famine strengthened the bargaining position of the peasants, especially those organized in collectives. This reading takes us nearer Ray's position. A common criticism of the Permanent Settlement was that it defined ownership right on land and devalued user rights. In reality, user rights were widely variable, and some of these superior user rights dated to the post-famine consolidation phase.

Unbroken population growth and migration of workers from the western uplands quickly restored the loss, and by 1850 began to put pressure upon the limited land resources of the delta. Even as the zamindars' property right in the land was defined better than before, auction and sale of zamindari increased, making their bargaining power weaker. Gradually these sales and subdivisions of large estates reduced, whereas population growth increased the demand for land.

Other large regions within eastern India had a very different history from the deltas. Assam and eastern Bengal did not suffer as bad a famine as did western Bengal, but an institutional change was in evidence. The Brahmaputra floodplains in Assam contained a stable wet-rice cultivation system reliant on compulsory military and labour service rendered by peasants in place of revenue remission. As the state structure weakened in the wake of military conflict in the second half of the eighteenth century, the service tenures decayed, with adverse consequences for the state's stability. After British takeover in 1826, a ryotwari settlement came into being. A more significant force of change came from the distribution of forested lands to tea planters under a new wasteland act, but the full effect of this development takes us beyond the book's timespan.

Orissa was under Maratha rule from the mid-eighteenth century until 1803. The regime relied on opportunistic revenue farming.[15] The states' desperate attempts to raise revenue from these regions, often with crude institutional means, owed much to the little income that could be had from the poor quality soil in the uplands in the first place. Transportation systems were either absent or in a state of collapse. On top of that, revenue was often farmed out to multiple claimants who then fought it out on the ground.

Western India

Frank Perlin says that military conflict in the eighteenth century stimulated the urban economy in western Maharashtra because soldiers spent more money on weapons and textiles.[16] Wars made somebody else worse-off and the soldiers better-off only if they survived. Many irregular soldiers earned nothing in between wars. Western Maharashtra did gain from tribute flowing in from Hindustan (Chapter 2).

The tribute stabilized what would otherwise have been a precarious fiscal system, one that was overly dependent on low-quality land, a tight labour market, and only a few tradable and taxable goods. The state became steadily poorer, more fractious, militarily weaker, and more indebted. Increasingly, it gave away its powers to the large holders of land grants inside western Maharashtra, and these grantees had limited access to the tribute money.

A chronological history of the peasant in the Maratha domain can build on the works of Mountstuart Elphinstone and James Grant Duff. These snapshots cannot be taken to represent all of the eighteenth century, but they are invaluable in drawing up a narrative of the later years. The key influences upon the peasants' economic conditions had not changed in any particular direction in the last 30 years of the Peshwa's rule. There is no evidence of changes in soil fertility, irrigation, sown area, migration, land market, grain trade, and bulk transportation. The indigenous revenue administration saw it to be in their best interest not to change the relationships in the village.

Grant's account suggests two general types of property rights in land, miras or permanent ownership and user right, and a variety of temporary user rights.[17] The Persian term 'miras,' literally heritage, is discussed more fully below. The miras right could be purchased, granted by the state officers or superior right-holders, or accrue from long usage (60–100 years of recorded occupation). The right was hereditary and transferable. Grant collected some sale deeds to claim that the miras right was saleable too. The deeds were not of sufficient number or frequency to suggest that sales were common. Miras, however, was secure from encroachment or arbitrary evictions.

Much of western India was a region scarce in labour and abundant in land. But groundwater was scarce and available between hard rock layers, land was of poor quality and required much effort expended over time to make it productive. Peasant labour, therefore, was valuable. Village officers protected these rights. 'Every village is a small state in miniature, and all the land in the country, with the exception of inaccessible mountains, or places wholly unfrequented, is attached to some one village. The boundaries of its lands are defined, and encroachments carefully resisted.'[18] A mirasdar, who had been absent for a long time, did not lose right over the property. And even absentees who remained untraced and did not claim any share of the produce for 60 years or more could return to the village and reclaim land if village records supported the claim.

Temporary rights were user rights without a long-established claim. These rights varied in the length of the contract and the amount of taxes collected. The two rights – miras and temporary – converged when a family had held temporary rights for a long time. The peasant offering to break new land or recultivate abandoned land would work under a temporary tenure. A stable state sure of its revenue officers' honesty and loyalty could adopt 'the usual means of very low and gradually increasing assessments' to develop cultivation in this way.[19] Temporary rights could also be found in land held by absentee mirasdars or by holders of military tenures (saranjam), merit tenures, and service tenures (inam).

Such forward-looking measures gave way from time to time to revenue farming, which produced quick results at the risk of upsetting the local order. Both Peshwa archives and the early colonial reports suggest a growing dependence of the state and warlords in the later years of the regime upon revenue farming arrangements.

They also note that the gifting away of the revenue offices did not crucially affect peasant property rights, even though there were attempts at times by the revenue officers to evict peasants.

Compared with western Maharashtra, our knowledge of conditions in Gujarat and Rajputana is somewhat limited. Dilbagh Singh's research on eastern Rajasthan suggests deteriorating agricultural conditions in the second half of the eighteenth century.[20] However, the picture is based on information on famines and warfare. Singh offers a detailed view of rural hierarchy and the relationship of a later time. In Amber, the first four decades of the eighteenth century saw expansion in cultivation and trade, whereas the death of Sawai Jaisingh in 1743 marked the onset of a turbulent time. After that, for almost 50 years, eastern Rajasthan suffered from attacks, famines, depopulation, depression, and trade disruption.

As the state became weaker and more dependent on resourceful local notables, a group of primary landlords, bhomias or bhumias, became more powerful than before. Consistent with the general pattern, the state and its agents offered secure rights to the peasants in most regions. Cases of dispossession for non-payment of revenue do not often appear in historical scholarship. The most common form of cultivation right in Mewar at the end of the eighteenth century was that of the Bhumia. Tod explained that the Bhumia was the tenant of the military lords and had a secure right to cultivate the soil, the security expressed in the term miras. The Bhumias organized in collectives that protected their rights to land. These rights survived political turmoil and change of regime. 'The Rana may dispossess the chiefs… he could not touch the rights emanating from the community.'[21]

Recent studies suggest a somewhat more complex scenario in rural Rajasthan in the late eighteenth century. There was not exactly a decline. The states in eastern Rajasthan grew increasingly anxious about controlling the peasant economy. This anxiety revealed itself in the shape of regulations and injunctions, and in turn, peasant communities' attempts to evade these measures. Simultaneously, the penetration of commerce and credit in the agricultural economy empowered some peasants and landlords.[22] Therefore, any impression that the peasantry suffered a political disequilibrium may still be in doubt.

Northern and central India

Like eastern India, the vast and ecologically diverse territory designated here as northern and central India did not follow one trajectory. Following Eric Stokes, three generalizations on peasant property in the Ganges-Jumna Doab, the most coherent subregion within northern India, seem possible.

First, the distinction between landlord and proprietor mattered. Landlord rights consisted of a rental share in exchange for military service, tax collection, and payment to the treasury. Proprietary rights consisted of cultivation rights. The two groups and the two types of rights often joined, not only in the landlord's demesne but also in those densely cultivated tracts of land where 'the landlord body dissolved into a body of proprietary cultivators.'[23] The landlord again disappeared in the less fertile and more water-scarce Bundelkhand. A small average product per person, and a small taxable income per person, made it harder for the landlord to extract enough income.

Second, for some time in the eighteenth century, a reshuffling happened in landlord rights, as many primary landlords or cultivating landlords had to confront the revenue farmers who had bought their way into tax collection rights. The former group, consisting mainly of Rajput lineages, survived the encounter, but suffered expropriation in some cases, more exactions at times, and almost everywhere, loss of control over tax collection rights. Where they survived, their scale of operation was reduced to the area over which they exercised cultivation right. The Awadh state and the Sindhias, increasingly dependent on the new groups that Stokes called 'magnates,' kept magnate power within limits. With the introduction of the Company's full proprietary titles, the magnates worked harder to strengthen their claim to ownership of the estates.

The third proposition concerns the groups of under-tenants who tilled the soil. Moving into informed speculation, Stokes said that in villages where the position of the primary zamindars was relatively secure, there was little change in the under-tenants' rights. The under-tenant position was also secure where cultivation did not yield a large surplus, and the secondary zamindar body was non-existent.

Did peasant property rights become more uncertain and exposed to rental pressure? Research on the Doab in the late eighteenth century suggests that this did not happen a lot. There was still an unexploited land frontier available in the submontane regions. The Chalisa famine of 1783–84 reduced the extent of cultivation and possibly the number of cultivators so that the end of the century more likely saw an extension of cultivation. Furthermore, the peasantry had at least three forms of defence against oppression. In the more insecure agro-ecological zones, the settled peasants organized themselves in communities, the members of which were connected by blood and marriage ties. These communities controlled common property resources, shared equipment, and shared tax payment obligations. In some villages, they contracted directly with the state officers and superseded zamindari right on the land. A second form of defence was the possession of arms. As discussed before, they supplied soldiers to both the regional army and increasingly to the Company's army. The third form of defence against extortion was migration.

In short, the structure of property rights in the Gangetic plains serves as the best illustration of the twofold pattern that this chapter began with – gentrification on the one hand and survival of peasants with little change on the other. There was limited entry and exit in both these spheres, as one would expect against broadly unchanged population growth (except after famines).

The main form of change in northern India came from the market. From the mid-eighteenth century, trans-regional demand for commercial products such as cotton, sugar, and silk grew. Indigo and opium soon joined these trades. There was an extension of cultivation. The volumes were limited, and the supply zones few and far between. Still, commercialization did induce inter-regional shifts in agricultural trade. As C.A. Bayly has shown, private resources such as labour and capital shifted from the Delhi–Agra region and Rohilkhand to the eastern Gangetic plains during the second half of the eighteenth century because the former region saw political instability, the decay of canals, and commercial decline. Thanks to the influx of merchant capital, migration of peasants, natural irrigation, and the Awadh and Benares states' relatively stable authority, cultivation grew in the eastern Gangetic plains. The agro-political landscape was not all uniform in the east, but all major subregions experienced growth in cultivation.[24]

Bayly suggests that parts of the western Gangetic plains experienced a fall in the water table due to climatic change in the eighteenth century.[25] The precise definition of the affected regions is not clear. If the conjecture holds, the increasing climatic stress added to the shift of resources towards areas with more stable resource conditions. Using Richard Fox's stylized account of the consolidation of Rajput peasant lineages, Bayly suggests that in the areas of agricultural expansion, hierarchical political structures emerged within the peasant communities that had led the move. New hierarchies served to achieve cohesion and discipline within the group and in negotiations with outsiders. Agricultural expansion stimulated nonagricultural enterprise. Consistent with these hypotheses, 'Benares was one of the fastest growing cities during the years 1750–90' (see also Chapter 6).[26]

Zones of expansion could throw tenancy contracts out of established custom. Meena Bhargava shows that when the Gorakhpur region in the eastern plains came into British hands in 1801, the gentry was made of Brahmin, Rajput, Bhumihars, and other upper castes and Sayyids, who had already monopolized the existing leases.[27] These classes dominated the land-ownership pattern that came into being after new property rights were introduced. The actual cultivators consisted of two inherited and hereditary rights to land, khudkasht and pahikasht, or permanent and temporary rights, respectively. The Company administrators debated the nature of the khudkasht right. Issues such as the extent to which it resembled ownership, or included implicit access to common property, or was hereditary, generated much discussion. The pahikasht was a less problematical category since these tenants had few privileges outside land use, but their case was complicated by the sheer numbers that had a technically insecure right.

Among the other major zones, Awadh, located in the middle Gangetic plains, contained some of India's most fertile lands. In the first half of the eighteenth century, it experienced agricultural and commercial expansion, stable and continuous rule, and the absence of warfare. Both political personages and capitalists migrated from the Mughal territories into Awadh.[28] The situation in the second half of the century was more disturbed. The Marathas showed that the Awadh state was militarily weak. Nor did it have the means to secure a stable contract with its main tax payers, the landlords and the peasants. The Company administrators noted that the state was losing its control over the taxpaying classes. The former ally, Rohilkhand, likewise had a brief phase of prosperity and stability in the middle decades of the century, deteriorating into a stateless chaotic insularity racked by a struggle for control.

Punjab fragmented into spheres of influence of military commanders. Between 1730 and 1760, Punjab saw invading armies cross and re-cross its borders on many occasions and was exposed to extortionate and imperialist moves by the Afghans and the Marathas on several of these. These conditions affected the agrarian order and disrupted trade and finance. One study claims that political fragmentation and disintegration did not change economic prospects in the second half of the eighteenth century.[29] The evidence on economic change is based on the inference that there was substantial continuity in local and regional institutions despite changes of rule.

Central India in this study consists of Bundelkhand, Malwa, Berar, and adjoining areas where Maratha factions ruled between 1730 and 1803. Maratha rule had only a thin presence, and the state officers collected what revenue they could from revenue farming arrangements and from tributary chiefs who stayed virtually independent. Governance was so thoroughly decentralized and the lack of information so complete that we cannot hazard any guess about long-term trends either in production or the institutional setup. For the territories under the control of the Bhonsale and Holkar branches of the domain, Berar and Chhattisgarh, little research has been done to reconstruct agrarian history. The lack of research reflects the scarcity of documents and the highly indirect nature of the rule. In the Raipur region of Chhattisgarh, the most fertile and well-cultivated part of Berar, the government gave away jagirs to the commanders. However, the jagir holders found it impossible to establish direct command over the estates' revenues.

In 1800, the government rented the subah of Chhattisgarh to a Maratha chief or subahdar, who gave out revenue contracts to substantial tenants, whose primary job was to collect rent from the peasants. This was done based on a plough tax, as there was not enough administrative control or information to establish a land tax. The tenants maintained small army units at their own expense. The subahdar's energy went to extracting rent from the tributary kings in the mountains, which could never be done smoothly. Conditions of the roads were poor, and the tenants taxed trades of all descriptions.

Nevertheless, some grain export did occur under Banjara leadership, who supplied the Maratha army. The remoteness and almost symbolic authority of the Maratha state in Nagpur were evident in the experience of a party of Company officers travelling (c. 1798) from Chunargarh to Rajahmundry. Although they carried the Maratha pass, the party was stopped every few miles by chiefs demanding a toll. These chiefs were, in theory, a tributary to the Marathas, but their actions revealed how little weight the pass carried in reality.[30]

Southern India

During the transition from Mughal to British administration, the revenue system of coastal Andhra region, formed of the Krishna-Godavari deltas and nearby areas, relied on tax farming. 'Little else is known from official records of how the government share was collected from the cultivators.'[31] Substantial cultivators and village accountants (karnams) were officially in charge of collecting and ascertaining village revenue and had access to the most fertile lands. Early colonial administrators reported that village officers coerced more impoverished peasants to make them cultivate more land than they were willing to do, to give up more grain for the state, or to meet the deficits of other villages. Against this backdrop, the Permanent Settlement started in 1803–4. Former revenue units were consolidated or broken up, and the rights to the taxes of these units changed into a legal property right. Were the peasants better-off? Not necessarily, though the start of major irrigation projects on the deltaic rivers in the 1840s changed the balance in their favour.

When the Company acquired Salem and Baramahal, the territory of uncertain extent ceded by Tipu Sultan in 1792 and located on Mysore's south-eastern border, the administrators carried out an exercise to discover the historical roots of property relations in the region. As in other areas, a hierarchy of farmers was discovered, and the hierarchy looked to be related to the position of landholders in the revenue system. Counterparts of the north Indian landlords were scarce in this region. But within the village, substantial farmers with access to more lands, better lands, and sometimes water sources were present.

Their rights to the lands were 'mirasi' rights. Miras was a Persian term popularized by Charles Harris, Collector of Tanjore at the end of the eighteenth century, to refer to what was then known as kaniatchi, a right to land that was saleable without permission from state officers. Being in theory saleable did not mean being sold often. Quite often, mirasi rights were rights not to a single plot but a share in the village land and changed hands. Sometimes the rightsholder was a group rather than an individual. The mirasi right, therefore, was often embedded in a notion of joint or shared right. Wealthier groups enjoyed such rights. States rewarded the headmen and community leaders with concessional land grants, and miras could arise from such functions.[32] The Company administration first tried to strike revenue collection deals with these people before moving to a direct contract with the cultivator.

With their firm commitment to unburdened ownership rights, most administrators did not like this form of joint tenure. Thomas Munro called it a system 'hostile to improvement,' meaning a barrier to the development of land and commodity markets. From 1827, ryotwari settlement in the Company's territories followed the rule of individual ownership right. Mirasdars or holders of mirasi tenure adapted to the change without significant disruption because their right was a quasi-private property. Prominent mirasdars became capitalistic landowning peasants. 'In political terms,' writes P.B. Mayer, 'the successful navigation of the mirasidars through the period of transformation ensured their continued place of dominance in rural society.'[33]

Underneath these semi-administrative classes, there were superior tenants, inferior tenants, and labourers. All classes of tenants were residents of the village where they worked, though some members of the subordinate tenant group worked outside their villages. The institutionalization of migrant rights aided peasants' circulation into a broader region, usually working on various tenancy arrangements. Further below, the labourers were like serfs or slaves. There was no distinct market for slaves in existence, but the right to own or use land for their subsistence was regulated.[34]

When we move from the dry Baramahal to the fertile and irrigated deltaic zone around Chingleput, lands that were ceded to the British by the Nawab of Arcot in 1760, we again encounter the mirasdar or kaniyachi. 'The Caniatchi,' wrote Tod, 'is the Bhumia of Rajasthan.'[35] However, the military service aspect had become weak in the Tamil country. The mirasi rights were often defined as a jointly held right in shares of village resources. It was not only a right over cultivable land but entailed with it shares of common resources.

In Baramahal and Chingleput, the introduction of the ryotwari tenure in the 1810s opened up a dispute over whose right should be privileged, the mirasdar or the tenant-farmer. The dispute moved through several phases between the 1810s, when the ryotwari was introduced, and the 1860s, when it had settled down to an established custom. The outcome of these disputes was a curtailment of the less tangible miras rights over the common property. Ownership rights sometimes went to the mirasdars, but mainly to the superior tenants.[36]

Further south in Tinnelvely or Tirunelveli, the mirasdar was analogous to a north Indian primary landlord. There was a hierarchy of rights between landowners and land users, mixed up with caste in the wet zones but more fluid in the arid zones.[37] In this region with a history of circulation of people, the spectrum of rights at the time of British occupation owed to the date of migration of peasants and the level of access to resources that the more recent migrants could expect. Consistent with this principle, in this semi-arid region, access to irrigation resources played a vital role in deciding the economic value of landed property.

Conclusion

Overarching a diverse pattern of change, five processes stood out. First, there was enormous fiscal pressure on all states in the late eighteenth century, which must have bore upon the village in some form. As far as we can tell, those landlords and peasant groups who could undertake the expansion of cultivable land gained, rather than lost, from being under pressure. The gains were not dramatic though.

The second process was demilitarization initiated by the new state. The more military power an agent possessed, the deeper was the change of circumstances for that agent. The weapon the new state wielded was the offer of ownership to the zamindar and similar magnates. The unintended consequence of the step was a disempowerment of the zamindar, not only militarily but also sometimes economically.

The third process concerns the peasant. Despite the states' growing bankruptcy, nowhere do we see evidence that the peasants became worse off. User rights to land were strong. It was relatively easy to migrate into and enter cultivation in an area where land was available. It was harder to exit cultivation because it was not easy to sell land. The physical conditions of cultivation did not change. Increasing fiscal pressure eroded the states' capacity to make worthwhile investments. In the presence of decaying roads, canals, dams, tanks, and retreating commerce in some regions, there was little the village could do in raising output or selling products. These conditions made the village in many areas impervious to political shifts. Villages in some of these zones retreated into a shell, protected from outsiders by peasant communities and primary zamindars.

Fourth, property right may have been secure, but the rights were poorly marketable. Colonial reforms deliberately aimed at the marketization of property by defining the property right as ownership alone. Did that make the peasant worse-off or better-off? Theoretically, it made the peasant worse-off in the zamindari area, but practically, most zamindars could not manage their estates without substantial peasants' collaboration. Elsewhere, clear ownership made no immediate or deep impact.

The fifth process concerns trade in agricultural commodities. During the timespan covered in the book, some zones saw a retreat of commerce, and others saw commercialization. The eastern Bengal delta, Benares, and Bihar were examples of market expansion. By contrast, mid-to-late-eighteenth century Punjab, Bundelkhand, Malwa, Chhattisgarh, Orissa, or Assam had too many unsafe and inefficient roads, were too distant from ports and markets, had too many local chiefs trying to establish transit duties, and a virtual absence of police and courts to actively join long-distance trade.

The conditions of business along the coasts were another matter, as we see in Chapter 5.

Notes

1 Paul Axelrod, 'Living on the Edge: The Village and the State on the Goa–Maratha Frontier,' *Indian Economic and Social History Review*, 45(4), 2008, 553–580. See also Frank Perlin, 'Of White Whale and Countrymen in the Eighteenth Century Maratha Deccan: Extended Class Relations, Rights and the Problem of Rural Autonomy Under the Old Regime,' *Journal of Peasant Studies*, 5(1), 1978, 172–237; Stewart Gordon, *Marathas, Marauders, and State Formation*, Delhi: Oxford University Press, 1994; and André Wink, *Land and Sovereignty in India*, Cambridge: Cambridge University Press, 1986.

2 Neeraj Hatekar, 'Farmers and Markets in the Pre-Colonial Deccan: The Plausibility of Economic Growth in Traditional Society,' *Past and Present*, 178(1), 2003, 116–147.

3 B.B. Chaudhuri, *Peasant History in Late-precolonial and Colonial India*, Delhi: Pearson Longman, 2008.

4 See discussion in David Ludden, 'Introduction,' in Ludden, ed, *Agricultural Production and Indian History*, Delhi: Oxford University Press, 1994, 1–23.

5 On hierarchy, Dilbagh Singh, The State, Landlords, and Peasants: Rajasthan in the 18th Century, New Delhi: Manohar, 1990; Narayan Singh Rao, *Rural Economy and Society: Study of South-eastern Rajasthan during the Eighteenth Century*, Jaipur and New Delhi: Rawat, 2002, 61–62.

6 For surveys of the scholarship, see, Tirthankar Roy, *The Economic History of India 1857–2010*, Delhi: Oxford University Press, Fourth Edition, 2020, Chapter 2; Burton Stein, ed., *The Making of Agrarian Policy in British India 1770–1900*, New Delhi: Oxford University Press, 1992; Dharma Kumar, ed., *The Cambridge Economic History of India, vol. 2, 1750–1970*, Cambridge: Cambridge University Press, 1983.

7 Rajat Datta, *Society, Economy, and the Market: Commercialization in Rural Bengal, c. 1760–1800*, New Delhi: Manohar, 2000.

8 Kumkum Chatterjee, *Merchants, Politics and Society in Early Modern India. Bihar, 1733–1820*, Leiden: E.J. Brill, 1996.

9 Price rise stands at odds with a claim that the reduced inflow of silver after 1765 caused a monetary contraction, Asiya Siddiqi, 'Money and Prices in the Earlier Stages of Empire: India and Britain 1760–1840,' *Indian Economic and Social History Review*, 18(3–4), 1981, 231–262.

10 *Change in Bengal Agrarian Society c. 1760–1850*, New Delhi: Manohar, 1979, 284

11 Richard M. Eaton, *The Rise of Islam and the Bengal Frontier, 1204–1760*, Berkeley and Los Angeles: University of California Press, 1993.

12 Datta, *Society, Economy and the Market*.

13 See, for further discussion and citations, Tirthankar Roy, *Natural Disasters and Indian History*, Delhi: Oxford University Press, 2012.

14 W.W. Hunter, *The Annals of Rural Bengal*, vol. 1, New York: Leypoldt and Holt, 1868. See also Datta, *Society, Economy and the Market*; Nikhil Sur, 'The Bihar Famine of 1770,' *Indian Economic and Social History Review*, 13(4), 1977, 525–531; N.K. Sinha, *Economic History of Bengal - from Plassey to the Permanent Settlement*, vol. II, Calcutta: Firma KLM, 1962.

15 Chaudhuri, *Peasant History*, 180–181.

16 'Proto-Industrialization and Pre-Colonial South Asia,' *Past and Present*, 98, 1983, 30–95. See 82–3.

17 J. Macleod, 'Extract of a Letter from Captain Grant, Political Agent of Sattara, to the Honorable M. Elphinstone, dated 17th August, 18919,' Mountstuart Elphinstone, *Report on the Territories Conquered from the Paishwa*, Calcutta, 1821, Appendix, xv-xxiv. The author is James Grant Duff (1789–1858), historian, army officer, and briefly, administrator. Elphinstone (1779–1859), scholar and administrator (Governor of Bombay and other positions).

18 James Grant Duff, *A History of the Mahrattas*, London: Longman, Rees, Orme, Brown and Green, 1826, vol. I, 22–23.

19 Grant Duff, *History of the Mahrattas*, vol. I, 315, reference to Peshwa Balaji Bishwanath, c. 1715.

20 Dilbagh Singh, *The State, Landlords and Peasants: Rajasthan in the 18th Century*, Delhi: Manohar, 1990.

21 James Tod, *The Annals and Antiquities of Rajasthan*, vol. 1 of 3, London: Humphrey Milford, 1920, 576

22 Dilbagh Singh, 'The Role of the Mahajans in the Rural Economy in Eastern Rajasthan during the 18th Century,' *Social Scientist*, 2(10), 1974, 20–31.

23 Eric Stokes, 'Agrarian Relations: Northern and Central India,' *The Cambridge Economic History of India, vol. 2, 1750–1970*, Cambridge: Cambridge University Press, 36–85, 39.

24 *Rulers, Townsmen and Bazaars: North Indian Society in the Age of British Expansion*, Cambridge: Cambridge University Press, 1983, 92–93.

25 Ibid., 84–86.

26 Ibid., 104

27 'Landed Property Rights in Transition: A Note on Cultivators and Agricultural Labourers in Gorakhpur in the Late Eighteenth and Nineteenth Centuries,' *Studies in History*, 12(2), 1996, 243–253.

28 Muzaffar Alam, *Crisis of Empire in Mughal North India: Awadh and the Punjab 1707–1748*, Delhi: Oxford University Press, 1992.

29 V. Sachdeva, *Polity and Economy of the Punjab during the Late-Eighteenth Century*, Delhi: Manohar, 1993.

30 J.T. Blunt, 'Narrative of a Route from Chunargarh to Rajahmundry,' *Asiatic Annual Register*, London: J. Debrett, 1801, 128–200.

31 G.N. Rao, 'Agrarian Relations in Coastal Andhra under Early British Rule,' *Social Scientist*, 6(1), 1977, 19–29

32 Tsukasa Mizushima, 'The Mirasi System and Local Society in Pre-colonial South India,' in Peter Robb, Kaoru Sugihara, Haruka Yanagisawa, eds., *Local Agrarian Societies in Colonial India: Japanese Perspectives*, Abingdon: Routledge, 2013 [1996], 77–146; David Ludden, *Peasant History in South India*, Princeton: Princeton University Press, 1985, 88, 90.

33 P.B. Mayer, 'The Penetration of Capitalism in a South Indian District,' *South Asia*, 3(2), 1980, 1–24.

34 Brian J. Murton, 'Key People in the Countryside: Decision-makers in Interior Tamilnadu in the Late Eighteenth Century,' *Indian Economic and Social History Review*, 10(2), 1973, 157–180. On ryotwari, Dharma Kumar, *Land and Caste in South India*, Cambridge: Cambridge University Press, 1965; Nilmani Mukherjee, *The Ryotwari System in Madras: 1792–1827*, Calcutta, 1962; A. Sarada Raju, *Economic Conditions in the Madras Presidency, 1800–1850*, Madras: Madras University Press, 1941.

35 Tod, *Annals and Antiquities*, vol. 1, 575.

36 S.S. Sivakumar, 'Transformation of the Agrarian Economy in Tondaimandalam: 1760–1900,' *Social Scientist*, 6(10), 1978, 18–39.

37 Ludden, *Peasant History*.

5

CONDITIONS OF BUSINESS

There were two worlds of commerce and industry about 1700. One of these looked inwards, towards the cities of the empire, sought markets, capital, labour, and security there, and moved goods overland along the major road and river transportation arteries of the empire. Its link with the seaboard and maritime trade was not insignificant, but it was not vital. The other world looked outwards, to the sea, was located on the seaboard, and protected by smaller kingdoms that survived thanks to geographical distance from the empire. The eighteenth century is a story of the attrition of one and the growth of the other. In the early nineteenth century, the seaboard cities took greater interest in and control over the overland trade in agricultural commodities.

The shift had limited potential to change average levels of living. Maritime trade was not significant in terms of scale. It was too small a business to make a difference. But, then, its meaning did not depend on how big it was. Seaboard trade's significance was in expanding choices for Indian business, in becoming an attractive alternative destination for the capitalist based in the interior. This choice crystallized in the eighteenth century, eventually initiating a slow convergence of land-based trade and sea-bound trade.

The narrative has several parts. One of the main ones is European trade on the coasts. Why is it significant to the story at all?

The meaning of early-modern trade: incorporation or transformation?[1]

Early work in the field by William Moreland and others relied on limited resources available from printed material and travelogues.[2] Such works nevertheless highlighted the role of Europeans in the Indian Ocean. These suggested the enormous importance of Indo-European trade for the economic emergence of Western

Europe and suggested a link between trade and the formation of an empire in India. The scholarship also showed that India supplied cotton textiles to both Asia and Europe. The trade was very large in scale, so large that the trade made artisans in Europe anxious about the competition. The older scholarship, however, was less specific on the role of Indians in Indo-European trade. Since the 1980s, research done in the field did much to advance our knowledge of different merchants groups and regional economies in shaping the maritime trade of Asia.[3] The newer works also shed light on other global dimensions of the textile export trade, for example, that the cotton cloths were paid for with silver imported from Spanish America, or that cloth was a means of payment in the slave trade in Africa.

What did all this mean? In the 1970s, and largely based on the old scholarship, Immanuel Wallerstein and the world systems school explained the significance of early modern trade. It was in India's 'incorporation' in a Europe-centred system of worldwide exchange.[4] It appeared that trade was a form of domination that differed only in form from the more full-scale European empires to emerge later. Later scholarship was good with the detailed picture but did not challenge the incorporation thesis. If anything, it indirectly corroborated it by suggesting that European merchants' power increased over time, culminating in an empire. In a marginally different account, the Indo-European trade of the eighteenth century represented a 'proto-industrialization' rather than an incorporation of Asia in Europe. That prospect of the emergence of indigenous capitalism was frustrated by the Industrial Revolution in Britain.[5]

The implicit persistence of the idea that Europeans swallowed up what was once an autonomous Asian capitalism is mostly a misreading based on the biased nature of the archival sources that exaggerate European role in trade. The knowledge of India and Indian business that we gain from the European trade archives does not penetrate more than a few miles beyond the coastline and only a little deeper into the deltas. The wealth and richness of the European information system tend to obscure the vast areas of ignorance that persist in this information system. River borne trade, inland market towns, caravan trade, institutional foundations of domestic trade, money markets, regional market integration, the uplands, the forests, the submontane zones, and much of the Deccan Plateau are subjects on which little systematic data exists and little work has been done. Unfortunately, indigenous sources are even less informative on these spheres, for reasons that we need not go into.

These rise-and-fall narratives of Indian business history invest the foreign trade from the coast with a meaning that it could not possibly have and bears little relation with the actual scale in which foreign trade worked. Maritime trade had always been vital to the coastal regions' economies, and its importance increased during Indo-European trade. But the trading regions themselves were little islands of enterprise, most of them had a highly seasonal character to boot, and a rural landscape bordered them. Foreign trade was not a force that could directly transform the Indian economy. Whether it signified incorporation or protoindustrialization is a meaningless play with words. It was irrelevant if we look at its scale.

TABLE 5.1 The relative scale of foreign trade, 1750–1913

	Export from India (m £)			GDP (m £)		Export-GDP ratio (%)	
						B/D to	B/E to
	A	B	C	D	E	C/D	C/E
1750–60	3.3	4.3	6.5	507.8	170.0	0.9–1.3	2.6–3.8
1860	28.9	28.9	28.9	507.8	507.8	5.7	5.7
1913	176.4	176.4	176.4	1367.1	1367.1	12.9	12.9

A. The estimated value (in million £) of the exports from India by the English, the Dutch, the French, and the Danish East India Companies combined. From Om Prakash, *European Commercial Enterprise in Pre-colonial India*, Cambridge: Cambridge University Press, 1998. See Table 3.3, pp. 98–9, for Dutch Company's export data (1750), Table 4.2, p. 120, for the English Company (1758–60, average annual), Table 7.1, p. 311, for the Danish Company (1754–63 average annual), and Table 6.4, p. 254, for the French Company (1755–64, average annual). The data reported in country-specific currencies. These are converted into £ by using The Marteau Early 18th-Century Currency Converter, http://www.pierre-marteau.com/currency/converter.html.
B. Export, assuming the total export of the four East India Companies formed 3/4th of total exports from the region.
C. Export, assuming the total export of the four East India Companies formed half of total exports from the region.
D. Assuming 0% GDP growth rate between 1750 and 1860. The range refers to the two assumptions about relative share of four companies in total export, the lower figure corresponds to 3/4th share and the higher figure to a half share. National Income of 1913 from S. Sivasubramonian, *National Income of India in the Twentieth Century*, New Delhi: Oxford University Press, 2000, Table 6.1, p. 396; National Income: 1860 is estimated assuming a 1% growth rate in real GDP in the prewar 50 years. The growth rate is approximately the same rate as implicit in the late nineteenth century income estimates available from Alan Heston, 'National Income,' in Dharma Kumar, ed., *Cambridge Economic History of India*, vol. 2, Cambridge: Cambridge University Press, 1983. The derived average rate from Heston was probably slightly above 1%, but I stick to 1% on the ground that underestimation of non-agricultural income was likely higher for 1860 compared with 1913. Price trend is assumed to be zero between 1750 and 1860. The basis for this assumption is the silver price of rice in Bengal taken from 'India prices and wages 1595–1930 (Allen and Studer),' http://gpih.ucdavis.edu/Datafilelist.htm, which yields a slope of zero value for these years. Between 1860 and 1913, the weighted price index rose by 60%, the figure reported is adjusted for the inflation. Price data from Michelle McAlpin, in Dharma Kumar, ed., 'Price Movements and Economic Fluctuations,' *Cambridge Economic History of India*, vol. 2, Cambridge: Cambridge University Press, 1983.
E. Assuming 1% GDP growth rate between 1750 and 1860. See also D above.

The most straightforward index of the scale of foreign trade in relation to the economy is the trade-GDP ratio. Table 5.1 presents a set of plausible numbers for this ratio. There is good data for the major European companies' exports from India. The companies were only one category of the market players, albeit the largest exporting firms in 1750. The data on European private trade and overland trade remains patchy. The best we can do is make alternative assumptions about how large these segments were relative to the companies. We next need to work out a plausible range of nominal GDP, and the best way to do so is to work backwards from the earliest direct estimates and use various assumptions about GDP growth for the period 1750–1860.

All these numbers are speculative, but Table 5.1 is as specific as we can be with the information that we now have. These numbers are not representative of the scale of maritime trade as such. We know nothing about the scale of coastal commerce, of the effects of international on intra-regional trade. It was in this sphere that most Asian traders were engaged, both before and after European entry. But it is a fair assumption that in 1750 the combined European operation was by far the larger in scale since almost all the other segments along the coast directly or indirectly depended on Indo-European trade.

The calculations establish that foreign trade formed a minor element in India's total economic activity in the mid-eighteenth century. For a realistic range of GDP growth, the trade-GDP ratio was less than 3% for 1750. 'Wherever we have specific information,' Tapan Raychaudhuri writes, 'it is clear that the Europeans' trade accounted for a mere fraction of the output and 'export' in any given centre of production.'[6] My calculations confirm Raychaudhuri's conclusion. It makes little sense to say that foreign trade could either shape livelihoods, or that the retreat of the Indo-European textile trade in the late 1700s or the early 1800s could cause much disruption anywhere. Foreign trade did not matter in that way.

If maritime trade was so small, then the relative scale of any one segment was still smaller. Of interest here is the Arabian Sea trade conducted from Konkan, which indigenous groups dominated throughout. The big merchants who dominated the trade from Surat or Cambay were exceptional figures in South Asia's commercial world. Not surprisingly, names like Mullah Abdul Ghafur or Virji Vora keep cropping up in almost every account of trade on the Indian coasts. They do because they were exceptions, not the norm.

Not only was foreign trade a small part of the economy of India, but it was also not of great consequence even within the core trading zones. Sushil Chaudhury's data suggests that the share of export in cloth production in the mid-eighteenth-century Bengal was around 20%.[7] Om Prakash derives a smaller ratio based on a more detailed reconstruction of the data.[8] For south India, Habib says that 10% of the textile looms were for export in 1800.[9] Some of the other estimates too are based on looms, which is a flawed index because it is highly unlikely that the looms making cloth for the Europeans were only making cloth for the Europeans and no one else; the export-production percentage based on looms must overstate the real proportion. I have estimated the share of income earned in textiles in Bengal's total income at 10% (1763).[10] Given that textiles represented the only important tradable from Bengal, the share of export in the region's income was around 2%. The share of total trade was 4% of income, touching the upper bound in the range shown in Table 5.1, but still small.

Of course, trade was one of the components of the non-agricultural economy, albeit one with considerable backward and forward linkages. How much do we know of the occupational structure as such? We should be justified in taking Bengal as the upper bound. The most plausible ratio for the proportion of working people engaged outside agriculture in Bengal has recently been estimated at 20%.[11] Contemporary estimates varied from 15 (James Grant, 1790), 20 (H.T. Colebrooke, 1804), to 19 (Francis Buchanan, 1800, Bihar districts). Furthermore, the proportion varied greatly between the western uplands, where little trade was carried on, and the lower deltaic districts, where village-based surveys often yielded percentages much higher than these. But even in lower Bengal, a certain proportion of the 'artificers' and manufacturers in any standard survey of occupations consisted of part-timers who also took part in agricultural work on the side. If the share of non-agricultural occupations in total employment was 20% in Bengal, an exporting region, the Indian average should be smaller.

Price statistics show the modest effect of Indo-European trade upon the domestic economy. By some datasets, prices in Bengal rose after the 1720s, suggesting European demand and bullion import. Chaudhury's reconstruction of price statistics disputes this conclusion and shows no secular and general increase in food-grain prices.[12] Om Prakash, too, suggests that the import of New World silver into India did not lead to a price revolution.[13] Prakash's reading is that there was surplus capacity in Bengal. My reading is that the tradeable sector was just too small.

There is little information available on trends in wages and earnings of the weavers who supplied the export sector. The currently available numbers pertain to levels of wages and are more like snapshots. Prasannan Parthasarathi says that the weavers earned exceptionally high wages.[14] If valid for the Kaveri delta where agricultural yield was high, that contention is not consistent with the work on weavers' wages in Bengal or with Prakash's point that there was surplus labour.

My point is not that foreign trade was unimportant, but that its importance cannot be found in reading European domination or in estimating its impact on the regional economies. These effects were negligible. There were two other facts that make the Indo-European trade meaningful. First, whereas Indo-European trade did not end the cleavage within the business world discussed before, between agriculture-bound and ocean-bound spheres, it created the potential to bridge the two worlds. Cities like Bombay, Calcutta, and Madras led this integration, after the textile export trade collapsed from around 1810.

Second, if the trade-GDP ratio was small, it rose after 1750. The scale of foreign trade increased enormously between 1750 and 1860. So large was the rise that, with any realistic trend in income growth, the relative share of trade in the earlier benchmark year must turn out to be small. If the trade-GDP ratio were to exceed 5%, either GDP growth rate would be higher than 2% per year between 1750–1860, or company trade was as little as 10% of total trade in 1750. In other words, to suggest that trade was of significant order in 1750, we need to assume either that the company's rule enabled extraordinarily economic growth or that the share in the trade of all the European companies combined was small. Both would be extreme positions.

The significance of that rise did not rest on what the European merchants were doing on the coasts. The significance was in drawing mass-produced and mass-consumed goods like food and cloth, into networks of overseas and long-distance trades. The growth drew upon the inclusion of agricultural commodities in the export basket and import of cotton textiles after 1820. It also drew on the Indian trading groups' enterprise. The coastal world of business had always been small in relation to the interior world, but the balance was upset and upset decisively in the eighteenth century. As the coastal-maritime world of enterprise expanded, it sucked in capital and labour from northern and western regions. The land-locked successor states sometimes supplied commodities and capital to this process, but they did not lead it. The Indian trading firms based in the port cities did. This was a paradigm shift in the history of Indian capitalism.

To see how economic power thus consolidated on the coasts, it is necessary to delve deeper into the history of the Indian Ocean trade itself.

The prehistory of the Indian Ocean trade

The well-known story of the first century of Indo-European trade deserves only a brief recap here.[15] The last half of the sixteenth century and the first half of the seventeenth century saw the coming together of two important trends in the political economy of South Asia: the ascendance of European traders and merchant firms in the Indian Ocean and the consolidation of three powerful Asian empires, the Mughal, the Safavid, and the Ottoman.

Between 1498, when the Portuguese mariner Vasco Da Gama circumnavigated the Cape of Good Hope to reach the Malabar Coast, and 1515, when the conquest and rule of Afonso de Albuquerque came to an end, the Portuguese had established a position of dominance in the major sea-lanes in the western part of the Indian Ocean. The key to this control was a string of fortified settlements set up in the Konkan, Persia, the Arab peninsula, and East Africa. Albuquerque's capture of Malacca in the Malay Peninsula in 1511 rearranged trade networks on the eastern side too. It now seemed to the Portuguese mariners that something like a state could be established on the waters. To take firm control of the spice trade, the Portuguese introduced a system of licensing. Asian ships had to pay taxes to carry any goods on the main routes, and were prohibited from the transportation of spices. These attempts to govern the sea routes led the Portuguese into conflicts with local traders and shipping. Arab-Portuguese frictions were already present and were now worsened by the licensing system. An effect of these conflicts was the gradual retreat of the Arab and the Chinese mariners, their place being taken by Gujarati ship owners and merchants in the western part, and Javanese trade and shipping in the eastern part of the ocean.

A second trend was political in origin. The major empires and states of Asia earned their taxes mainly from the land. But knowing that overseas trade was profitable, a lucrative source of taxation and a source of coveted foreign articles, they were interested in seaports. Hormuz on the Persian Gulf, a string of ports on the eastern Mediterranean, and Surat, Hooghly, and Masulipatnam in India were partially developed and governed by the major seventeenth-century states in Asia. Overland trade to and from these centres grew in volume. Despite a rise in transaction costs for the Asians after Portuguese ascendance, the joint outcome of European participation and empires' formation was 'general prosperity in trade all around the ocean.'[16] Portuguese control, far from restraining trade, connected the segments of the ocean better and increased the scale of trade.

The entry of the English and the Dutch (c 1600) into the Asian waters occurred on a different principle from the Portuguese. Whereas the Portuguese enterprise was in theory coordinated by the court, the English and the Dutch enterprises were organized around companies, supported by the respective courts. The English East India Company's shareholders were merchants and bankers of the City of London, and the Dutch company was owned by shipping cartels. The London capitalists long felt frustrated that the Ottoman Empire and its friends, the Genovese and Venetian merchants, could regulate the Mediterranean route from Europe to India. Emboldened by naval successes scored over the Spanish in the Atlantic, the merchants decided to sponsor voyages in the east following the sea route.

Rather than engaging in warfare, the English and the Dutch opened diplomatic missions with the states in India and Indonesia and sought trading privileges in return for an implicit promise to keep the Portuguese at bay. That the English company traded under a Crown monopoly charter helped diplomatic negotiations. Whereas the Portuguese had established colonies, the merchant companies sought permission to own warehouses in the Asian ports. Although the English and the Dutch were rivals in trade and even came to blows on several occasions, they managed to pose a united front against the Portuguese. By 1650, they had greatly weakened Portuguese influence in the Indian littoral, almost reducing it to irrelevance. By then, the Dutch had consolidated their influence in the Indonesian archipelago while maintaining a large operation in India. The trades in these two directions were complementary because Indonesian spices were often paid for with Indian cloth. The English, by contrast, concentrated on India.

From the middle of the seventeenth century, the English Company had been following in the footsteps of the Portuguese by trying to set up their own ports on the coast. A sense of insecurity was pervasive in the likelihood of Dutch attacks, or harassment by the provincial rulers. Political turmoil in England, the uneasy relationship between the Crown and Parliament, and the company's ambiguous position within these disputes, also cast their shadow.

The firms wanted to secure their position on the seaboard by erecting defences around their settlements. The officers sought from the local states the license to become a landlord. The decision to own forts was usually taken by the officers stationed in India against London's orders. There were three successful negotiations and many abortive attempts. The successes led to the establishment of Madras (c. 1632), Bombay (c. 1661), and Calcutta (1690). Madras was purchased from the small Chandragiri kingdom. Bombay was a gift from the Portuguese, and Calcutta, located inside the Bengal province of the Mughal Empire, was leased from a vassal of the provincial ruler. All of these sites had unsteady beginnings as trading ports. After all, Bombay was a rival of the much bigger port Surat, Madras of Masulipatnam, and Calcutta of Hooghly. Madras managed to draw a lot of trade away because Masulipatnam had been declining for some time due to the Golkonda state's weakness. Calcutta attracted Indian merchants and bankers from the second quarter of the eighteenth century. Bombay came into its own after the gradual decay of Surat set in from 1760.

These three ports represented strengths that were quite unique. They represented a distinct business culture in India. Whereas Surat and Masulipatnam had belonged to states that lived mainly on land taxes, the Company towns were ocean-bound and had no ties with the land. Bombay, Calcutta, and Madras were ports where seafaring merchants, rather than landlords and warlords, governed and made laws. These were, therefore, sites attractive to Indian merchants, bankers, artisans and labourers as well. There was always work to be had. The landlord of these ports was interested in sponsoring these livelihoods. And custom was less a force than in the interior in negotiations on prices and wages.

Still, in 1700 it would not have been easy to foresee a future where these ports acted as steps to build an empire. Continuing political troubles at home made the Company cautious and risk-averse. Its business privilege, which was a monopoly charter granted by the Crown, was under attack from private traders, even from its own employees, who wanted the charter to be withdrawn. At the turn of the eighteenth century, the company did have to deal with a rival firm, which had support both in London and India. The relation between Indian business firms and the Indian rulers was based on established protocols and the service the Indian firms rendered in funding royal debts and commuting taxes into money. The Europeans did not enjoy such goodwill, nor were their services so useful. In return for the license to trade, they had to pay money to the Indian kings. These gifts were a source of irritation to the Company officers. On the other side, the expectation that the kings would take sides in the rivalry between European firms annoyed the kings. There were numerous European privateers and pirates in the Arabian Sea, whom the Company officers clandestinely patronized. Piqued by the protection that the European pirates received from these patronage networks, the emperor, Aurangzeb, came close to ending English trade in Surat and Bombay.

Notwithstanding these obstacles, in the middle decades of the 1700s, the new business world's potential effects were beginning to become evident (Map 5.1).

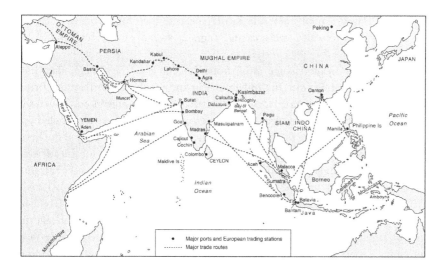

MAP 5.1 The Indian Ocean trading world, routes and ports, 1700.

Indian Ocean trade: the eighteenth century

Three tendencies deserve notice. First, Bengal became the main field of investment of the English – now British – East India Company, which was becoming the largest of all European firms in India. By 1750, two-thirds of the major companies' total export went by the Company. The composition and direction of trade had changed too, towards several new products sourced from Bengal, indigo, saltpetre, and opium being the main examples. The company was developing a significant interest in Chinese tea, and the vast quantities of silver bullion that it imported were partly diverted into the East Asia trade. Calcutta was again a convenient port of transit between Europe and China, and it became a vital one in the trade when Bengal opium began to be used as a means of payment in China trade.

Bengal had advantages, such as the low price of food and cheap transportation along the deltaic rivers. The larger of the river systems could be used to move cargo to and from northern India at a relatively small cost, enabling the Europeans to access saltpetre and indigo. Bengal had many highly skilled textile artisans. Behind the shift of business focus, there was also a change in the European consumption pattern. From coarse cotton, or painted and printed cotton, in which the Coromandel coast excelled, there was a relative shift in demand towards fine white cotton or muslins. Bengal artisans and local cotton growing tradition were good with muslins. The larger significance of the shift of the Company towards Bengal was that Bengal politics and British enterprise were becoming interdependent.

The second big development of this time was the breaking up of the Mughal Empire. Warfare broke out in the interior from the second decade of the eighteenth century. By mid-century, hundreds of wealthy Indian merchants and bankers from the western part of the Gangetic plains migrated to the Company towns. The exodus was of a significant scale in Bengal, where repeated Maratha raids raised insecurity in the commercialized western borders. Some of these merchants who came to Calcutta played a mediatory role in the company's dealings with the regional state. Later generations of merchants and migrants would partner with the British private traders.

The third significant change arose from the entry of the French East India Company. A late entrant into the Indian Ocean and much smaller than the British Company in terms of business scale, the French were a formidable military force, emerging as the British's principal rivals in regional politics. The rivalry spilled over into territorial wars during the War of Austrian Succession (1740–48) and the Seven Years War (1756–63, see also Chapter 2). On both occasions, the local leaderships took opposite sides in Bengal and Carnatic's succession disputes and palace intrigues. The British emerged victorious in these battles, leading to the Treaty of Paris in 1763, which all but destroyed French ambitions in India. The French Company was wound up, restarted, and wound up again during the Napoleonic wars. During this mid-eighteenth-century Anglo-French conflict in India, both companies' local leaderships defied the directors' instructions. The quiet drive towards autonomy had reached a decisive point. From now on, the local employees, the Royal Navy officers, stationed to protect the ports, and their friends, the private traders, called the shots in deciding the East India Company's policies in India.

The culmination of the three tendencies was military and political domination of the Carnatic and Bengal. For well over a decade after 1765, when Bengal was acquired (see Chapter 2), the administration was divided between the local ruler and the company. The company had little effect on governance. It did have an immediate effect on the balance of payments, however. The long dependence upon silver to pay for Indian exports ceased. The company now began to use land revenues to pay for exports instead and borrowed more locally. Between 1757 and 1787, official statistics recorded little silver import into India (see also Chapter 3). These volumes probably underestimated the true extent of silver import. The private merchants were doing large volumes of business and imported silver on private account, which is not well-recorded. Furthermore, the drop also reflected that the company was beginning to experience some success with selling British goods in payment for Indian goods. The British goods that sold well at this time were manufactured iron, instruments, cannons, and guns.[17] Also, greater defensive expenditure led the company to spend more of its local revenues on heads other than overseas trade.

The company's military adventures in north India in the 1770s received censure from lobbies in the Parliament, especially the critics of the monopoly charter. British provincial mercantile and industrial interests, from whose ranks came many of the leading private traders, joined these criticisms. Adam Smith gave the misgivings a philosophical foundation in his *Wealth of Nations* (1776), suggesting not only that monopoly was a bad market principle, but also, with reference to the Company, that a firm that ran a state would fail both as a firm and as a state. The company ran up a huge debt and borrowed from Parliament, against stricter Parliamentary regulation upon governance in India. An abortive regulating act of 1773 was succeeded by the more comprehensive India Act of William Pitt (1784), which created the administrative setup to establish Parliament's authority over the Indian territories acquired by the company.

The India Act confirmed the Company's role as a ruler in India and devalued its role as a trader. In revisions of the charter in 1793, private trade was given significant formal privileges. The company raised a voice in protest, but there was no effective opposition. Nor was the opposition more than symbolic in 1813, when the monopoly was withdrawn from the Company's India trade. For decades before the change, the monopoly had operated merely in name.

Private traders

By 1750, the company had almost given up the long-running battle to suppress private merchants. Indeed, the close relationship of patronage and protection between the local officers and the growing number of private traders made disciplining the latter an impossible project. Among these people, some were the firm's employees, and some knew the officers well or were in their good books. A substantial number of these enterprises were in the nature of covert joint ventures with the officers.

These partnerships raise a question about the character of the firm. Some scholars suggest that the chartered companies can be compared with the modern multinationals, insofar as both shared strategies that enabled the managers to economize on transaction cost and reduce opportunism by agents.[18] Others suggest that unlike a modern multinational firm, the company did not have a unitary command-and-control structure. Its overseas enterprise combined modern joint-stock principle in raising money and pre-modern partnership in management. The partners were the City of London merchants on one side and peripatetic sailors, soldiers, and officers on the other side. These two classes were not friendly at home. But the sailors and soldiers joined the venture on the promise that they could trade on the side. The latter group had to make friends in India, deal with hostile kings and untrustworthy agents, and were more aggressive, knowledgeable about local conditions, and opportunistic than the shareholders. As the local officers became involved in Indian politics, they often acted against the London bosses' instructions.[19] The private traders and the local agents' economic interests converged, and the military success of one made the other bolder than before. The conflicts with the Bengal state between 1756 and 1763 concerned taxation of European private trade. The dispute blew up into a battle because the officers sided with the private traders. Similar issues cropped up in Awadh in the 1760s.

After the company took over power, private traders moved more freely and some of them started enterprises that bore new kinds of risk. After 1813, artisans joined the now much larger pool of merchants and fortune-hunters coming to India. Since iron was already a major import from Britain to India, and yet iron ore and charcoal were both available in plenty in the foothills of the Chotanagpur, several ventures started up in iron smelting in these areas from the 1770s. Dockyards near Calcutta employed European capital. In the 1790s, interest in indigo and cotton processing in Caribbean-style plantations also attracted much interest. The largest group among private enterprises was engaged in commodity trade – opium, indigo, cotton, saltpetre, and a few other articles – and set up banks and insurance businesses to fund such trades. Almost all of them formed of Indo-European partnership. With firms like the famous Carr-Tagore enterprise in Calcutta, the Indian partner supplied the capital, and the Europeans supplied the management. The history of these hybrid partnerships is now well-researched. So are the shocks that finished off many of them in the 1830s and the 1840s.[20] The shocks came from commodity trade speculation and price fluctuations, blowing up into banking crashes that pulled many healthy businesses down.

Not all firms disappeared during these episodes, and the many that weathered the shocks laid the foundation for industrialization in the late nineteenth century. Yet, the easy road to bankruptcy in the trade, as well as artisanal enterprise, showed that such ventures faced poor access to information, insufficient hedging, high trade costs, the risk of insider lending, small reserves, and above all, a narrow, imperfect, and expensive capital market. When crashes became imminent, the money dried up. At the same time, the land became an attractive alternative investment in Bengal, as zamindari taxes became more affordable.

The Company state in the early nineteenth century was not particularly friendly to these European enterprises. By 1800, the company itself had changed its identity from a body of merchants to a government. Many individual officers were still known to the entrepreneurs, but extending overt support was frowned upon. As a ruler, the company lived on land tax like any other Indian regime and was deeply opposed to European interference in the property relations in the countryside. Only after the 1830s was the land law relaxed enough to allow Europeans to hold large landed property. The firm also tried to block the grant of banking charter, which was an important channel for transferring remittances.

If the European private traders had a varied experience, the fate of the Indian merchant operating in the Indian Ocean after European ascendance was also a mixed one.

Indian Maritime Merchants

Ashin Das Gupta offered three useful observations on the Indian Ocean merchant in the eighteenth century. First, big merchants who owned ships and operated like business firms in their own right stood on their ground until the early eighteenth century. European traders were not yet the dominant players in maritime trade. However, the relative fall in the Ottoman, Mughal and Persian states' economic situation may have affected Arabian sea trade, and in turn, affected these merchants. Second, a change in the direction from intra-Asian trade to Asia-Europe trade benefited merchants working as partners and agents of the company. Third, subsequent to European dominance, there was a redefinition of Indo-European relationships, older forms of partnership giving way to newer forms.

Who were the Indian merchants we are dealing with here? The decline story does not apply to all categories of Indian traders. It applies to a class who owned ships, employed large volumes of capital, and made the relatively longer voyages between Surat and West Asia, or in the east, between Bengal or Coromandel and Southeast Asia. In the Arabian Sea, these substantial merchants carried valuable cargo, and often received special treatment onboard other ships and ports. Smaller in scale were the merchants who did not own vessels and often worked as principal merchants' agents.

Below them were many small-scale merchants who carried generic cargo. Shipping was an important marker in this hierarchy. The conjunction of trade and shipping marked out the big players who were potential rivals of the European firms. One of the reasons for the vitality of Indian shipping was that it charged lower freight rates than the European ships. However, there were not many merchant firms that owned ships for shipping was not a popular field of investment. The ships were individually owned, and while insurance covered the goods, it did not cover the ships.

The big merchants did not enter the India-Europe trade because the Europeans had more knowledge of transoceanic navigation and consumer markets in Europe. Their understanding of charts, maps, ocean currents, instruments, routes, and their technique of making sturdier and larger ships carrying guns on board was superior to that of the Indian maritime merchants. Indians were good navigators, but they did not venture beyond the Indian Ocean. A particular advantage that this global reach gave the Europeans was access to Spanish silver.

But these differences do not explain why the big Indian firms had to give way even on the Indian coasts. Das Gupta offered an answer by disputing the Dutch historian of Indonesian trade and society, Jakob Van Leur. In 1955, Van Leur had said that European and Asian trades used distinct business organizations. Maritime trade in Asia was carried out mainly by people who hawked from port to port. The Asian merchant was a peddler, the trade was confined to luxuries, the composition had remained changeless for centuries, and powerful noblemen controlled traders. As a commercial world, it was 'irrelevant to later capitalist development.'[21]

Trade, Das Gupta showed, was not confined to luxury articles but served the demand of common people. The ruling powers along the littoral depended on the seafaring merchants, even partnered with them.[22] If peddler conjures up the vision of a small player, there were many exceptions to that benchmark among the ship-owning merchants of Surat. And yet, many did share a dependence on spot markets and auction type sales and aversion to building long-lasting contractual arrangements and lasting institutions. '[I]t is possible that they remained pedlars somewhere deep in their minds.'[23]

Another big difference was that Indians operated within family firms, whereas the Europeans formed joint-stock companies. Personal honesty and cooperation among kins were essential to the commercial success of the Indians. This was limiting, for when merchants came from different communities, the reliance on personal ties did not lead to the 'consciousness of being men of the same calling.'[24] They could not form professional collectives. Merchants were potentially vulnerable to political pressure. A particular effect of such divisions was the fragmentation of the financial market. The financial system could perform most routine tasks, but could not meet crises, for 'money was not pooled together even within Surat.'[25] Despite a great deal of bargaining and large transactions in the commodity market in Surat, the competition was not free because of information and entry barriers.[26]

In Das Gupta's reading, the decline of the Indian merchant marine's top end was not an outcome of European competition. Instead, the decline began when the local rulers increased pressures on them to fund wars. Merchants were 'hounded to death by ruthless political pressure in the second half of the 18th century.'[27] The stress was especially acute in those leading ports which formed parts of empires. Those who 'faced extinction at the hand of Indian administrators exchanged that dangerous position for a constricted existence.'[28]

Perhaps the most decisive advantage the European companies possessed stemmed from the joint-stock system. The form of management allowed the British Company to pool vast amounts of money and use the economies of scale available in overseas trade. It could build an elaborate infrastructure consisting of forts, factories, harbours, and ships. Joint-stock also made them better risk-takers. Most Indian traders spread risks by dealing in a variety of goods in auction-type exchanges. Thanks to its capacity to absorb risks, the company dealt in a few goods, which it bought on a large scale. Being specialized, it needed to contract with a specific set of suppliers year after year and to pay out vast sums of money as advances. Contractual sale of goods was not unknown in India before, but a contractual sale on such a scale by a single firm had no precedent. Finally, the Europeans operated in a more integrated financial market than did the Indians, allowing for a larger scale of investment, greater capacity for risk absorption, and higher capital intensity. Their ability to procure silver in larger quantities, for example, owed to the presence of well-developed financial markets in Europe at this time. In India, banking was less developed, money passed through fewer hands, and interest rates were higher.

Applying these ideas, we can understand why, with the decline of Mughal power, in the eighteenth century, Surat's mercantile community was 'no longer dominated by a few merchant princes possessing enormous wealth and commanding influence in political circles and local administration.'[29] Instead, there were many merchant firms of similar circumstances. Possibly taking advantage of this levelling down, 'the EIC and VOC split the broker's portfolio of responsibilities and employed several merchants, each with a particular assignment.' Overall, the agents and partners of the Europeans grew more dependent on that particular custom. This image of a levelling of Indian merchants in Surat during the twilight of the Mughal Empire should be valid, at least in broad outline, in several older ports. The fortune of Masulipatnam, the most important port of the Coromandel in the seventeenth century, fell quickly because its prominence had been too dependent on the strength of the Golconda state.[30] With both Surat and Masulipatnam, merchants and bankers shifted to Bombay and Madras, respectively.

While the top end thus declined after 1700, numerous groups benefited from expanding Indo-European trade along the coasts. The Company ships did not transport materials and supplies, such as grain or timber, between points on the Indian coasts. They did not even shuttle between the three Company ports often. And yet, the growth of these towns, the rising volume of shipping in them, and warfare in the interior greatly increased the demand for coastal transportation. The gap was filled by indigenous shipping. Demand also increased for ship repair services. Chhaya Goswami shows that Gujarati merchants from Kachchh continued without serious disruptions into the nineteenth century by using diaspora and community networks.[31] Others like the Parsis of Surat and Bombay, though not a traditional business community, utilized new opportunities readily and effectively.

Among other groups that directly gained from European ascendance were those merchants who contracted with the European companies.

Agents and associates

The companies and the private traders needed to hire agents to procure the goods. The negotiation process between large firms on the seacoast, and thousands of artisans in the countryside was a complicated affair. Contracts and contract enforcement engaged the Company officers daily and filled the pages of the 'consultation books' maintained in the factories. In the early 1600s, much purchase in overseas trade was made via the spot market. However, contractual sales increased in importance, especially after cotton textiles became the companies' main investment. Initially, the contractors were influential people; some were warlords on the Coromandel coast. But in the eighteenth century, the typical contractor was either a local textile merchant, or a weaver-headman, or a combination of both.

Contracts were often made for a whole year and entailed giving out large sums of money as advance payments. The specifications of the quality of cloth, the designs, and the volume, were very detailed, which increased the risks of disputes on delivery. Disputes occurred on both the quality and the quantity of delivered goods. Such negotiations, contracts, and disputes had no Indian precedents, and therefore, they were not protected by any Indian law. Legally, the companies could do little when the contracts were wilfully disregarded.

To avoid such situations, the British Company recruited its chief agents carefully. They were often individuals who held power over the artisans. At the same time, they were more knowledgeable about the production site than were the company's officers. Being more powerful or more informed than both parties, the agents could become more of a liability than a help. Therefore, the Company officers disliked this dependence and distrusted their closest partners in the trade, but they could not do without them either.

In the conventional historiography, there is ambivalence and uncertainty about these transaction costs. Most studies tend to overlook the non-performance of contracts or see it as a sign of the artisans' bargaining power.[32] Another strand in the literature contends that there were risks but that the East India Company's ascendance as a government could lead to a coercive way of enforcing contracts.[33] Both are valid but limited theses. The bargaining theory overlooks that the companies had neither enough policing power nor the information to monitor performance. If the weavers or the agents decided to cheat, there was little legal penalty that the firm could impose on them. The beginning of governmental control did address one weakness, the lack of policing power. But it did not remedy the legal vacuum or solve the asymmetric information problem. At the beginning of the nineteenth century, these two problems continued to plague the private traders too. A third view is that these problems shaped the evolution of business organization in the 1800s and even made the Company officers more interested in protecting profits by taking a share of power.[34]

All European firms operating in India worked through an Indian agent or broker. Sometimes, the broker belonged in a commercial group. Several of them used the relationship as a springboard for entry into trade. The broker had complex managerial responsibilities. The broker was responsible for the enforcement of contracts between the firm and the artisans. Although initially a contractual relationship, it took on political tones when the company ran into fights with local powers and needed the broker as an influential ally. From the 1720s, both on the Coromandel coast and in Surat, '[t]he beginning of [a] new equation between merchants, companies and the state' was thus visible.[35] When Anglo-French rivalry broke out in the middle of the century, the chief brokers were an ally and informer.

Some of the Parsis of western India acted as brokers of the company. By 1820, many more were prominent as shipwrights and merchants in their own right. They began as carpenters, entered shipbuilding and repair in Surat and Bombay towards the end of the eighteenth century, and ended as merchants themselves. A well-developed artisanal apprenticeship system that ensured that the master-builder status continued down the family lines helped develop these skills. They were among the first Indian merchant and seafaring people to have gone to England to train in shipbuilding. Such exposure mattered during the transition from sail to steam in the 1840s. The Parsi master-builder made the change quite smoothly.

Their established position as shipwrights and their knowledge of timber supplies from Malabar launched groups of Parsis as potential players in the emerging Indo-China trade. When the company began its withdrawal from Indian trade (after 1813) and twenty years later, from China trade (the charter ended in 1833), the Parsi shippers bought up some of the ships and refitted these for coastal or China trade. Wars with China (1839–42) and Burma (1824–6) saw these ships being used for supplies. Already Indian opium had emerged as the main export to China, and the proceeds from opium sale funded huge quantities of tea imported from China to the Atlantic. The Parsi shippers played a significant role in cargo transportation in the Bombay-Canton and the Calcutta-Canton routes.

The Company and the private traders also relied on Indian bankers. In particular, two services were quite crucial, conversion of Spanish money into Indian money and remittance of funds between Indian regions. Reputation mattered in the business of valuation of the coins in a world where almost all valuable coins were made of alloys of gold and silver. Therefore, there were not many players in this business. Later in the eighteenth century, the company's own revenues were transmitted across the three presidencies (the main territorial divisions) using bankers' drafts drawn on Indian banking houses. Again, reputation was crucial. These services were developed relatively more in western India than in the east. The main centres of indigenous banking were Surat and Ahmedabad. A number of large firms also existed in the cities of the Gangetic plains. Some of them had risen in political power thanks to extensive tax farming. From the late eighteenth century, the eastern region's merchants and bankers invested in zamindari estates.

On the other hand, some types of banking, because of its close and growing dependence on the regional states, also faced obsolescence, even hostility, in the new regime. The chief banker of Bengal in the 1750s, the Jagatseth, was a big firm, but its prominence stemmed from the weakness of the state under which it worked. It was big because of the government license that it had enjoyed to coin money, change money, and commute taxes. Although a friend of the Company, the Jagatseth lost relevance rapidly as the former consolidated its fiscal administration and unified the currency.

Big business did deals with hundreds of thousands of textile artisans, the real foundation of Indo-European trade in the eighteenth century.

Artisans

The major textile supply regions for the European traders were Bengal, Coromandel, and Gujarat. Of the three, Gujarat was accessed first, Coromandel next, but Bengal dominated the trade in the eighteenth century. Leading histories of the European companies and regional economies have concentrated mainly on Bengal and Coromandel.[36] The Gujarat scholarship has only recently been catching up.[37] There were significant similarities between these regions in their trading systems. In all, the export textiles were made in large villages located not far from the port city. These clusters did not situate deep into the interior. In general, transportation overland was both costly and unreliable, and therefore, it made sense to offer weavers some incentive to relocate near the warehouses. There was, therefore, a gradual tendency for textile manufacture for export to gravitate towards Calcutta and Madras. Although both cities were homes to merchants and agents, the artisans did not move into the urban core, preferring to stay in the periphery of the towns probably to enjoy the lower cost of living and better quality of life there. These then resembled 'urban villages,' a concept dealt with more fully in Chapter 6.

The exporting rural hubs in Coromandel and Bengal were home to an elite class of weavers, who contracted supplies with the companies' agents and brokers and enjoyed a great deal of authority locally. Their power derived from the ability to negotiate with several companies simultaneously, the ability to trade on the side, and facility with European languages. The spinning of cotton yarn was done locally by hand, and cotton did not grow in the same areas where textile production was taking place. The task of spinning engaged domestic workers. The headmen directly or indirectly took care of cotton supplies to this dispersed labour pool. They could abuse their authority to oppress those making textiles. P. Swarnalatha shows that the weavers accepted a headman's authority more readily when he was seen as a caste-man and contested the authority when he was from outside the community.[38]

The transition to colonialism in Bengal and south India brought changes in business organization. The transformation reduced competition of other European corporate bodies in the textile market, increased the stranglehold of the Company officers and private traders upon the textile artisans, and secured contractual obligations between weavers and British merchants, at times by violent means.[39] The abuses weakened the position of headmen and master weavers well before imported cotton textiles cut the ground from beneath their feet.

Compared with the artisans who supplied Indo-European trade, the much bigger group that served the home market and sold goods entering the overland trade remains under-researched. Thanks to the custom of wealthy warlords and landlords, urban crafts were concentrated in the Gangetic plains. The artisans made carpets, brass articles, fine pottery, and wool and silk garments, among other goods, in urban workshops and factories. The consumers owned some of these factories, emulating the practice of the imperial household.[40] Inside the factories, teams of male artisans arranged in hierarchical master–apprentice relationships executed orders. Almost all other contexts of production were dominated by household labour and allowed more women to work in industry.

These skilled urban crafts did suffer from weaker state power but did not disappear. Some recovered as urban crafts after British takeover of the Indo-Gangetic Basin regions. Many sources report the existence of urban workshops and factories in the same region from the early to mid-nineteenth century, bearing the same name as workshops did in the Mughal times (karkhana). These reincarnations were more commonly found in the eastern Gangetic plains, but a smattering of them remained in the old Mughal towns, suggesting that there had never been a total extinction of these skills and modes of working. There was, nevertheless, a significant change. The articles produced by these units now served a growing export market or urban middle-class market. The factories were either owned by the masters themselves (a partial convergence with the family firm) or owned by export merchants rather than by aristocratic and wealthy consumers as in the past.

Not enough is known about artisans in the princely states. One exceptional work sheds some light on the subject.[41] Jodhpur's territory was mainly arid, with a patch of irrigated area located in its eastern half. Strategically positioned on overland trade routes, the state was home to many merchants and bankers, who consumed many skill-intensive manufactures made in the cities. These capitalists thrived owing to the fiscal weakness of the state. A key point of emphasis of the study is the difference in political organization between the cities and the countryside. In both contexts, artisans had developed community institutions of dispute settlement, and the state respected their autonomy with respect to civil law. But comparatively speaking, the rural artisans were less organized and more exposed to the landlords' arbitrary exercise of power and exploitation. By contrast, the town artisans could employ community solidarity more effectively.

Like these artisans, much overland trade and the traders connected with it remained far removed from Indo-European trade. And therefore, overland trade maintains a shadowy presence in most archival sources. Important changes did happen in this sphere.

Internal Overland Trade

The commercial efflorescence in Mughal India depended on the road cum river based transportation arteries along the Ganges and the Indus. Though not navigable throughout their lengths, the rivers enabled the movement of bulk goods such as grain, sugar, salt, and cloth, and valuable goods like silks and spices, far more cheaply in northern India than in southern India. The plains themselves afforded wheeled traffic and short-haul caravans. These arteries along the Ganges and the Indus joined in Punjab, where trans-Himalayan caravan routes met, giving rise to large seasonal fairs and spot markets on the outskirts of Delhi and Lahore. Several roads led out of northern India towards Afghanistan, Persia, and Central Asia. The mountain passes could accommodate sheep and horses, but not camels and bullocks. Therefore, the carrying capacity of the trade was not large. Given the transit cost, the trade concentrated on low-bulk, high-value articles, such as silk and wool.[42] Also, from across the mountains, there came horses, which were essential to warfare.

What happened to these systems during and after the eighteenth century is an open question. In the eighteenth century, the two significant overland segments of which we have some knowledge were transporting valuable articles such as Bengal silk to north India and beyond India. The bullock caravans carried grain to the coasts and cotton to the textile-producing areas. Sushil Chaudhury said that the Asian merchants who organized overland trade along the Ganges-Jumna plains and exported many artisanal goods from this region operated on a bigger scale than overseas trade. The claim is credible, and usefully questions the tendency to over-stress the European element in regional commerce.[43] Against this picture of growth, there are many reports of local decline of commerce. One sign of local decline was the migration of groups closely linked to the Indus-Ganges routes during Mughal times towards the successor state capitals and the ports.

In the historiography of early-colonial India, there is a sharp polarization of views about trading conditions between 1800 and 1857. 'The dramatic expansion of trade along the Ganges,' wrote Tom Kessinger, 'was the most significant develop-ment for north India's economy after 1757. With the return of peace to the upper Ganges valley in 1801, an enlarged flow of goods began to move down-river, facili-tated by relatively low transportation costs and attracted by the link to the world market via Calcutta.'[44] Another study of the Indo-Gangetic region observes that for some time before the railways began in the 1860s, there were signs of 'expanding commerce, population growth and cultivated acreage extensions … Market con-nections with the recently annexed Central Provinces and the Punjab were improv-ing, bullock carts were replacing pack animals, canals were being introduced into the western Doab and steamboats on to the Ganges below Allahabad.'[45]

It is necessary to be cautious about the 'dramatic' element in Kessinger's account. Market integration was a slow tendency, frequently disrupted by crop failure and sharp changes in trading conditions. In the current state of knowledge, it is hard to estimate price convergence trends precisely. Realistically, price integration on an India-wide scale was a distant and post-railway prospect, whereas within subregions like the Ganges artery, price convergence may have occurred.

At the opposite end, we hear about a 'great' depression between 1825 and 1856 in the Madras Presidency and over a shorter span in the same region that Kessinger wrote about.[46] 'The early nineteenth century, wrote C.A. Bayly, 'saw a clear cyclical crisis in the economy.'[47] Depression scholars attribute the process to a monetary contraction caused by an outflow of silver on the government account, and point at a price depression as proof of a depression. The argument of a monetary contrac-tion is weak because the government was such a small part of the economy that the claim that it could cause depression by sending remittances abroad is not credible. In practice, silver flowed in via trade surplus and flowed out via government pay-ments. These should at best balance one another, except that private transactions are almost always underestimates. There is in any case no direct measure of money demand to show if there really was a monetary contraction. Price trends tell us little about the period 1800–1858. The data on trends in prices are contradictory. Prices of grain were steady in some accounts and rose in some other accounts.[48] Robert Allen and Roman Studer compile grain prices for eight markets in eastern and northern India; this dataset shows that the average price rose in the first half of the nineteenth century.[49]

It is unnecessary to choose between these two competing stories – the growth of markets and the decline of markets. The more likely scenario is that commercialization progressed faster in northern India because colonial expansion happened earlier and in an already highly commercial region, and because the trade and transportation costs were smaller in this region than in the south. The only barrier to trade was political and military, which reduced with the advent of British power. The same factor was weak in south India. It might have been weak also in areas where bankrupt kingdoms ruled, like Awadh.[50] The persistence of transit duties too was less of a problem in north India than in the south.[51]

In *Rulers, Townsmen, and Bazaars*, C.A. Bayly described 'the intermediate groups that were consolidating themselves between state and the peasantry' in the late eighteenth and early nineteenth-century eastern Gangetic plains.[52] The groups that the study concentrates on include the Khatri, Agarwal, Oswal, and Maheswari families. They were Hindu merchants, lived in small towns, and through their associations, corporations, and temples retained a degree of continuity in how they lived and did business. British expansion in the area did not disrupt their social cohesion or economic importance. I would add that market integration over the Indo-Gangetic Basin as colonialism expanded enabled the merchants and bankers access the produce of a larger region, lower transaction costs, and new investment opportunities.

Nearly all the merchant-banker groups that Bayly and others write about were immigrants from western and northern India. The Mughal invasion of Bengal was followed by the migration of Punjabi Khatri individuals into eastern India. They resettled as court officers, military officers, and landholders under some of the larger landed estates. In the 1750s, Amirchand or Umichand, a Khatri merchant, was one of the company's principal agents in Bengal.[53] Khatris were prominent in Calcutta as brokers and agents of European firms, though some were later replaced by the Marwaris in that role.[54]

If the Khatri move into Calcutta began as partners of the Mughal Empire, the Marwari merchant and banking firms' migration followed a more commercial logic. The most prominent of these firms originated in Rajputana, where the east–west trade routes had offered them business opportunities, and the princely states offered them legal autonomy and immunity. From this base, in the eighteenth century, some of them migrated to Indore and Hyderabad. But the implicit guarantee of security was not enough, or the business opportunities dried up, for around 1800, these firms displayed a preference for the British territories.[55] With Indore, Marwari merchants, who were involved in the inland trade in Malwa opium, formed a link between Bombay and central India. From early in the nineteenth century, Marwari entry into Calcutta enlarged in scale and diversified in business interest.

The early nineteenth century offered many opportunities to a port-city-based trader. Marwari merchants, as mentioned before, formed a link between Bombay and central India. Gujarati and Parsi merchants based in Bombay, or with a significant presence in that city, conducted the export trade in cotton. A growth in cotton export trade from Bombay port to China from the end of the eighteenth century encouraged migration of Parsi, Bhatia, and Marwari business families to the city. They brought with them experience in Asian trade and overland trade. British victory over the Marathas in 1818 brought a vast tract of cotton growing region into direct link with the city, and export market.[56]

Besides the exportable, opium, indigo, and cotton, there were goods traded in the domestic economy, like grain and imported cotton cloth and yarn. Thomas Timberg's history of the Marwaris describes the ancestry of Omkarmal Jatia (1882–1938), a close associate of the Andrew Yule group of industries in Calcutta. In 1838, when a branch of the firm shifted to Calcutta, its main operation was in Khurja and in grain trading.[57] After the railways opened, Calcutta became the transport hub for domestic grain trade and the move paid off. Similarly, the ancestors of the Calcutta Marwari group Goenkas worked in partnership with the firm of Pantia Ralli, which was to emerge as a major grain trader.

From about 1820, a growing quantity of cotton yarn and cloth was being imported from Manchester into India. From three million pounds in 1820, the volume of yarn import reached 31 million in 1860 and stabilized there. Cotton cloth import increased from zero in 1820 to 825 million yards in 1860, about 40% of total cloth consumption.[58] The importation of textiles of such order ended many artisan livelihoods. On the other hand, it was a huge benefit to the consumer and provided enormous scope to Indian merchants by transporting cloth and yarn from the ports to the interior and marketing it. Since per head consumption of cotton cloth was rising through these years, the expansion of trade volume outweighed some decline in the trade in handmade cloth. Again, the business of marketing imported cloth in the interior was in Indian hands, and began from the port city. Nearly all the large Marwari firms of Calcutta in the early nineteenth century functioned as agents of import houses.

Another rising field of investment was financing agricultural commodity trade, discussed in the next section.

Banking, finance, and modern forms of agency

Despite the claim by historians of medieval India that banking and commerce flourished in the imperial realm, it remains difficult to find concrete information on the firms. The business history of Mughal India makes few references to specific entrepreneurial figures or specific firms.[59] We do know something about the circulation of money among the nobility or among the city merchants. There were Agra bankers in the seventeenth century, their main clients being the military-political elite of the same cities.[60] Perhaps the only actual firm that there is good data on, thanks to its complex relationship with the British, was the Jagatseth in eighteenth-century

Bengal. But theirs was an unusual story. The firm of Jagatseths held the license to carry on various monetary functions that should ordinarily be done by the state. They were big and powerful to the same extent that the Bengal Nawab's hold on the monetary system was precarious. Yet, money was valuable in Bengal because of Indo-European trade. Not surprisingly, this great firm declined within a few years of the political transition in Bengal.

Political actors joined trading at times. Sanjay Subrahmanyam says that '[d]ealings between the Mughal state, nobles, and the trading economy took several forms,' and in particular, the ruling order 'themselves at times took a substantial interest in trade.'[61] Some warlords owned ships.[62] That is not necessarily a sign of robust capitalism, however. We should remember Adam Smith, who believed that merchants running a state were a bad deal for competition. Courtiers running ships could have the same effect. The missing biographical material makes it difficult to judge whether politicians doing trade crowded out independent actors or that they were too few to matter. In any case, enterprise of this kind had apparently weak link with banking.

Finance was a field where big changes had begun to happen in the 1700s. In the 1770s and 1780s, Benares, Surat, Peshwa's domain, and in Company's Bengal, large banking firms were present, and we have more than a cursory knowledge about them thanks to Peshwa's and Company's archives. From these statist records, we know that Gopal Das and his son Manohar Das of Benares sent messages congratulating British power and victory and lent money to the company in times of need, that the Jagatseth supplied textiles to the British traders and changed money for them, that Arjunji Nathji of Surat arranged remittances for the company, that a group of bankers handled the Peshwa's enormous debt, and that Haribhakti functioned as a banker to the state of Baroda. Some of these firms, like Haribhakti, rose to prominence thanks to revenue farming. These records suggest that the main business of the bankers was funding wars and political actors (see Figure 5.1).

This, however, is a bias that the archives create. Less than a century later, private Indian banking's main business had changed radically to financing commodity trade. Political clients disappeared from the account books, and yet the banking business did not disappear. When did the change happen? When did it begin? The logical answer is that it happened along with India's political transition, which had this twofold effect, impoverishment of many political actors and the creation of a much wider geographical space over which commercial connections could be remade.

Most Indian bankers who lived in Benares, Mathura, Kasimbazar, Baroda, or Pune did not do deposit banking. Their main business was financing trade and lending to known clients with substantial assets. 'In origin all indigenous bankers appear to have been traders and merchants. The profit arising out of trade provided them with the necessary funds to start their banking business.'[63] Several of them probably dealt more with political actors in the unusual conditions of 1770–1800, but this was a transient phase at best. Their 'multifarious commercial activities' had survived this phase.[64] 'The main advantage possessed by the eighteenth-century

FIGURE 5.1 Home of banker in Ajmer, 1858. The sketch of a palatial home of a Rajputana banker for a London newspaper. © Antiqua Print Gallery/Alamy Stock Photo.

commercial groups,' write a study on Benares, 'was their ability to command resources across a much greater distance.'[65] This is evident in the branch locations of Gopal Das Manohar Das firm. Of the twenty branches reported, ten were in British territories. In the 1920s, a banking enquiry committee in Bihar province surveyed urban bankers and recorded the history of a leading Marwari mercantile firm, Debi Prashad. The firm had started near Patna as a banker in 1840. It drew in deposit accounts from the rich Indian residents and northern Bihar's European community.[66] Descriptions of great Marwari firms of Calcutta, Jabalpur, Delhi, Patna, and Bombay, suggest that many family firms migrated to these emerging hubs of trade and administration (around 1840–50) to find clients among merchants and service workers.

By 1900, the business of indigenous banking was firmly tied to agricultural commodity trade. The significance of the mass migration of Marwaris, mainly bankers, can be seen in this light. The port cities, Bombay, Calcutta, and Madras, were the financial hubs, where the biggest bankers were based. In the late nineteenth century, several interior cities had emerged as financial hubs on the back of substantial grain trades. Among the big players were the Khandelwal banking houses of Mathura, the Oswal bankers of middle Bengal, Srimali, and Porwal bankers in Ahmedabad, Maheswari bankers in Jabalpore, not to mention warehouse owners in market towns, transporters, jute balers and cotton ginners. Still, the port cities were the centres of the financial markets.

Why the port city? At the top end of the scale, indigenous firms and Indo-European corporate banks collaborated a lot, reducing risks for both parties. The large firms funded other bankers who moved money in the interior. The business of remitting money from the centre to the branches relied on the drafts known as hundi. The corporate banks accepted hundis issued by the city firms, hence the attraction of the port city.[67] Over the nineteenth century, the city offered other fields of investment, like stock-broking, bullion trade, and commodity futures. Much of that development happened after the book's timespan, but had begun earlier.

Towards the end of the timespan, a new and promising field was opening up to Indian entrepreneurs – agency. Huge building projects like the Ganges Canal in the 1840s, the railways after 1853, and the dams that came up on the south Indian river deltas needed to hire thousands of people. Nowhere were they hired directly by the engineers, supervisors, and foremen. Their direct employers were a group of contractors, who committed to deliver labour and perform the required tasks. Labour contractors also operated on a large scale in the supply of indentured work-ers to Mauritius, Assam tea plantations, Mysore coffee plantations, and tea workers in Ceylon. Not all flows were fully active before 1857, but most had already begun. With few exceptions, the contractors were Indians. Although a few came from busi-ness background, most were middle-class individuals who saw in labour contract agency a promising field of enterprise.[68]

Much of this dynamism was a feature of the Indo-Gangetic Basin. In south India, the turn of the century was a more disruptive time, starting with the fall of caravan trade.

Mobile transporters of southern India

Major caravan routes took off from market points located on the Ganges and the Indus and went towards central, western, and southern India. Along these roads, bullock caravans were managed by specialist carriers known as the Banjaras or Lambadas. The origin of the Banjaras remains a matter of speculation. There is no doubt about their value to the commercial world of the arid interior and forested uplands of southern-central India, which had few navigable rivers, and few roads suitable for wheeled traffic until the railway era. The presence of bullock caravans in these regions was recorded from the fifteenth century when the Delhi Sultanate's influence began to spread southwards. However, the caravan runners acquired a special prominence during organized military campaigns in the Deccan between 1670 and 1818. For this reason, the East India Company records and contemporary travel narratives contain much valuable material on them.[69]

Caravan trade in the Deccan Plateau was stimulated in two distinct ways, which benefited the Banjaras.[70] The first of these was the necessity to supply raw cotton to the cotton textile manufacturing clusters along the coasts. Much of the cotton that entered long-distance trade came from western India and moved east towards Bengal and Coromandel. The trade was so established that around 1800, the company's attempts to procure cotton for export, which meant trying to divert cotton away from the domestic routes, did not succeed. Only much later in the mid-nineteenth century did these attempts begin to succeed. By then, the reduction in hand-spinning had made domestic demand for cotton much smaller. This cotton was exported from Calcutta to China late in the eighteenth century, not a small business, but not much is known about it.

The second stimulus was the supply of grain to the armies on the march. The major powers in the Deccan Plateau– the Marathas, Hyderabad, and Mysore – all relied on Banjara caravans for the subsistence of the soldiers. They did so because, unlike the Company, none had easy access to seaports that could transport grain supplies from the rich deltas. In return for their services, the regional states offered the Banjaras freedom of movement. The Company had more choice about grain transportation, thanks to its ports. But when engaged in battles deep inside the Deccan Plateau, it was still reliant on the same groups and needed to negotiate with the Banjaras in much the same way as did the others.

All these changes put immense pressure on the Banjara groups towards the end of the eighteenth century. There were several groups in operation. Despite their theoretical neutrality, prolonged military rivalries inevitably spilled over into rivalries between groups allied to different armies. Questions of loyalty became paramount, and incentives were offered, and punishments meted out in constant efforts to divert supplies away from enemy armies. The idea of diplomatic immunity did not go far in the late 1700s Deccan. Furthermore, grain was not always available. Indeed, it was almost impossible to obtain grain during the great famines of 1770 and 1783. It needs to be remembered that the Banjaras were purely transporters and did not possess stationary storage capacity. In fact, they were barely visible in permanent markets as traders.

A Company document estimated that the bullock caravans that carried grain, cotton, and salt between north and south India and across the Deccan Plateau, that is, the combined carriage capacity of the two major Banjara camps Rathor and Bartia numbered 170,000 bullocks about 1790.[71] The average load carried by a medium-sized bullock was 75 kgs.[72] The overland system's carrying capacity at the very peak of its development was a little over 10,000 tons, which was a tiny fraction (less than 1%) of the possible south Indian grain output of several hundred million tons. For comparison, in 1901, the main south Indian railway companies' cargo amounted to over five million tons. If we add the Great Indian Peninsular Railway, which connected Bombay with the western part of the Deccan plateau, the number will rise to eight million tons. This was an increase of 800 times. Production in the region would have increased between these two benchmarks, but possibly not even doubled. In short, if the level of trade in the railway era represents a peak level of commercialization, the level in the earlier benchmark year was not much commerce to speak of. These comparisons would be misleading when the caravans carried valuable goods. The bullock caravans' main business was not silk, gold, or wool, but grain, cotton and salt. As far as grain was concerned, a contemporary assessment for Bengal, that 'except in cities, the bulk of the people is every where subsisted from the produce of their own immediate neighbourhood,' held true in the eighteenth century for the Deccan.[73]

The insignificant percentage that overland trade forms of grain demand suggests that in peacetime, the Banjaras were not an effective or important player in the grain markets. And yet, the estimated volume was large enough to feed warring armies. The total numbers engaged in the major Deccan conflicts were not large at any time, usually well below a hundred thousand people in each case. For such numbers, 10,000 tons could mean half a year's rations. In short, the Banjaras could not stimulate general market activity, but they were a critical aid to warfare.

As a result of this significance, the eighteenth century ended with a sharp rise in demand for these mobile transporters' services together with steadily increasing pressure to politicize their services. Equally, with the end of warfare in southern India, there came a time when the Banjaras faced growing irrelevance. Later in the nineteenth century, the railways and the enclosure of the common lands as farms or forests deprived them of markets and pastures and pushed many to disreputable livelihoods the state connected with criminality.[74]

Conclusion

In the historiography of Indian business in the eighteenth century, materials stored in the European trade archives have played so large a role that it is easy to exaggerate the scale of overseas trade and believe that early-modern Indo-European trade saw the start of a one-sided relationship like the empire that it engendered. The truth is that Indo-European trade was too small to dominate anything. The significance of the eighteenth-century commercialism lay elsewhere.

It can be found in a movement towards an integration of the overland and the maritime. Far larger in scale than Indian cotton textiles exported by the companies was the potential scale of trades in agricultural commodities, mass-consumed textiles, coastal and Indo-Chinese trades. These potentials were explored more fully in the early nineteenth century. Increasingly, merchants and bankers based in the port cities funded these trades or organized these. More Indians than Europeans dominated the trades.

If Indo-European trade mattered at all in business history, its relevance was an indirect one. The port cities were the making of Indo-European trade. In the late eighteenth century, businesses based in the Mughal sphere declined as the commercial cities depopulated. On the other side, bankers and merchants began to diversify from, say, raw silk to raw cotton. By 1830, indigenous merchants were entrenched in almost all of the major commodity trades in the region, cotton, grain, cloth, opium and indigo. The Company ports and a few interior towns well-connected with the seaboard, like Patna or Ahmedabad, were hubs of consumption and centres of services essential to long-distance trade. The railway network that started being built from the 1850s was a logical next step to integrating the interior order and the port city.

One of the key factors behind an asymmetric response of business to the new political-economic order was urban decay in northern India. Chapter 6 places this episode in context.

Notes

1 I use 'early modern' as a preparatory, scene-setting, time.
2 William H. Moreland, *India at the Death of Akbar: An Economic Study*, London: Macmillan, 1920; and *From Akbar to Aurangzeb: A Study in Indian Economic History*, London: Macmillan, 1923.
3 The pioneering works were the histories of the organized European enterprise. See Holden Furber, *John Company at Work*, Cambridge, MA: Harvard University Press, 1948; Tapan Raychaudhuri, *Jan Company in Coromandel, 1600–1690: A Study in the Interrelations of European Commerce and Traditional Economies*, The Hague, Martunus Nijhoff, 1962; Charles R. Boxer, *The Portuguese Seaborne Empire, 1415–1825*, London: Hutchinson, 1969. K.N. Chaudhuri's influential contributions helped form a conception of the Indian Ocean as a totality. See especially, Chaudhuri, *Trade and Civilisation in the Indian Ocean: An Economic History from the Rise of Islam to 1750*, Cambridge: Cambridge University Press, 1985; and *Asia before Europe: Economy and Civilisation of the Indian Ocean from the Rise of Islam to 1750*, Cambridge: Cambridge University Press, 1991. Important overviews and collections should include Kenneth McPherson, *The Indian Ocean: A History of People and the Sea*, Delhi and Oxford: Oxford University Press, 1998; Denys Lombard and Jean Aubin, eds., *Asian Merchants and Businessmen in the Indian Ocean and the China Sea*, New Delhi: Oxford University Press, 2000; Ashin Das Gupta and Michael N. Pearson, eds., *India and the Indian Ocean*, Calcutta: Oxford University Press, 1987; Om Prakash, *The New Cambridge History of India; Vol. II.5. European Commercial Enterprise in Pre-colonial India*, Cambridge: Cambridge University Press, 1998. For important regional studies, see Ashin Das Gupta, *Malabar in Asian Trade 1740–1800*, Cambridge: Cambridge University Press, 1967; Surendra Gopal, *Commerce and Crafts in Gujarat, 16th and 17th Centuries: A Study in the Impact of European Expansion on a Pre-capitalist Economy*, New Delhi: People's Publishing House, 1975; Sinnappah Arasaratnam, *Merchants, Companies and Commerce on the Coromandel Coast, 1650–1740*, Delhi: Oxford University Press, 1986; Om Prakash, *The Dutch East India Company and the Economy of Bengal, 1630–1720*, Princeton: Princeton University Press, 1985; Sanjay Subrahmanyam, *The Political Economy of Commerce: Southern India, 1500–1650*, Cambridge: Cambridge University Press, 1990; Sushil Chaudhury, *From Prosperity to Decline: Eighteenth-Century Bengal*, Delhi: Manohar, 1995; Lakshmi Subramanian, *Indigenous Capital and Imperial Expansion: Bombay, Surat and the West Coast*, Delhi and Oxford: Oxford University Press, 1996; Prasannan Parthasarathi, *The Transition to a Colonial Economy: Weavers, Merchants and Kings in South India, 1720–1800*, Cambridge: Cambridge University Press, 2001. Recent collections of research and surveys of the field can be found in Giorgio Riello and Tirthankar Roy, eds., *How India Clothed the World: the World of South Asian Textiles 1500–1850*, Leiden: Brill, 2009; Tirthankar Roy, *India in the World Economy from Antiquity to the Present*, Cambridge: Cambridge University Press, 2012; and David Washbrook, 'India in the Early Modern World Economy: Modes of Production, Reproduction and Exchange,' *Journal of Global History*, 2(1), 2007, 87–111.

4 'Incorporation of Indian Subcontinent into Capitalist World-Economy,' *Economic and Political Weekly*, 21(4), 1986, PE28-PE39.

5 Proto-industrialization refers to a growth of manufacturing in semi-rural clusters serving distant markets. Frank Perlin, 'Proto-industrialisation in Precolonial South Asia,' *Past and Present*, 98, 1983, 30–95.

6 'Inland Trade,' in Tapan Raychaudhuri and Irfan Habib, eds., *The Cambridge Economic History of India, vol. 1: c. 1200-c. 1750*, Cambridge: Cambridge University Press, 1983, 335.

7 Chaudhury, *From Prosperity to Decline*, 174–5

8 Om Prakash, 'Bullion for Goods: International Trade and the Economy of Early Eighteenth Century Bengal,' *Indian Economic and Social History Review*, 13(2), 1976, 159–86.

9 'Studying a Colonial Economy—Without Perceiving Colonialism,' *Modern Asian Studies*, 19(3), 1985, 355–81.

10 Tirthankar Roy, 'Economic Conditions in Early Modern Bengal: A Contribution to the Divergence Debate,' *Journal of Economic History*, 70(1), 179–94.

11 *Ibid.*

12 Chaudhury, *From Prosperity to Decline*.

13 'Bullion for Goods.'

14 'Rethinking Wages and Competitiveness in the Eighteenth Century: Britain and South India Compared,' *Past and Present*, 158, 1998, 79–109.

15 For a longer summary, see 'Indian Ocean Trade,' in Roy, *India in the World Economy*.

16 Ashin Das Gupta, *The World of the Indian Ocean Merchant 1500–1800*, New Delhi: Oxford University Press, 46.

17 H.V. Bowen, 'Sinews of Trade and Empire: The Supply of Commodity Exports to the East India Company during the Late Eighteenth Century,' *Economic History Review*, 55(3), 2002, 466–86.

18 Ann M. Carlos and Stephen Nicholas, '"Giants of an Earlier Capitalism": The Chartered Trading Companies as Modern Multinationals,' *Business History Review*, 62(3), 1988, 398–419.

19 Holden Furber, 'Review of A. Mervyn Davies, *Clive of Plassey: A Biography*,' New York: Charles Scribner's Sons, 1939, *American Historical Review*, 45(3), 1940, 635–7.

20 See, for example, Anthony Webster, *The Twilight of the East India Company: The Evolution of Anglo-Asian Commerce and Politics, 1790–1860*, Rochester: Boydell and Brewer, 2009; Blair B. Kling, *Partner in Empire: Dwarkanath Tagore and the Age of Enterprise in Eastern India*, Berkeley and Los Angeles: University of California Press, 1977. Also, Tirthankar Roy, *A Business History of India: Enterprise and the Emergence of Capitalism from 1700*, Cambridge: Cambridge University Press, 2018.

21 Das Gupta, *World of the Indian Ocean Merchant*, 92.

22 See also C.A. Bayly and Sanjay Subrahmanyam, 'Portfolio Capitalists and the Political Economy of Early Modern India,' *Indian Economic and Social History Review*, 25(4), 1988, 401–24.

23 Das Gupta, *World of the Indian Ocean Merchants*, 98.

24 Ibid., 131.

25 Ibid., 100.

26 Ibid., 101, 127.

27 Ibid., 108.

28 Ibid., 169.

29 Ghulam A. Nadri, 'The English and Dutch East India Companies and Indian Merchants in Surat in the Seventeenth and Eighteenth centuries: Interdependence, competition and contestation,' in Adam Clulow and Tristan Mostert, eds., *The Dutch and English East*

India Companies: Diplomacy, trade and violence in early modern Asia, Amsterdam: Amsterdam University Press, 2018, 125–149.

30 N. Kanakarathnam, 'Maritime Trade and Growth of Urban Infrastructure in Port Cities of Colonial Andhra: A Study of Masulipatnam,' *Proceedings of the Indian History Congress*, 75, 2014, 690–696.

31 Chhaya Goswami, *Globalization before its Time. The Gujarati Merchants from Kachchh*, New Delhi: Penguin, 2016.

32 Prasannan Parthasarathi, *Why Europe Grew Rich and Asia Did Not: Global Economic Divergence, 1600–1850*, Cambridge: Cambridge University Press, 2011.

33 Om Prakash, 'From Negotiation to Coercion: Textile Manufacturing in India in the Eighteenth Century,' *Modern Asian Studies*, 41(5), 2007, 1331–68.

34 R.E. Kranton and A.V. Swamy, 'Contracts, Hold-up, and Exports: Textiles and Opium in Colonial India,' *American Economic Review*, 98(5), 2008, 967–89; Roy, *India in the World Economy*; and Tirthankar Roy, *East India Company: The World's Most Powerful Corporation*, Delhi: Allen Lane, 2011.

35 Citation from Radhika Seshan, 'From Chief Merchant to Joint Stock Merchant: A Comparative Study of Kasivirana and Pedda Venkatadri, Chief Merchants of Madras,' *Proceedings of the Indian History Congress*, 70, 2009–2010, 347–353.

36 Prakash, *Dutch East India Company*; Raychaudhuri, *Jan Company in Coromandel*; Arasaratnam, 'Weavers, Merchants and Company: The Handloom Industry in Southeastern India 1750–1790,' *Indian Economic and Social History Review*, 17(3), 1980, 257–281; Subrahmanyam, *Political Economy of Commerce*; Parthasarathi, *Transition to a Colonial Economy*; Chaudhury, *From Prosperity to Decline*; Hameeda Hossain, *The Company Weavers of Bengal: The East India Company and the Organization of Textile Production in Bengal, 1750–1813*, Delhi: Oxford University Press, 1988.

37 Ghulam A. Nadri, *Eighteenth-Century Gujarat: The Dynamics of Its Political Economy, 1750–1800*, Leiden: Brill, 2009; Pedro Machado, 'A Regional Market in a Globalised Economy: East Central and South Eastern Africans, Gujarati Merchants and the Indian Textile Industry in the Eighteenth and Nineteenth Centuries,' in Giorgio Riello and Tirthankar Roy, eds., *How India Clothed the World: the World of South Asian Textiles 1500–1850*, Leiden: Brill, 53–84.

38 P. Swarnalatha, 'Revolt, Testimony, Petition: Artisanal Protests in Colonial Andhra,' *International Review of Social History*, 46(1), 2001, 107–29.

39 Parthasarathi, *Transition to a Colonial Economy*; and Prakash, 'From Negotiation to Coercion.'

40 Tripta Verma, *Karkhanas under the Mughals, from Akbar to Aurangzeb: A Study in Economic Development*, Delhi: Pragati, 1994.

41 Nandita Prasad Sahai, *Politics of Patronage and Protest: The State, Society and Artisans in Early Modern Rajasthan*, Delhi: Oxford University Press, 2006.

42 The trans-Himalayan trade with Central Asia has been studied by Scott C. Levi, *The Indian Diaspora in Central Asia and Its Trade, 1550–1900*, Leiden: Brill, 2002, 30–1, and Levi, 'India, Russia and the Eighteenth-century Transformation of the Central Asian Caravan Trade,' *Journal of the Economic and Social History of the Orient*, 42(4), 1999, 519–48. Also, on overland trade, Sushil Chaudhury and Michel Morineau, eds., *Merchants, Companies and Trade: Europe and Asia in the Early Modern Era*, Cambridge: Cambridge University Press, 1999.

43 Chaudhury, *From Prosperity to Decline*.

44 Tom Kessinger, 'Regional Economy (1757–1857): North India,' in Dharma Kumar, ed., *Cambridge Economic History of India*, vol. 2, Cambridge: Cambridge University Press, 1983, 242–270.

45 Ian Derbyshire, 'Economic Change and the Railways in North India, 1860–1914,' *Modern Asian Studies*, 21(3), 1987, 521–545.

46 P.J. Thomas and B. Natarajan, 'Economic Depression in the Madras Presidency (1825–54),' *Economic History Review*, 7(1), 1936, 67–75; Asiya Siddiqui, 'Money and Prices in the Earlier Stages of Empire: India and Britain 1760–1840,' *Indian Economic and Social History Review*, 18(3–4), 1978, 231–261.

47 C.A. Bayly, 'State and Economy in India over Seven Hundred Years,' *Economic History Review*, 38(4), 1985, 583–596, cited text on 590.

48 For evidence of price stability, see Siddiqui, 'Money and Prices.' For evidence of price rise, see Ehtesham Uddin Ahmad, 'Agricultural Production and Prices in Late Nawabi Awadh (1801–1856),' *Proceedings of the Indian History Congress*, 69, 2008, 603–611.

49 https://gpih.ucdavis.edu/Datafilelist.htm (accessed 15 December 2020).

50 Ahmad, 'Agricultural Production,' on the dismal conditions in Awadh.

51 Thomas and Natarajan, 'Economic Depression,' on south India.

52 C.A. Bayly, *Rulers, Townsmen and Bazaars: North Indian Society in the Age of British Expansion, 1770–1870*, Cambridge: Cambridge University Press, 1983, 6–7.

53 John R. McLane, *Land and Local Kingship in Eighteenth-Century Bengal*, Cambridge: Cambridge University Press, 1993, 177.

54 Thomas Timberg, 'Three Types of the Marwari Firm,' *Indian Economic and Social History Review*, 10(1), 1973, 3–36.

55 Ibid.

56 Archana Calangutcar, 'Marwaris in the Cotton Trade of Mumbai: Collaboration and Conflict (Circa: 1850–1950),' *Proceedings of the Indian History Congress*, 73, 2012, 658–667.

57 Timberg, 'Three Types of the Marwari Firm.'

58 Tirthankar Roy, 'Consumption of Cotton Cloth in India, 1795–1940,' *Australian Economic History Review*, 52(1), 2012, 61–84.

59 For a survey that reflects this weakness of the scholarship well, see Karen Leonard, 'The "Great Firm" Theory of the Decline of the Mughal Empire,' *Comparative Studies in Society and History*, 21(2), 1979, 151–67.

60 Irfan Habib, 'Usury in Medieval India,' *Comparative Studies in Society and History*, 6(4), 1964, 393–419.

61 Sanjay Subrahmanyam, 'The Mughal State - Structure or Process? Reflections on Recent Western Historiography,' *Indian Economic Social History* Review, 29(3), 1992, 291–321.

62 For a set of examples from Golconda, see Sanjay Subrahmanyam and C.A. Bayly, 'Portfolio Capitalists and the Political Economy of Early Modern India,' *Indian Economic Social History* Review, 25(4), 1988, 401–24.

63 Kamala Prasad Mishra, 'The Role of the Banaras Bankers in the Economy of Eighteenth Century Upper India,' *Proceedings of the Indian History Congress*, 34(II), 1973, 63–76. See also C.A. Bayly, 'Das Family,' *Oxford Dictionary of National Biography*, https://doi.org/10.1093/ref:odnb/75041 (accessed on 20 January 2021).

64 G.D. Sharma, 'Business and Accounting in Western India during the Eighteenth Century,' *Proceedings of the Indian History Congress*, 46, 1985, 308–315.

65 Vinod Kumar and Shiv Narayan, 'Colonial Policy and the Culture of Immigration: Citing the Social History of Varanasi in the Nineteenth Century,' *Proceedings of the Indian History Congress*, 73, 2012, 888–897.

66 Ibid., 158.

67 On the interdependence between the two types of bank, see Amiya Kumar Bagchi, 'Transition from Indian to British Indian Systems of Money and banking 1800–1850,' *Modern Asian Studies*, 19(3), 1984, 501–519.

68 On two contexts of contracting before 1857, Rita P. Bhambi, 'Great Indian Peninsula Railway Company and its Contractors (1853–1871),' *Proceedings of the Indian History Congress*, 73, 2012, 880–887; Jan Lucassen, 'The Brickmakers' Strikes on the Ganges Canal in 1848–1849,' *International Review of Social History*, 51 (Supplement 14), 2006, 47–83.

69 Bhangiya Bhukya, *Subjugated Nomads: The Lambadas under the Rule of the Nizams*, Hyderabad, Orient Blackswan, 2010.

70 Captain John Briggs (Persian interpreter in the Hyderabad court), 'Account of the Origin, History, and Manners of the Race of Men called Bunjaras,' *Transactions of the Literary Society of Bombay*, vol. I, London: John Murray, 1819, 170–197. See also, R.G. Varady, 'North Indian Banjaras: Their Evolution as Transporters,' *South Asia*, 2(1), 1979, 1–18; and Joseph Brennig, 'Textile Producers and Production in Late Seventeenth Century Coromandel,' *Indian Economic and Social History Review*, 23(4), 1986, 333–55. On the nineteenth century, useful references to the Banjaras can be found in Ravi Ahuja, ' "Opening up the Country"? Patterns of Circulation and Politics of Communication in Early Colonial Orissa,' *Studies in History*, 20(1), 2004, 73–130; and N. Benjamin, 'The Trade of the Central Provinces of India (1861–1880),' *Indian Economic and Social History Review*, 15(4), 1978, 505–14.

71 Cited by Briggs, 'Account of the Origin.'

72 H.T. Colebrooke, *Remarks on the Husbandry and Internal Commerce of Bengal*, Calcutta, 1804, 163.

73 Ibid., 161.

74 Bhangiya Bhukya, '"Delinquent Subjects": Dacoity and the Creation of a Surveillance Society in Hyderabad State,' *Indian Economic and Social History Review*, 44(2), 2007, 179–212.

6

TOWNS

The rise and fall of towns illustrate state formation, state collapse, changes in the relationship between business and politics, and the evolving links between the ports and the interior. A key pattern in eighteenth-century India was an initial fall and later recovery of towns in the Indo-Gangetic Basin, whereas the coastal commercial centres experienced a steady rise. This chapter sets out to study the general character of the urban reshuffle. A model of urbanism wherein politics was the chief attraction to business in an earlier era was superseded in the new world by a model of urbanism where business attracted new business. There was a change from political towns to business towns.

In this account, the emerging places like the colonial ports were emerging not because of the concentration of power but the remarkable conjunction of maritime trade and a cosmopolitan business class. With such foundations as these, in the nineteenth century the ports could stay at the frontiers of globalization. Ports on the Indian Ocean littoral moved money and commercial skills around between them; they were hubs of services like finance, but they were not necessarily garrison or temple towns anymore. The chapter tells the prehistory of that emergence.

It is necessary to start with a definition of the 'town' in the period in question.

What was a town around 1700?

The boundary between the town and the countryside was always blurred.[1] Still, in imperial north India, nine characteristics often occurred together in a town – a garrison, a fort, courts of justice, a police force, a big bazaar, settlements of skilled artisans, bankers, a transit point in long-distance trade, and a large mosque. In other words, in those settlements where these features occurred together, population density increased sharply. In south India, the towns did not necessarily possess all of these features. Some of them displayed different ones, such as a temple that served as a cultural and manufacturing hub. They were also smaller in size compared to those located in the Gangetic plains and were few and far between. Clusters of villages specializing in an industry like handloom weaving sometimes acquired town-like features; that is, they became hubs of administration, attractive places for migrants, commerce, and banking. Despite this difference, the north Indian constellation of features marking a convergence of the economic, cultural, and spiritual capitals helps make sense of the urban history in all regions. It helps us understand why towns were so crucial for business.

In both north and south India, town and country were interdependent. The village delivered taxes, food, and mercenary soldiers, and the political elite who lived in the cities protected property rights on land and sponsored the extension of cultivation. Therefore, the town lived on rural resources, and the village lived on urban power. Towns were concentrations of skilled and capital-intensive services. For example, one business that had an unambiguously urban bias was banking. The largest banking firms financed long-distance trade, helped with remittances, and gave loans to rich clients. They engaged in rural credit indirectly by funding other bankers or merchants.

The chapter says that towns like these declined after the mid-eighteenth century, unless they had commercial advantages, whereas towns with commercial advantages rose. In more detail, the breakup of the Mughal Empire and the rise of new states saw the core urban zone shift from the western part of the Indo-Gangetic Basin eastwards, to Bihar, Bengal, Benares, and Awadh. The rise of new regimes out of the old Mughal provinces of Awadh, Hyderabad, and Bengal stimulated urban growth. None of these new capitals was as large as the imperial cities at their best, but they grew in size and diversified in occupation. The three ports where the Company was a landlord experienced a similar increase in population and incomes. Madras and Calcutta's rapid growth stemmed from the trade that the Company directly engaged in and their attraction for the Indian capitalists who migrated from the interior and other decaying ports. Bombay gained from Surat's troubles; Madras from the decline of the Golkonda state and its chief port Masulipatnam, and Calcutta from the disturbances in western Bengal and the attrition of Hooghly. Away from these grand trajectories, agricultural trades encouraged the emergence and growth of market towns, places that traded in cotton, food, and cloth and were located nearer the sources of supply of these goods.

These new dynamics redefined the town. The model of political town formation gave way to a new model of commercial town formation. Towns did not need to have all those nine features to remain relevant.

How large was the urban population?

The seventeenth century

The Aligarh school description of north India suggests a relatively high urbanization level, an outcome of the high proportion of the gross output of land taken as taxes and channelled to the centres of military and fiscal administration.[2] These urban centres were home to soldiers, artisans, service workers in the courts' employ, and bankers and merchants investing money in overland trade and remittance businesses. Three towns – Agra, Delhi, and Lahore – had populations of 400,000 each at their peaks. There was a whole cluster of smaller places – Budaun, Kanauj, Bayana, Sambhal, Mathura, Lucknow, or Benares – living on commerce and service, sometimes a specific staple or tradable good (indigo in Bayana), as well as on military settlements.

There is a contrary picture too. Stephen Blake says that 'the economy of Mughal India was agrarian-based; 90–95 percent of the population lived in small villages…' The main constituents in the fiscal administration and the urban economy were military personnel than capitalists.[3] The three principal cities of the empire were large no doubt, but thanks to their military and political importance. Towns that did not have such importance were too small to matter. The economic drive towards urbanization was relatively weak. Similarly, K.N. Chaudhuri designates Lahore, Delhi, Agra, Patna, Burhanpur, and Ahmedabad, the 'primate cities' of the empire, that is, cities many times larger in size than the next largest, indicating a high degree of concentration.[4] These towns were the core, drawing in resources, the rest of the region being a dependent periphery without much urban dynamism of its own.

There is yet a fourth interpretation, one that suggests that India was a collection of autonomous regional segments, each with its own set of towns. B.G. Gokhale divides India into six regional systems that conducted more trade within themselves and with outsiders than between each other. 'Each was dominated by a large urban center serving a vast area rich in agricultural and industrial production,' as well as a state that commanded sufficient power to run a stable fiscal administration. The six systems and the corresponding urban centres were: Bengal–Bihar (Dhaka–Patna), Agra, Punjab (Sialkot–Multan), Deccan (Burhanpur), Madras (Cochin), and Gujarat (Surat and Ahmedabad).[5]

Seaports do not appear at all in the Aligarh-Blake-Chaudhury descriptions. And while they do appear in Gokhale, they tend to be classified as part of an inland region. Surat in the above scheme appears in Gujarat, whereas it was a Mughal port and its main business relied neither on Gujarat nor on north India, but on the Arabian Sea. Surat's significance rested on its access to the Red Sea and the Persian Gulf, and as a port of embarkation for the hajj pilgrims. I emphasize the autonomy of the seaboard towns; these were a product of trade and not of states, and functioned semi-autonomously from the influence of the inland states. These different urban spaces did get more closely connected, but that was an effect of the emergence of the East India Company as a state.

There is, nevertheless, a point of agreement. Whether we start the construction of the big picture with the empire or with the regions, one fundamental reason for urban concentration was 'the complementarity of economic nodality and political attributes.'[6] There was mutually reinforcing growth of military and political power and economic activities. Many European descriptions of interior towns – such as Delhi, Agra, Lahore, Burhanpur, Ahmedabad, or Dhaka – observed the simultaneous presence of four attributes within each one of these places: a market that sold the

MAP 6.1 Overland trade routes and trading towns, 1700.

produce of a large hinterland, a cosmopolitan collection of merchants and bankers, a seat of administration, and a large garrison complete with a well-defended fort. The settlement of troops and their commanders made a town attractive to the merchants, bankers, and skilled artisans. A further dimension has been added to this list – religious endowments. 'Rulers constructed religious monuments and civic institutions that simultaneously functioned as commercial centers.'[7] Thus we obtain the constellation of nine features characterizing the town in our times (see the beginning of the chapter).

Such a politically driven urbanism suggests that with political decline, towns would decline too. It further suggests that political upheavals might not affect businesses so much, because businesses could leave. Warlords, whose interests were tied to land, could not leave so easily and were affected more. Did these things happen? (Map 6.1)

TABLE 6.1 Population estimates for selected towns

	1660–80	1800–25	1850	1860–70	1891	1941
Agra	400,000	60,000	66,000	149008	168,622	647,073
Delhi	400,000	100,000	152,406	154417	192,579	700,000
Lahore	400,000	100,000	95,000	98,924	176,854	671,659
Lucknow		300,000	300,000	284779	265,000	259,798
Benares		582,000	200,450	175188	219,467	203,804
Pune		110,000	75,170	118,836	161,390	158,856
Hyderabad		120,000	200,000		124,057	500,623
Patna			284,132		165,192	300,000
Madras				427771	452,518	518,660
Calcutta			413,182	377924	741,144	1,043,307
Bombay	10–50000	180,000	586,119	816562	821,764	979,445

Sources: See text, and India, *The Imperial Gazetteer of India*, vol. 8, Oxford: Clarendon Press, 1908, 410; Walter Hamilton, *The East India Gazetteer*, London: John Murray, 1815, 114, 204, 678; Tom Kessinger, 'Regional Economy: North India,' in Dharma Kumar, ed., *Cambridge Economic History of India, vol. 2, 1757–1970*, Cambridge: Cambridge University Press, 1983, 265–6; Irfan Habib, 'Studying a Colonial Economy—Without Perceiving Colonialism,' *Modern Asian Studies*, 19(3), 1985, 355–81; Muhammad Umar, 'Indian Towns in the Eighteenth Century—Case Study of Six Towns in Uttar Pradesh,' *Proceedings of the Indian History Congress*, 37, 1976, 208–218; Edward Thornton, *A Gazetteer of the Territories under the Government of East India Company and the Native States on the Continent of India*, London: W.H. Allen, 1854; India, *Statistical Abstract relating to British India*, various years, London: HMSO.

What do the numbers show?

Nearly all contributors to the subject agree that numbers are hard to find even for the largest cities. In this scenario, the occurrence of outlandishly large figures suggests that those who reported these data did not know where a town began or where it ended. If we ignore the outliers, five points can still be made (Table 6.1). First, the premier cities in the Indo-Gangetic Basin depopulated in the eighteenth century. Second, there was growth of small towns in the same broad area. Third, towns in the Deccan Plateau were individually too small to alter the general picture. Hyderabad and Pune were about 100,000 in size; Mysore was about half this size as far as we know. Fourth, decline in the interior was far outweighed by growth in the three ports held by the Company. The fifth proposition is perhaps the most surprising one. If we take a long view and extend the town size data well into the twentieth century, it is clear that somewhere from the mid-nineteenth to the mid-twentieth century, the interior towns started regaining their prominence; some of them did so quite dramatically.

The main site of this reshuffle was late Mughal northern India. Although statistics to measure this are hard to find, that fact has not deterred historians from making bold statements about the proportion of the urban population in this region and how the ratio changed in the eighteenth century. Stephen Blake believes that the percentage of the urban population in seventeenth-century India was about five. James Heitzman writes, 'Measured against estimates of total South Asian population between 100 and 200 million around the year 1750, we may posit an urban population then between 10 and 20 per cent of total population (I am inclined to accept a figure of about 20 million urban dwellers).'[8] Since the three major cities of northern India did not contain a population exceeding 1.2–1.4 million in total, and since these were by far the largest, a figure of 20 million is an exaggeration. Even a long list of the towns of the Gangetic plains would not yield more than 20 identifiable large urban sites. The rest were insignificant as population concentrations. In any case, the level of urbanization in the western Gangetic plains was 8–10% in 1800. The figure of 20% in 1750 should imply an improbably large decline in the urban population in the late eighteenth century. Equally, the assumption of 5% in 1700 would suggest a rise in urbanization while leaving the exact period of the increase unspecified. I side with a third alternative – that there was a fall, but not a dramatic one.

Bad numbers permit a choice of extremes – in this case, between bleak desolation and energetic economic growth. We can do better with examples.

De-urbanization: Delhi, Agra, Lahore, Dhaka

There is little controversy that these primate cities declined, and they declined because politics was vital to their economy. Delhi, Agra, and Lahore had a population of 400,000 each in 1700, which reduced to 100,000 each by 1800. These places had expanded in the seventeenth century as their command over fiscal resources increased. Their decline began with the outbreak of rebellion, warfare, fiscal decay, and migration of capital, from the end of the seventeenth century. The formal and more visible disintegration processes of the empire did not begin until the second, or even the third, decade of the eighteenth century. But the seeds of a decline had already been sown.

If we take a long enough view, decline would be too strong a word to describe what happened in these cities. Lahore, the first capital of the Mughal Empire was situated on the well-cultivated banks of the Ravi. The town consolidated its position by becoming a transit point in overland trade between the Indian plains and the trans-Himalayan markets. Its commercial importance stayed intact until the 1730s. After that, foreign invasion and warfare drove many of its wealthy residents to Amritsar. Lahore re-emerged in the last quarter of the century as the second town in the Sikh confederacy under Ranjit Singh. It was 'still a town of considerable size, with a good bazar,' but little long-distance trade and banking remained.[9]

Delhi, the sultanates' capital from the thirteenth to the early sixteenth century and again the capital of the Mughal Empire from 1648 until 1858, had a similar fate in the 1700s as it steadily lost access to its tax base and was repeatedly sacked. Delhi's ruins were the most remarked upon by nostalgic noblemen travelling between Hindustan and Afghanistan on a journey to Persia.[10] Interestingly, invaders from Afghanistan and Persia were two significant factors behind Delhi's woes. The images are evocative but do not add any insight into an economic history narrative. Delhi carried enough strategic and symbolic value to re-emerge as a major urban centre, but that was a much later affair.

Agra was the bigger business centre in the trio, apart from being the empire's capital for a century. Agra illustrates the effect of the military contests in northern India better than Delhi and Lahore. Agra was the nodal point connecting trade from eastern India with that from Rajputana and Malwa. It was the point where trade along the Ganges and Jumna axis left the rivers and took the roads towards the Gulf of Cambay or towards Persia. Located in a cotton and indigo producing area, Agra was advantageous to the textile industry. These strengths did not disappear, even as the town's political status changed. Agra ceased to be the imperial capital in 1648. Within 20 years, the large agricultural and commercial province of which Agra was the centre faced a Jat uprising. The resultant warfare was intermittent, and a truce of sorts was in effect in 1721. However, the truce broke in the wake of Nadir Shah's invasion of Delhi (1739). In the 1750s again, Agra was in the vortex of the rivalry between the Afghans and the Marathas. The town was alternately under the Mughals (until 1757, 1773–83), the Marathas (1757–61, 1772–3, 1784–1803), the Jats (1761–8), the British (1803–), and effectively without a government between these years. According to Jadunath Sarkar, the prominence of the town as a business centre stayed intact throughout the turmoil thanks in part to the exodus of wealthy capitalists from Delhi to Agra. This assessment needs qualification. The hinterland of the town was severely squeezed as major trade routes to the west, and the east came to be controlled by rivals.[11]

Away from the pivot of the military contests, numerous former administrative-cum-commercial centres went into decay in the eighteenth century. If Delhi, Agra, and Lahore were in the line of fire, in the provincial capitals, there was not much insecurity of life. Still, these places were slowly starved of trade, tax income, and state sponsorship for civic institutions as moneyed capital and skilled labour began to leave. Dhaka was temporarily the capital of the Mughal province of Bengal. When the capital shifted to Murshidabad (c. 1703–12), Dhaka was saved only because of strong European interest in muslins still made in the town's vicinity. The presence of the European companies and private traders buying this cloth for export continued into the nineteenth century. It is hard to date precisely when this business began to become unprofitable. By 1830, Dhaka experienced the same fate that Murshidabad, and before it, another Bengal capital Rajmahal, had suffered – political irrelevance. An official visit in the 1850s found 'all its splendid buildings…, the palaces of the ancient newaubs, the factories and churches of the Dutch, French, and Portuguese nations, are all sunk into ruin, and overgrown with jungle.'[12] Burhanpur and Ahmedabad, like Dhaka, were capitals of large Mughal provinces in the seventeenth century and had grown as commercial and manufacturing centres, points of caravan trade, and military settlements. Both suffered a similar fate in the eighteenth century, even though population estimates are unavailable to judge the extent and timing of the decline.

The emergence of regional capitals: Lucknow, Benares, Patna, Hyderabad, Pune

As the Mughal Empire collapsed, there was a shift in urbanization from the west or middle of the Indo-Gangetic Basin towards east and south. In the emerging towns, politics was still a crucial axis. But revenue farmers and bankers had more say in running states. This was in continuation of an earlier trend, the development of firmer ties between the imperial capital and the local commercial centres.[13] In the second half of the eighteenth century, the commercial centres gained in wealth and power.

The emerging towns were distinctive in several ways. The constant need to finance warfare added to the scale and nature of the economic services offered. Bankers had rich clients, and yet they needed to mitigate the risks of lending to cash-strapped warlords by means of tax farming, commodity trade, or money-changing. The smaller towns could not rely on a tribute flow from outside the core region. The Peshwa's dominion did depend on such a flow, but it dwindled as the Maratha states in Malwa, Bundelkhand, and Gujarat assumed independence. Furthermore, the local elite defined the character of the towns to a great degree and made each different from the other. The Brahman rulers of Pune, for example, left their mark all over the town and made it culturally speaking poles apart from Hyderabad, whose rulers saw themselves to be carrying the legacy of the Mughal nobility.

C.A. Bayly's work suggests a shift of urban enterprise in the Gangetic plains from the second half of the eighteenth century. As the Mughal Empire crumbled after 1740, the process made way for regional centres of power in Rohilkhand, Awadh, the Jat domain in Haryana, Punjab under the Sikhs, Bundelkhand and Malwa under the Marathas, Benares under a Bhumihar Brahmin landlord, and in Bengal under the East India Company. Between 1700 and 1800, Benares and Lucknow expanded to 200,000 people each. In the same period, Delhi, Agra, and Lahore had become smaller; but their de-urbanization only meant a relocation of private capital, first to Lucknow, Benares, and Patna, and eventually to Calcutta. The towns in the new zones tended to be governed by semi-independent bodies consisting of merchants and the landed gentry. The partnership between the Jagatseth, the Nawab, and prominent zamindars in Murshidabad was an example. The disintegration of that partnership leading to the end of the rule would suggest that the successor-state model was fundamentally not very stable.

A Mughal provincial town, Patna was located advantageously on the Ganges and on one of the main arteries of goods traffic between Bengal and Agra. The imperial decline did not affect Patna profoundly, since already in the first half of the eighteenth century, it had become a point of transit in Indo-European trade. Throughout the eighteenth century, Patna gained from a steady migration of rich landlords, merchants, and artists. The 'disintegration of Mughal Empire and repeated incursions of Persian and Afghans under Nadir Shah and Ahmad Shah Abdali stimulated the process of immigration of aristocratic families, merchants, poets, artists and saints to Patna.'[14] There was a temporary halt to the process at the turn of the

FIGURE 6.1 Patna Golghar. A huge granary bult in 1784 as famine insurance on Warren Hastings' orders, the Golghar also testifies to the crucial importance of this town as a grain trading centre. © CPA Media Pte Ltd/Alamy Stock Photo.

nineteenth century. After that Patna's economic emergence resumed on a different basis – commodity trade protected by the power of British-ruled Bengal (Figure 6.1).

The commercial importance of the town strengthened a few years after the Company assumed diwani, with the growth of two businesses vital to the regime's survival: saltpetre and opium. Kumkum Banerjee shows that the business axis shifted from the west to the east in the late eighteenth century.[15] The resurgence was due to new foreign and domestic trades led by European capitalists in eastern India. The Bihar plains integrated seamlessly with the trading system of Bengal. Situated in a fertile plain, Patna was the node of a vast grain trading network that built up from small market towns to transport hubs to the major market and grain storage points, chiefly Patna again. Capital and credit flowed down the hierarchical structure, reaching the remotest villages that had some marketable surplus. A part of the profits of trade and finance was retained by the towns at the bottom of the commercial pyramid. The list of these expanding and emerging market towns included Bhagalpur, Purnea, Dumraon, Sasaram, and Bakhtiyarpur.

Anand Yang's study of Patna shows that a late-eighteenth-century boom based on revenue-farming, banking, and manufacturing, came to an end around the middle decades of the nineteenth century with decay of artisanal production. But after that shock, trade, and finance revived again in the town, now based on agricultural trade and finance. Patna was a major centre of the new face of trade and banking in the late 1800s and a representative case.[16]

The hypothesis that there was active migration of moneyed capital out of the imperial core receives confirmation in Karen Leonard's work on banking in Hyderabad. In this view, the 'great firm' migration from the heart of the empire hastened the empire's collapse by starving it of credit. Whether or not migration of great firms can be considered evidence for a theory of imperial collapse is controversial. It is not clear which variable – trade collapse, state collapse, and migration of capital – was the cause and which the effects.[17] The fact of a migration is robust enough.

The fortunes of the regional centres were not necessarily secure, as the example of Lucknow suggests. When Asaf ud-Daula relocated his capital from Fyzabad to Lucknow (1774), 'bankers and men of property accompanied the court.'[18] A rich state produced a rich aristocracy and, consequently, wealthy capitalists and skilled artisan communities. But being located in the middle of a vast fertile agricultural zone that yielded the highest level of taxes in India, the region was exposed continuously to demands made by the Maratha forces. Unable to meet this threat, the state became a dependency of the Company.

The state's subsequent history is one of extortion by the Company together with inefficiency and wastage of the money that remained. In the second half of the eighteenth century, there was a sharp decline in trade in urban manufactures in the Awadh territory. Customs realized by the state fell in 1785 to 20% of what it was 30 years before. In Allahabad, in Tanda, and in the capital Lucknow itself, manufacturing and trade were believed to be much reduced in scale. According to one report submitted in 1787, the fall occurred due to the efforts of the Company to cut competition by force in almost all major trades of the region, mainly cloth.[19] The privileges that the Company had exacted from the dependency led to a fall in customs revenues; these revenues were not large to begin with. The other factor behind the fall was the reduction in trade in the region as a whole, especially trade in Agra and Delhi's direction. The report successfully restored 'free' trade in the region after 1787, but by then, the state's authority was so reduced that customs continued to be evaded anyhow. By the early nineteenth century, the aristocracy was ruler only in name. When the Company eventually assumed power in Awadh (1856), trade had revived, and the state had weakened further.

As the shadow of the empire receded from Benares, the greatest of all Hindu pilgrim centres, the town went through a small-scale construction boom. Temples, bathing and burning ghats, monasteries, schools of learning, and palaces were built with Maratha and Rajput princes' donations. Its importance as a pilgrim centre increased. Together with the wealthy consumers who lived here, this factor stimulated the production of luxury handicrafts, chiefly brassware, and silk textiles. A rural stretch sandwiched between two business towns located 50 miles apart, Mirzapur and Benares, and conveniently located on the Grand Trunk Road developed as a hub of cotton and woollen carpet manufacture. In the nineteenth century, railway connection further strengthened these three foundations of the Benares economy: religion, education, and crafts.

The rulers of the emerging towns retained and deliberately recreated some of the features of the old regime. They sponsored the settlement of skilled artisans, settled garrisons and their commanders, built a walled and fortified area, and large markets. Periods of sustained peace would strengthen all of these elements by keeping intact taxes flowing into the capital. Providers of skilled services such as scribes, bankers, and artisans formed the middle class. Even the poorest among these three, the town artisans, still commanded vastly more prestige and power than the artisans in the villages. Such power had a corporate basis. Nandita Sahai's research on late-eighteenth-century Jodhpur reveals strong caste-based associations of artisans in the capital town. These bodies no doubt gained from proximity to the court.[20]

In the new capitals, commerce and banking thrived, as they had in the Mughal Empire, on the back of a fiscal system that lived on land tax and tribute from dependencies. Leonard's study of Hyderabad draws the picture of a flourishing commercial-cum-financial centre that concentrated wealth in an aristocracy living on land taxes.[21] Pune was another example. Shivaji was interested in the town, but it was the Peshwa who adopted Pune as the Maratha dominion's capital in 1730, and elevated it to 'the nerve centre' of contemporary Indian politics.[22] Chitpavan Brahmins, and Bhats, migrants from the western coastal towns which had fallen under the influence of Muslim naval captains known as Sidis, joined as officers of the court and enriched the religious and intellectual life of the town. Tributary payments to the core sustained this superstructure. Although not a major trade centre, without easy access to long-distance trade routes and located in a semi-arid agricultural tract, the town continued to grow in economic importance thanks to the state's prosperity. The military machine was not directly managed by the state but farmed out to chiefs. These commanders, in turn, financed their participation in the wars by raising loans. Pune, therefore, also developed a money market geared to wars.[23]

B.G. Gokhale observes that the two characteristics of eighteenth-century Pune, military-fiscal origin, and the systematic use of religion as a state ideology, made Pune a special case: 'We have no instance of another such large town of this character in the urban history of India. Poona reflected the mores of a lifestyle dominated by Brahmanical ideas to a much greater extent than any other town.' Gokhale estimates that as much as 10% of the Peshwa's revenues, a staggering sum of money, went towards religious institutions. On a smaller scale than in Mughal Empire, the end of the Maratha dominion between 1803 and 1818 led to urban decay. With the decline of the dominion and the loss of tributary flows at the end of the century, the banking business also shrunk. In 1815, when it was still ruled by the Peshwa, Pune 'better answers the description of a large village than a town.'[24] But the same source also wrote that the town had a large bazaar. Although not destined to become irrelevant, Pune remained on the brink of obscurity for many decades before its re-emergence as a centre of administration.

Similar examples of desolation recur from the outlying branches of the dominion. When Cuttack came into British hands from the control of the Nagpur rulers, early European visitors to this Orissa town believed that the town had suffered a long depopulation and de-commercialization because of over-exaction by the state.

Gwalior and Baroda may also have experienced a similar period of inertia at the turn of the nineteenth century.

Quite a different order of urban emergence occurred on the seaboard.

The ports: Surat, Bombay, Calcutta, Madras, Karachi

Port cities, as I said before, were qualitatively distinct from the inland ones. They drew their sustenance from the sea, and not from land tax or the armed groups that managed the fiscal system. Equally, states based on such groups did not take much interest in the sea. Much of the analytical discussion on urban shifts misses this cleavage in the character of the towns.

The Mughal Empire owned ports. Surat and Hooghly were the main ports at the turn of the eighteenth century. But ports were not a vital resource for the Empire. Nor were they vital to the peninsular states of the seventeenth century. The states wanted to have access to the sea but would have found it too costly to secure it in most cases. Their survival lay inland in cultivation. By the 1800s, this picture had changed beyond recognition. Three port-based towns controlled the interior militarily speaking. Population growth reflected this significance. By 1760, Calcutta and Madras were far larger in population than most Indian towns of the time.

And yet, in the 1760s, their value as base camps in a conquest could hardly have been foreseen. When in the late eighteenth century, these towns became engaged in territorial campaigns, they were much larger and more diversified and more cosmopolitan as business hubs than their counterparts in the interior. In other words, colonial conquest did not make them crossroads of trade. Their status as hubs of trade enabled colonial conquest. Such conjunction of wealth, power, and global orientation were unprecedented in the region, just as unprecedented was the concept of an empire started by seafaring merchants. In the nineteenth century, when many interior states disappeared, the imbalance had increased. Not only did Bombay, Calcutta, and Madras draw capital and labour from all over India, but other places where the Company had firm control and with easy transport access also experienced similar growth. For example, Kanpur, Allahabad, Patna, and Karachi experienced growth by joining in the maritime trade that had been the source of prosperity for the Company port cities. In the 1850s, most large-scale Indian trading and banking firms had bases both in these places and in one or more of the ports.

The early history of the three ports is too well known to be repeated in detail. Charles II received ownership of the Bombay Island from the Portuguese in 1661 and transferred the estate to the Company seven years later. Taking possession of the new estate was not easy against hostility from the Portuguese settlers and the Dutch East India Company, who did not like the deal. States on the Konkan littoral were individually weak but could still cause trouble to the Company's ships offshore. The Mughal admirals, the Sidis, and the Marathas under Shivaji threatened the port. English politics cast an adverse shadow upon the future of the port (see Chapter 5). On top of all these troubles, Aurangzeb had a spat with the governor in Bombay over European pirates in the Arabian Sea. Bombay survived these problems, but it was in no position to become a strong contender to Surat until the beginning of the eighteenth century. Only the subsequent decline of Surat, which was poorly defended against both Maratha and pirate attacks, turned the balance of advantage in favour of Bombay.

Calcutta's early history parallels that of Bombay. About 1690, an officer and, temporarily, the leader of the Company establishment in Bengal, Job Charnock, secured from the ruler of the province permission to build a fort on the river Hooghly. The settlement might have remained an irrelevant one to the future of either Bengal or the Company but for two circumstances, the breakout of war in Europe (1740–60) that pitted the French against the English in Bengal; and Maratha forays into western Bengal that drove large numbers of Bengali businesses and service workers to Calcutta (the 1740s). French reverses in south India, together with these indigenous merchants' collaboration, helped the English take over Bengal between 1757 and 1765.

As Chapter 5 shows with the example of the Khatris and the Marwaris, the decline of the Mughal Empire with the consequent disruptions to trade in the core imperial zone pushed traders and banking firms to migrate into the capitals of the successor states in central, southern, and eastern India. Merchants engaged in overland trade were no longer able to operate freely or safely. As a result, the trade between the big cities and their hinterlands, as well as trade connected with the system of taxation, were much reduced in scale. This was the unstable commercial zone from which merchants and bankers fled in the second half of the eighteenth century. The flow into Calcutta from the north was almost certainly much larger in scale than that into any of the others.

Madras was the earliest of the three settlements, and despite French occupation in 1746, it survived the eighteenth century without significant setbacks to its political and economic importance. Its economic importance derived mainly from the cotton textile trade, which was contracted out to large weavers' settlements within the town's reach. Like Calcutta, Madras experienced growth in population as indigenous businessmen, some connected to textiles and some not, came to live there searching for security and higher returns to investment.

Bombay was in direct competition with the largest of the old Indian ports. Its economic advantages would not have been obvious to indigenous businesses in the early 1700s. Bombay's importance in the first half of the eighteenth century owed more to defence than trade. Its population was small compared with those of Calcutta and Madras. Despite efforts by local governments to increase trade and invite settlement, it did not draw much capital away from Surat. The profits of trade did not justify the expense incurred to hold this settlement. The town's resource base was small until new territories were acquired in the 1770s in exchange for participation in the Maratha succession conflicts. Even though better defended than Surat, Bombay was still exposed to attacks by a Maratha navy. Above all, compared with Surat, it had little indigenous commercial infrastructure to enable a continuous supply of textiles and other goods for its trade.

There was one advantage that the town enjoyed, however. It had better access than did Surat to timber from the forests of Malabar. And therefore, Bombay was better situated for shipbuilding. During a decisive period of Surat politics, several carpenters and weavers left the town to settle in Bombay. The Parsi carpenters recreated a shipbuilding industry that eventually surpassed the scale of the industry in Surat. In the 1740s, the master shipbuilder, Lowji Wadia, was the chief contractor for the repair and construction of ships for the Company. At the same time, three other sizeable Parsi merchant houses possessed the timber contact (Chapter 5).

In the first half of the eighteenth century, new conflicts developed, and collaborations were forged within Surat's 30,000 strong merchant community. Already at the turn of the century, when the town was yet to feel the effects of the breakup of the empire, piracy off the coast by European privateers had led to a series of disputes between the European companies and the Indian merchants of the town. Reprisals by the Mughal court were avoided by an agreement to supply protection to convoys of trading ships. But the solution satisfied neither the British Company, who thought it was expensive, nor the local merchants, who thought it was inefficient. In this atmosphere of unfriendliness, a few Parsi families emerged as trusted agents of the English. Rustom Manock was the pioneer in building this collaboration. Unusually resourceful and a skilled negotiator, he managed to gain officers' trust in the Surat establishment and create a captive pool of artisans who supplied goods in time and of the required quality.[25]

The agency of the Rustom Manock family became disputable because of the perennial suspicion that the agents were not entirely trustworthy and that they tried to intimidate other merchants. A short-lived move to cut out the Parsis from the agency had to be given up in the 1720s when Manock's son went to London to plead his case with the Company's directors and won a decision in his favour. It is likely that in deciding in favour of Manock's claim to the continued custom of the Company, London directors and sections within the Surat council took into account the changing politics. Maratha invasions in Gujarat disrupted the flow of food, tax revenue, and textiles into the town, and disputes between merchants threatened to become explosive under the decaying town administration. Merchants rallied under their respective communities or sided with the empire or the local ruler. The only community that did not have an alternative to siding with the English was the Parsis. The prospect of partnerships between Parsi coastal merchants and the European traders, therefore, was an asset to the Company in the hostile environment of the 1730s.

The Company effectively occupied Surat from 1759. Already, a diversion of trade and shipping towards Bombay had begun. In the 1720s and 1730s, European factors stationed in Surat complained of the decline in shipping from the town. For the British, this was an argument for a full-scale shift towards the safer port of Bombay. As Mughal authority over Surat crumbled, the town's economic hinterland shrunk in scale, and local political actors were left without effective control from above. The chances of disputes between Indians and Europeans increased, inducing the Europeans to blockade the port on several occasions.[26] The events leading up to the capture of the Surat castle by the British in 1759 have been the subject of a debate concerning the relationship between the Company, the town administration, and the Hindu and Jain merchants and bankers who had their base of operation in Surat. The point of the debate is whether the occupation followed a partnership or a conflict between business interests.[27] Irrespective of the conclusion, there can be little doubt that Surat was a special case. While facing a similar source of decay as elsewhere in the empire, it was unique in being a major port and having a cosmopolitan urban environment.

In the second half of the century, Bombay eclipsed Surat. But Surat did not become irrelevant. Lakshmi Subramanian has shown that it continued to be important, if on a different political and economic foundation, in western India's subsequent business history. Even as maritime trade dwindled to insignificance, trade and banking links between northern India and western India increased in the late eighteenth century. The resurgence was an outcome of the growing remittance business between the two zones and the growth of new trades with China, both an indirect result of the ascendance of the Company in Surat and Bombay. In these developments, the indigenous bankers played a leading role, and they also supplied political support to the Company when it made its authority over Surat formal in 1800.[28] Surat was also involved in trade with East Africa, exchanging cotton goods for ivory. Although Surat's position in the Arabian Sea trade changed, the cotton-for-ivory exchange continued.[29]

The last major seaport to emerge was Karachi, which started as a conduit for the Indus river cargo towards the end of the eighteenth century. Karachi was a minor port that lived on the Red Sea trade. About 1790, Karachi's population was 10,000, mainly merchants and mechanics, who traded with Muscat, Surat, Bombay, Malabar by sea and overland by camels with Kandahar and Kabul. As Karachi did not have any timber of its own, an important import item was timber from Malabar. Previously the site of a mud fort and not much more, the region's population retained a military bearing, always going armed. By the 1840s, Karachi was beginning to participate in Indo-European trade. In 1843, Sind had come under British control, a demilitarization process began, and Karachi started to become a rival port to Bombay.

Were the colonial places qualitatively a different kind of settlement from the indigenous ones? They were clearly different in that they were mainly business towns. Urban history explores another dimension of distinctiveness, ethnicity, and settlement pattern.

The morphology of the port town: one world, two worlds, many worlds?

Historical geographers try to identify the key features of the colonial towns.[30] These works make frequent use of the word 'hybrid' and try to give the word analytical content. Hybrid means a dualistic world consisting of a 'white town' centred around the fort and a 'black town' supplying food and labourers to the former. The two worlds did a lot of trade between them but never mixed socially. The same rules did not initially govern them. Indeed, 'these two sections of the town — the European and the Indian — shared little in the way of social or economic institutions.'[31] The indigenous part of the colonial town drew symbols of sustenance from indigenous towns. For example, a study of Madras shows how the Indian population in Madras tried to recreate the centrality of the temple so characteristic of the urbanism of the region.[32] An interesting question for historians is whether the ethnic dualist model is valid only for the Company towns or applied equally well to the Mughal imperial ones, where again the rulers were wealthier migrants.

This picture of a sharp separation is probably over-stylized. It is problematic for the eighteenth century. Heterogeneity rather than uniformity marked both spaces.[33] The so-called black town usually had a certain number of European artisans, sailors, and workers who had married into Indian society. And in its business dealings, the white towns were so heavily dependent upon prominent Indian merchants and bankers' partnership that certain proximity was bound to develop between them.

There were also state efforts to bridge the gap. Susan Neild has called Madras a city of villages, emphasizing that suburban Madras had roots in, continued dependence on, and occasional conflicts with, the precolonial agrarian society that lay on its borders.[34] Ravi Ahuja has shown how a 'city of villages' transformed into a real city during the eighteenth century under the combined impetus of appropriation of land, migration, rising property prices, and the formation of a bureaucratic apparatus set up to define and regulate property rights.[35]

The ethnic-dualist model would seem to be an exaggeration also to a business historian who should find systematic exchanges, partnerships, mutual dependence, and interpenetration between these spheres. People of mixed ethnicity pose a problem. Through much of the eighteenth century, Calcutta was an Indian place with a difference. It was Indian because its population was drawn mainly from indigenous traders and artisan communities, with a smattering of Europeans among them. The town was home to an Armenian community. It was home to the Indo-Portuguese peoples. Many European artisans lived and worked here. None of these groups belonged in the European elite. Before it industrialized, Calcutta's European business was as much Indian in outlook as it was European, and the distinction was not as sharp as we may imagine if we look at urban history with an imperial history lens.

These cities then provided fertile grounds for Indo-European collaborations in governance, business, and intellectual activity. The literate sections of the city collaborated with the government that formed after the transfer of the Diwani and the private European merchants who did business from Calcutta after the Company's trading interests dwindled. Kapil Raj, who calls late-eighteenth-century Calcutta a 'contact zone,' shows how the intellectual enterprise, initially built on administrative need for legal officers versant in indigenous law, at the same time progressed towards the study of language, natural philosophy, medicine, botany, and social customs and practices.[36] The contact was not arm's length; there was a mutual exchange of information and ideas, which prepared the bed for a latter-day intellectual efflorescence in the city.

By the end of the century, Calcutta's wealthy residents consisted of many European tradespeople and mechanics. Peter Robb calls them 'European residents of a middling kind.'[37] In Robb's description of the society, drawing on a private diary written in the 1790s, many people here lived a speculative sort of life on borrowed money. Fortunes could be made in innovative new businesses. Equally, often fortunes were lost in speculation over risky enterprises. Most took unusual risks and financed their ventures with money loaned to them at high rates of interest. Since escape into the interior was not an easy option, if not impossible, the risk for the creditor was small. And yet, through this chaotic flux, a new institutional order was emerging as '[p]rivate credit was being drawn into relations with the law and the state.' Debt contracts were recognized in the Company court, and employment contracts were beginning to receive a legal form and legal recognition. Contract enforcement might involve the use of physical force among Indians and Europeans. So easily did violence draw on both Indian and British tradition that '[i]t would be wrong to consider it characteristically colonial.'

Towards the end of the eighteenth century, private traders and Company sponsorship encouraged a number of significant industrial ventures in lower Bengal. Charcoal iron smelting on a large scale, ship repair and dockyard, indigo manufacture, and salt manufacture are perhaps the most well-known examples. Indigo, salt and iron were resource-based enterprises and needed to locate themselves deep in the countryside where these resources were available relatively cheaply. But the firms that entered these industries needed to be in close touch with Calcutta in order to secure loans, access ports, and in the case of iron, secure markets. Even if of rudimentary construction, the only existing docks came up on the river Hooghly in Calcutta.

Between 1790 and 1850, some of these ventures went bankrupt and were given up, especially in iron. Some registered success, such as indigo. Others such as shipping and shipbuilding continued despite frequent bankruptcy. And still others such as salt were taken over by the state for fiscal reasons. Collectively, they created the foundation for bigger things to come in the late nineteenth century. In this way, the growth of joint-stock banking, insurance, contracts, deep shaft mining, steam engines, and an urban lobby seeking fast and safe transportation into the interior emerged, laid the foundation for an industrialization to follow.

Market towns

With the political unification at the turn of the nineteenth century, there emerged another pathway of urbanization, the consolidation of the market towns and more exchanges between them. Neither politics nor garrisons drew migrants to these places. Business alone, and increasingly, opportunities for education, were the attractions. In the process, new and old settlements in the Gangetic plains revived and were reincarnated. Textile clusters in south India re-emerged.

Kanpur in the Indo-Gangetic Basin had a similar trajectory to that of Patna. Until the end of the eighteenth century, the town had little commercial importance except as the site of a Company trading station. In 1778, Kanpur also became a military station, situated there to defend the Awadh territories and to keep a watchful eye on the Nawab. The eighteenth-century ended in this fashion. Subsequently, Kanpur's military importance increased, and so did its attraction to European businesses supplying provisions and goods to the garrison. The convenient location on the river stimulated grain, hide, and the cotton trade in the bazaars. On these foundations, an extensive tanning and textile factory industry developed later, making Kanpur the second most industrialized inland town after Ahmedabad.

The model of the emergence of commercial towns was present in the successor states as well. As one account of Marwar has shown, many small places in the late eighteenth century developed around only one resource, a large market in grain.[38] In what is now the southern part of Andhra Pradesh, earlier ruled by tributary kings allied to the Mysore or Maratha states, a similar pattern of market-oriented urbanization dependent on grain trade emerged in the late 1700s.[39] Such urbanization was the outcome of improved links between markets and producing zones.

Another pattern of trade-driven urbanization was developing in the Kaveri delta around a cluster of large villages, the pattern that David Ludden calls 'early modern textile urbanism' and illustrates with Kanchipuram and Tirunelveli.[40] In this description, 'farming, manufacturing, war, finance, and commodity trades came together' in these large villages. Tank-irrigated agriculture sustained extensive grain production and trade. Temples validated the power of the rising mercantile and artisanal groups. Skilled artisans were organized around strong caste associations. And merchants and agents took part in long-distance trade.[41]

The convergence of different types of towns based on economic interests was reinforced in the nineteenth century when the railways and new agricultural trades revived the comparative advantage of some of the old imperial towns. The journey of the Mughal cities into obscurity continued in the early nineteenth century but began to slow after that. Some of the regional capitals carried on with an illusion of power under the rule of the princely states. But some others were coming back into business. Delhi, Agra, and Lahore bounced back after the railways connected them with the ports and with the main routes of overland trades along the Ganges and the Indus in the mid-nineteenth century. All began to see rise in population (Table 6.1), a rise that eventually far exceeded in scale anything these places had seen during their days as imperial capitals. Likewise, Ahmedabad, Dhaka, and Cuttack survived the turmoil in politics. Dhaka and Cuttack rapidly increased in population in the late nineteenth century, thanks to their situational advantage and the re-emergence as administrative centres.

According to Ludden, textile urbanism came to an end in south India, with the end of the Company trade and peasantization of the rural landscape. Still, not long after these tragic developments, the towns that had once led the textile trade saw a huge resurgence in handloom weaving. The industry now served domestic consumers. In 1930, the Kanchipuram industry was many times larger than what it was in 1700. Patronage fell, while the adaptive capacity strengthened, now with eyes on new trades.

Conclusion

This chapter set out to study the general character of the urban reshuffle. The fact of a reshuffle has been noticed, especially in the Gangetic plains.[42] Most studies limit the scope of the argument to north India. I suggest a broader and more qualitative change. A model of urbanism wherein politics was the chief attraction to business in an earlier era was superseded in the new world by a model of urbanism where business attracted new business. There was a change from political towns to business towns. As these towns grew and diversified, they acquired agglomeration economies, sustained by knowledge of jobs and opportunities, availability of skills, education, and security.

In this account, the emerging places like the colonial ports were emerging not because of the concentration of power but their economies of scale, initially based on attraction as trading hubs. With such foundations as these, in the nineteenth century the ports could stay at the frontiers of globalization. Ports on the Indian Ocean littoral moved money and commercial skills around between them, they were hubs of services like finance. They were not garrison or temple towns mainly.

To a capitalist hailing from Punjab, Gujarat, or Rajputana, or a skilled artisan from the Gangetic plains, the attraction of the Company towns, and these new urban centres, derived as much from the advantages of cheap markets for finance and skills, as the protection afforded by the garrisons stationed there. The consumption of the aristocratic classes living there was an unimportant factor. In this way, early modern India saw the decline of one model of urban formation and the growth of another. The new principle of urbanization was not based on elite sponsorship, but on diversification of the livelihood base, from trade to finance to education. Merchant sponsorship of public goods joined with state investment in infrastructure and administration to strengthen the agglomeration economies of these towns.

The politics of colonialism, of course, was not unimportant. As Chapter 5 showed, political integration connected markets and offered scope to trading and banking firms to set up branches in many more places from before. During high imperialism of the late nineteenth century, the empire connected port cities from Aden to Bombay to Rangoon to Singapore to Hong Kong. Thanks to that connection, business communities moved capital around between these places. By this benchmark, the emergence of the successor states had a limited and sometimes transient effect on urban dynamism.

What was the magic ingredient in commercial urbanism? What does agglomeration economies mean? Information is one part of the answer. In the past, 'systems of communication, often centring on interpersonal, caste, and religious ties, were the key to trade,' and this was so especially because commercial intelligence passed through community channels. Before the eighteenth century, these systems of communication were not necessarily urban-centred.[43] Remote temple towns that represented the places of origin and religious ties for mobile merchant communities continued to exercise a great influence on the pattern of enterprise, flow of information and credit, and the migration of merchants across the subcontinent's vast spaces.

This link was becoming weaker in the new world. Port cities and other commercial towns became homes to large and settled bodies of merchants doing novel businesses to develop a degree of autonomy and distance from the places of origin. The later growth of railways and telegraph strengthened that association between towns and capitalism. Novel forms of market information concentrated in these towns.

Chapters 2–6, then, present narratives of rise and fall. What was the net effect on how people lived?

Notes

1 David Ludden, *An Agrarian History of South Asia*, Cambridge: Cambridge University Press, 1999, 145–7.

2 For a discussion and the necessary citations, see C.A. Bayly, 'State and Economy in India over Seven Hundred Years,' *Economic History Review*, 38(4), 1985, 583–96. See also for a mainly descriptive study, H.K. Naqvi, 'Progress of Urbanization in United Provinces, 1550–1800,' *Journal of the Economic and Social History of the Orient*, 10(1), 1967, 81–101.

3 Stephen P. Blake, 'The Urban Economy in Pre-modern Muslim India: Shahjahanabad, 1639–1739,' *Modern Asian Studies*, 21(3), 1987, 447–71. I draw on the discussion in Sanjay Subrahmanyam and C.A. Bayly, 'Portfolio Capitalists and the Political Economy of Early Modern India,' *Indian Economic and Social History Review*, 25(4), 1988, 401–24.

4 'Some Reflections on the Town and Country in Mughal India,' *Modern Asian Studies*, 12(1), 1978, 77–96.

5 'Ahmadabad in the XVIIth Century,' *Journal of the Economic and Social History of the Orient*, 12(2), 1969, 187–97.

6 Chaudhuri, 'Some Reflections.'

7 Stephen F. Dale, 'Empires and Emporia: Palace, Mosque, Market, and Tomb in Istanbul, Isfahan, Agra, and Delhi,' *Journal of the Economic and Social History of the Orient*, 53 (1–2), 2010, 212–29.

8 'Middle Towns to Middle Cities in South Asia, 1800–2007,' *Journal of Urban History*, 35(1), 2008, 15–38.

9 Walter Hamilton, *The East India Gazetteer*, London: John Murray, 1815, 489.

10 See Z.U. Malik, 'The Core and the Periphery: A Contribution to the Debate on the Eighteenth Century,' *Social Scientist*, 18(11/12), 1990, 3–35.

11 *Fall of the Mughal Empire 1789–1803*, vol. 1 of 4, Calcutta: M.C. Sarkar, 1932–50, 324–5.

12 Edward Thornton, *A Gazetteer of the Territories under the Government of the East India Company, and of the Native States on the Continent of India*, London: W.H. Allen, 1854, 64.

13 Iqtidar Alam Khan, 'The Middle Classes in the Mughal Empire,' *Social Scientist*, 5(1), 1976, 28–49.

14 Nripendra Kumar Shrivastava, 'Contribution of Trade and Commerce in the Trend and Pattern of Urban Growth of Patna (1657–1765),' *Proceedings of the Indian History Congress*, 71, 2010–2011, 327–334.

15 'Grain Traders and the East India Company: Patna and its Hinterland in the Late Eighteenth and Early Nineteenth Centuries, *Indian Economic and Social History Review*, 23(4), 1986, 403–29.

16 Anand A. Yang, *Bazaar India: Markets, Society and the Colonial State in Bihar*, Berkeley: University of California Press, 1998, Chapter 5.

17 For a discussion of the debate around such problems, see Karen Leonard, 'Indigenous Banking Firms in Mughal India: A Reply,' *Comparative Studies in Society and History*, 23(2), 1981, 309–13.

18 Hamilton, *East India Gazetteer*, 497.

19 G.H. Barlow's commission, cited by Purnendu Basu, *Oudh and the East India Company*, Lucknow: Maxwell, 1943, 134–5.

20 'Artisans, the State, and the Politics of Wajabi in Eighteenth-Century Jodhpur,' *Indian Economic and Social History Review*, 42(1), 2005, 41–68.

21 'The Hyderabad Political System and its Participants,' *Journal of Asian Studies*, 1971.

22 B.G. Gokhale, 'The Religious Complex in Eighteenth-Century Poona,' *Journal of the American Oriental Society*, 105(4), 1985, 719–24.

23 V.D. Divekar, 'The Emergence of an Indigenous Business Class in Maharashtra in the Eighteenth Century,' *Modern Asian Studies*, 16(3), 1982, 427–43.

24 Hamilton, *East India Gazetteer*, p. 677.

25 David L. White, 'Parsis as Entrepreneurs in Eighteenth Century Western India: The Rustum Manock Family and the Parsi Community of Surat and Bombay,' University of Virginia PhD Dissertation, 1979.

26 Ashin Dasgupta, *Indian Merchants and the Decline of Surat c. 1700–1750*, Wiesbaden: Franz Steiner Verlag, 1979.

27 Michelguglielmo Torri, 'Surat during the Second Half of the Eighteenth Century: What Kind of Social Order? A Rejoinder to Lakshmi Subramanian,' *Modern Asian Studies*, 21(4), 1987, 679–710; Lakshmi Subramanian, 'The Eighteenth-Century Social Order in Surat: A Reply and an Excursus on the Riots of 1788 and 1795,' *Modern Asian Studies*, 25(2), 1991, 321–365.

28 Lakshmi Subramanian, *Indigenous Capital and Imperial Expansion: Bombay, Surat and the West Coast*, Delhi: Oxford University Press, 1996.

29 Martha Chaiklin, 'Surat and Bombay: Ivory and Commercial Networks in Western India,' in Adam Clulow and Tristan Mostert, eds., *The Dutch and English East India Companies: Diplomacy, trade and violence in early modern Asia*, Amsterdam: Amsterdam University Press, 2018, 101–24.

30 For an example from geography, see Meera Kosambi and John E. Brush, 'Three Colonial Port Cities in India,' *Geographical Review*, 78(1), 1988, 32–47.

31 Thomas Metcalf, *An Imperial Vision: Indian Architecture and Britain's Raj*, Berkeley: University of California Press, 1988, 8. See also P. J. Marshall, 'The White Town of Calcutta under the Rule of the East India Company,' *Modern Asian Studies*, 34(3), 2000, 307–31.

32 Susan J. Lewandowski, 'Urban Growth and Municipal Development in the Colonial City of Madras, 1860–1900,' *Journal of Asian Studies*, 34(2), 1975, 341–360.

33 Rebecca M. Brown, 'The Cemeteries and the Suburbs: Patna's Challenges to the Colonial City in South Asia,' *Journal of Urban History*, 29(2), 2003, 151–72; William Cunningham Bissell, 'Between Fixity and Fantasy: Assessing the Spatial Impact of Colonial Urban Dualism' *Journal of Urban History*, 37(2), 208–29; Swati Chattopadhyay, 'Blurring Boundaries: The Limits of 'White Town' in Colonial Calcutta,' *Journal of the Society of Architectural Historians*, 59(2), 2000, 154–79.

34 Susan M. Neild, 'Colonial Urbanism: The Development of Madras City in the 18th and 19th Centuries,' *Modern Asian Studies*, 13(2), 1979, 217–46.

35 'Expropriating the Poor: Urban Land Control and Colonial Administration in Late Eighteenth Century Madras City,' *Studies in History*, 17(1), 2001, 81–99.

36 'The Historical Anatomy of a Contact Zone: Calcutta in the Eighteenth Century,' *Indian Economic and Social History Review*, 48(1), 2011, 55–82.

37 Peter Robb, 'Credit, Work and Race in 1790s Calcutta: Early Colonialism through a Contemporary European View,' *Indian Economic and Social History Review*, 37(1), 2000, 1–25.

38 B.L. Bhadani, 'Land Tax and Trade in Agricultural Produce in Seventeenth Century Western Rajasthan,' *Indian Economic and Social History Review*, 29(2), 1992, 215–25.

39 David Ludden, 'Spectres of Agrarian Territory in Southern India,' *Indian Economic and Social History Review*, 39(2–3), 2002, 233–57.

40 Ibid.

41 Ludden, 'Spectres of Agrarian Territory'; Prasannan Parthasarathi, *Transition to a Colonial Economy: Weavers, Merchants and Kings in South India, 1720–1800*, Cambridge: Cambridge University Press, 2001.

42 Naqvi, 'Progress of Urbanization,' 84; Tom Kessinger, 'Regional Economy: North India,' in Dharma Kumar, ed., *Cambridge Economic History of India, vol. 2, 1757–1970*, Cambridge: Cambridge University Press, 1983, 265–6; Bayly, *Rulers, Townsmen and Bazaars*.

43 Howard Spodek, 'Studying the History of Urbanization in India,' *Journal of Urban History*, 6(3), 1980, 251–95. See also Spodek, 'Rulers, Merchants and Other Groups in the City-States of Saurashtra, Around 1800,' *Comparative Studies in Society and History*, 16, 1974, 448–70.

7

LEVELS OF LIVING

So far, the story of who gained and who lost from the grand transition of the eighteenth century has focused mainly on the big players – warlords, landlords, merchants, and bankers. Did ordinary people gain? Chapter 4 expresses doubt that the peasants' level of living could change either way. Is that a sound view?

The attempt to answer these questions will face two problems. The first problem is diversity. General interpretations of the time tend to be coloured by the political transition, creating the risk that we may impose too much uniformity upon a territory with no essential unity. India did not exist as one political, economic, and environmental entity in the eighteenth century. Conditions of living and parameters of economic change varied substantially between regions. Some of these regions were as large as a mid-sized European country. In the arid central Indian and Deccan uplands, states were poor; in well-watered zones, states were richer (measured in tax per person or tax per square mile). The seaboard was more exposed to long-distance trade. The urban and semi-urban settlements located in the big deltas saw flourishing textile production and export trade develop in the eighteenth century. Much of the countryside was unlikely to have seen such developments. Given such diversities, any generalizations about averages will be misleading.

The second problem is sources. Contemporary sources cover trade, taxation, and warfare better than standards of living. The English and the Dutch sources deal with a small segment of the larger trading world. Historians have tackled this problem by using wages and land yield as proxies for average condition. These datasets suffer from dreadful sampling bias issues. I will contend in this chapter that the basis to predict significant shifts in the average in any direction remains weak. That does not rule out shifts between regions or livelihoods.

The wage studies

In 1968, a contributor to a debate on Indian economic history presented a freehand drawing depicting India's economic condition over 300 years. The picture showed a steady decline in the eighteenth century.[1] The oldest tradition in quantitative history among Indian scholars made use of stylized wage series and confirmed just such a fall in the levels of living. Based mainly on Dutch reports of wages paid out to unskilled and semi-skilled labourers in the Mughal establishments (Rs. 3–10 per month), and what the Dutch factory paid out to a similar class of workers, an Indian historian of the interwar period, Brij Narain, concluded that the ordinary wage earners were lavishly well off in the Emperor Jahangir's time (1605–27) compared with Narain's own (1929).[2] In 1927, real wages were less than 20% of the 1627 level. The 'labourer' of 1627 needed no more than one-third the earning to feed a large household, leaving two-thirds 'for ghee, milk, vegetables, salt, sugar and clothes.' Many of these items were absent from the budget even of the rural rich 300 years after.

The leading historian of precolonial India, William Moreland, had already used some of the same sources, and his conclusion was different.[3] He estimated wage rates to be somewhat smaller in the earlier years, and inclined towards the view of Francisco Pelsaert and other contemporary European travellers that the 'common people' in the seventeenth century were 'poor wretches' whose lives were little better than that of 'contemptible earthworms.'[4] With such a baseline as this one, any change should be a change for the better.

If there was a decline, when did it happen? If we take Tapan Raychaudhuri's freehand drawing, the fall occurred between 1689 and 1813, followed by recovery. If we believe, after Frank Perlin and others, that the eighteenth century was a time of robust capitalism and colonial rule cut short the process, there should be a rise in 1700–1813, followed by a fall after 1813. In one reading, British colonial rule stemmed the downslide; in another reading, colonial rule caused the downslide.

The validity of either conjecture rests too heavily on wage data, which is of doubtful value. The wages used by most writers were paid in a labour market about which we know nothing. And yet, reading anything from wage trends requires that knowledge, for otherwise we would not be able to say if a certain trend reflects changes in wages or changes in the mode of payment. It is also necessary to be sure that the nature of the task paid for did not change.

A study of labour and employment by a leading expert on Mughal economic history says that there was not one but several broad classes of workers around 1600. There were the domestic servants in the imperial households, skilled artisans and labourers in imperial and aristocratic establishments, agrestic slaves, and rural servants.[5] The study then says that with the rural servants, 'customary entitlements to land and wages in cash and kind were inextricably mixed up,' implying that the cash wage would not say anything meaningful about how the village elite valued their work or paid for it. On domestic servants, the study says that 'the practice of holding back wages was apparently quite common.' This would imply that many workers were in debt to their employers or paid in kind. In the countryside, 'the caste system in the shape of general repression of the "untouchables" … influenced the level of wages.' And universally, 'women's labour is largely unremunerated in terms of money, and is often subsumed in family income, obtained by men of the household,' even when the women worked side by side with the men in the same tasks. In short, there were 'innumerable social divisions among Indian labouring classes.'

In theory, it is possible that a high wage paid to even an ordinary worker in Mughal India contained implicit payment to the family's labour. Fast forward 200 years, and in most worksites, men and women were usually paid separately. Of course, comparing these two wage rates we should see a fall. That means nothing. Neither Brij Narain, nor the later historians who used Mughal data acknowledged the problems of comparing wage rates in this way. Reacting to issues like these in early-modern China, Kent Deng and Patrick O'Brien reject the entire procedure of using wages over time to read long-term patterns of change in living standards.[6] I share their view that wage-based measures of change in levels of living are little better than 'unfounded guess-work.'

Prasannan Parthasarathi has revived the tradition of wage-based studies more recently.[7] Sashi Sivramkrishna uses the wage data from Francis Buchanan's surveys.[8] These studies and others like these were inspired by a specific question derived from the comparative history debate known as 'divergence,' whether Indian workers were worse-off or not compared with British workers before industrialization began.[9] Since that is not my question in this book, I will not comment on these works.

These works do not deal with trends directly. Still, it is evident that with a high set of wages as the benchmark, the nineteenth century could only see a massive fall in real wages, a disaster for which colonialism must be held guilty. Unfailingly all current works using wage data find that living standards fell in South Asia region since 1600, though one work finds that the trend slowed from 1750.[10] A nationalist dream, the thesis of prosperous workers falling into poverty is rejected by the best time-series data on wages that we now have. The dataset shows that agricultural labourers saw a slow betterment of their level of living in the early nineteenth century. That conclusion casts further doubt on what wages might have meant in the early-modern times.[11]

Wages should bear a relationship with productivity, especially productivity in agriculture, the main livelihood. What do we know about the productivity of land?

Land yield

Geography influenced agricultural livelihoods before the twentieth-century green revolutions. In terms of agro-ecological conditions, five major sub-regions in the Indian subcontinent can be distinguished, the submontane, the western desert and savannah, the floodplains of the two great Himalayan river systems (the Ganges and the Indus) or the Indo-Gangetic Basin, the peninsular uplands, and the seaboard. Of these five zones, the submontane lands had been largely forested, before parts of the forests were cleared for tea cultivation and timber extraction in the nineteenth century; and the desert and savannah sustained only pastoralist groups. In the other three zones, settled agriculture was the norm, the main source of living, and the main contributor to taxation. All were dependent on the monsoon rainfall for their main crop. However, conditions of irrigated agriculture and the prospects of increasing intensity of cultivation or crop diversification varied enormously.

On average, the floodplains and the seaboard had better soil in most places than the peninsular, being loamy and nutrient-rich, and with easier access to groundwater. The peninsular was deficient in both respects, except in narrow river valleys. A further distinction was the quantity of rainfall received on average. In that respect again, the peninsular was relatively deficient. Rainfall fell away in the western parts of the Basin or Punjab, giving rise to savannah conditions. Punjab, however, had huge rivers fed by snowmelt. Proximity to these perennial rivers could potentially create good agricultural conditions. By and large, the monsoon-dependent peninsular rivers provided a more limited and uncertain source of water.

Thanks to the ability to produce valuable grains such as wheat and rice and the availability of a larger agricultural surplus and easier transportation, the floodplains emerged as seats of powerful imperial states, overland trade, and flourishing urban centres. By contrast, the Deccan Plateau that dominates the map of the peninsular was an agriculturally more impoverished zone, growing locally consumed millets, and exposed to the threat of harvest failure.

Given the diversity, it is necessary to read any evidence on land yield with reference to specific regions. One cluster of studies exists on conditions in the Gangetic plains. A well-known work on north India by Ashok Desai estimates the ratio between average consumption in Akbar's time and average consumption in the 1960s by assuming that consumption was roughly proportional to the agricultural value-added per worker.[12] Consumption in the seventeenth century was found to be between 40 and 80% higher than in the 1960s. The exercise used *Ain-i-Akbari* (1595) figures for average productivity per acre and person in major crops in different qualities of land. Even if we treat the samples to have come from north India alone, it would seem that agricultural yields were higher in the seventeenth century than in the mid-twentieth. Desai presumes that through these three centuries, population growth and extension of cultivation to inferior lands reduced yields per acre and per worker, and in turn, reduced consumption and levels of living. Later re-examination of the dataset suggests a downward revision in the estimates and a position closer to William Moreland's that 'the average cannot have been greatly different from what it is today.'[13]

The British Indian state started collecting crop yield data systematically from the late 1800s. Most yield figures from times before come from the highly fertile and well-watered lands of the Indo-Gangetic Basin or southern deltas, creating an upward bias in impressions of the early-modern average yield. 'One striking fact about Indian agriculture in precolonial and early colonial days is the very high yield per acre,' writes Tapan Raychaudhuri.[14] Raychaudhuri cites Daniel Buchanan's estimate of rice yield, 200 seers per bigha (700 kgs/acre) in the central Bihar plains c. 1800, as evidence. Comparisons between these numbers that pertain to 1600–1800 and the figures from late-nineteenth-century survey statistics usually lead to the inference of a decline in the productive power of land between precolonial and colonial India. Another set from south India offered by Parthasarathi confirms high natural yield initially and suggests a possible decline in yield in the nineteenth century. Parthasarathi cites yield figures for paddy in late-eighteenth-century deltaic south India (708 kgs/acre) nearly double the average yield in Tanjore in 1906.[15] Raychaudhuri and Habib report three estimates of rice yield from Tanjore that average 650 kg/acre. This is again significantly larger than those derived from later surveys.[16]

A decline in yield is not implausible. C.A. Bayly suggests that climatic change imposed increasing ecological stress in the Delhi–Agra region in the mid-eighteenth century. A recent paper on the genesis of world inequality builds partly upon this conjecture.[17] Could climatic shocks affect the trend in yield, though? A natural experiment can answer the question. The last quarter of the nineteenth century saw El Nino famines and droughts, but there was no trend shift in land yield on this occasion. This is a robust finding because the yield data come from proper sample surveys. The eighteenth century need not have been any different from that pattern. Further, a universal failure of rain is a relatively rare occurrence, and the effect of partial loss of rain depends on where the rains failed. The two actual instances of famine that we know something about were the Chalisa (1783–4) and the Bengal famine (1770), both affecting regions that were relatively abundant in rainfall, with better irrigation, and were agriculturally developed. Overall, the link between El Nino events and permanent shifts in agrarian production conditions is unpromising.

A different kind of ecological stress was in evidence from the nineteenth century in the western delta and the uplands of Bengal. With extension in cultivation, and changes in the course of the rivers, lands were degraded, even lost. It is almost certain that in some areas, the process had begun in the previous century. This process was partly endogenous to the agrarian order in that it was a result of more intensive cultivation. Could that cause diminishing returns, even an actual fall in yield? That it could is too strong an inference.

If the proximate factors behind agricultural yield were resource conditions and technology, we should not expect any change. There is no significant evidence of either a dramatic improvement or a deterioration of technologies and resource endowments in agricultural production to warrant expectations of a rise or a fall in yield. The overwhelming dependence of the agricultural output on rainfall and soil did not reduce anywhere in the subcontinent during the eighteenth century. The available options for human intervention in reducing the risks of agriculture were few, and there is no evidence that new options became available during this time. Some of the existing assets, like canals and embankments decayed in the eighteenth century. But the effect of the capital loss upon land yield is unknown. Overall, crop regimes remained more or less unchanging.

There is little evidence showing that attempts to raise land productivity occurred on a sufficiently large scale anywhere in the subcontinent in the eighteenth century. The critical resource in this climatic regime was water, not land. Canals anywhere and wells anywhere except parts of the Indo-Gangetic Basin cost enormous amounts of money. The states did not reveal any capacity or interest to invest money on a large scale. The most valuable form of proprietary rights in land was held by the jagirdars (holders of military-fiscal tenure) and the zamindars (landlords), 'whose involvement in agricultural production was virtually nil.'[18]

B.B. Chaudhuri, in a recent assessment of the eighteenth-century economic history scholarship, suggests that any expectation of changes in land productivity is not only speculative but also implausible on the ground that those in command of money, power, and therefore, superior access to potential gains, were too distant from the production system.[19] Their task was to overcome a binding ecological constraint, the scarcity and high cost of extracting water from underground and storing water. Depending on rainfed agriculture and the consequently unregulated flow of moisture made controlled use of manure virtually impossible and thus restrained the level of manure usage in Indian agriculture. A high risk of monsoon failure made private investment risk averse and limited in scale. No wonder that '[t]he eighteenth century did not produce a break in the agricultural technology of India.'[20] Again, in the western Deccan, 'private investment in technological improvement or irrigation remained rather limited. The ecological context made the returns on agriculture risky and substantially lower than those available in the politico-military arena. High net-worth risk-prone individuals were typically investing in the political-military process rather than agriculture, because of the massive difference in returns.'[21]

The high natural yield figures I cited earlier were then an exception present only in some districts of the deltas and floodplains. In general, resource endowments limited technological options, and warfare diverted resources away from productive investment.

The missing yields of dryland crops is a big gap in this discussion. The main problem with of translating any one region's dataset into a reliable average for the subcontinent is that no attempt has been made to collate data on productivity in arid crops such as sorghum in the eighteenth century or even productivity in dry area rice as compared with irrigated rice. Although Raychaudhuri considers that the numbers obtained from the western Gangetic plains cannot be dismissed as 'errors of observation,' using them out of context could lead to errors of analysis. Any analysis of grain yield needs to be sensitive to the large variation that ordinarily occurred between districts in respect of yield, a variation that owed mainly to the quality of soil and available groundwater resources. Groundwater conditions and, related to these, the intensity of manure application could change dramatically between even contiguous districts. Between the alluvial flats, the uplands, and the seaboard, the difference was exceedingly wide. To take a later survey, in rice, the range within Bengal was 1:3 (1900). In rice again, the range in Madras was about 1:2 (1906). In wheat, the range was 1:4 (1870).[22] The higher numbers cited in the earlier one-off estimates represented the situation in the wet zones. From the late nineteenth century, official statistics overcame various ambiguities caused by regional diversity and calculated 'standard yields' based on crop-cutting experiments, standardized the unit of measurement, and collected figures for every district.

Notwithstanding Abul Fazl's magnum opus (Ain-i-Akbari, c. 1595), Mughal India had no dataset comparable in representativeness. A comparison between one-off numbers taken from irrigated lands in 1600 or 1800 with the later averages cannot lead to any sensible result.

The unit of measurement is also often left unclear in the scholarship. The available estimates of yield of the principal crops, for example, winter rice, suffer from two kinds of ambiguities about the unit. First, it is not clear whether the estimates referred to unhusked paddy or husked rice. It is necessary to observe that all available market prices are prices of rice so that we need to know yield in terms of rice. Ordinarily, the proportion of rice was about 60% that of paddy. Second, whereas all estimates refer to the units maund for weight and bigha for land area, the definition of these two units varied over time and between regions until official metrology in the late 1800s created uniformity.[23] To see what difference units could make, assume that the Buchanan figure cited earlier referred to unhusked paddy and the unit of land was the raiyati bigha. The rice yield from the Patna and Gaya region cited by Raychaudhuri translates to 330 kgs/acre, which is identical with the average yields in these districts in the late nineteenth century. Similarly, the high Tanjore numbers, if scaled down on the assumption that the original figures had referred to rice in the husk, would be similar to those found in agricultural surveys in the early 1900s.

What difference could regional variation make? Let us illustrate the point by using a set of numbers taken from eighteenth- and nineteenth-century Bengal. Consider first the extent of dispersion around the average in two datasets on 1860–1900, when reliable and comprehensive sample surveys were conducted for the first time in history in Greater Bengal.[24] These datasets suggest that the average yield of rice in Bengal was in the range of 410–440 kgs/acre (444 in 1866 and 409 in 1901). The earlier of these is a report by William Hunter prepared after the 1866 Orissa famine. His district data suggest that the lowest yields occurred in northern Bihar (Purnea 285), whereas in deltaic Bengal, the yield reached 571 kgs/acre (Rajshahi). According to official data in 1901, the latter of the two sources, the 'standard' land yield of Purnea was 276 kgs per acre, seven lower Bengal districts 550, and the average for all of Bengal 409. In both cases, the average for Bengal was 75% of that of deltaic Bengal. It is not inconceivable that rice yields sometimes exceeded 600 kgs for individual plots in the delta. But the average was still considerably below these high figures.

Given that the period 1750–1860 did not see any noteworthy mechanical or biological change in the manner of paddy cultivation, if we assume that a similar level of dispersion in yields characterized 1750 as in 1860, that is, assume neither inter-regional convergence nor divergence, the result would be an average yield substantially smaller than those commonly cited in the before–after comparisons. We have located four estimates of a 'large' rice yield from the late eighteenth and early nineteenth centuries.[25] The observers were based in deltaic lower Bengal. In all cases, the unit of measurement can be ascertained. These four estimates are (in kgs/acre) 396, 444, 634, and 543. The two numbers in the middle come from H.T. Colebrooke. The average of these numbers, 540 kgs, lies near what official statistics found to be the standard yield of deltaic Bengal a century later. Rajat Datta reports four other estimates from lower Bengal. The units of measurement are not defined. On the assumption that these figures referred to rice in the husk, large maund, and small bigha, the average yield was 633 kgs/acre.[26] These observations are the highest yield we can obtain for the eighteenth century, and they all came from the most fertile districts of the floodplains. But these high yields of 1760–1800 were near the high yields of 1860–1900. On the assumption that there had been no inter-district convergence or divergence in the intervening years, the earlier low yields and the later average low yields would be similar as well. And therefore, the average yield would not have changed at all.

To conclude, once the units are adjusted for, and the existence of a range is factored in, the inference that the grain yields were on average higher earlier than the nineteenth-century ones looks unlikely. There may not be anything wrong with the numbers, but to be able to use them, we need to know the dispersion around these numbers. The more acceptable hypothesis is that productivity did not change in the direction of either rise or fall in the eighteenth century. There may have been ecological stress and diminishing returns, but the effects could not be serious.

There have been a few attempts to infer levels of living based on population and income.

Population and income

An older scholarship tried to draw inferences on levels of living and especially the effect of subsistence shocks on levels of living by studying demographic data. Urbanization is a complex subject that deserves a separate and longer treatment (see Chapter 6). Reading population data is not an easy task either. In one view, there was small but positive (less than 1%) population growth in the seventeenth century.[27] In another re-examination of the pre-census (pre-1872) evidence, the population grew at around 1% in early nineteenth-century Bengal, a somewhat higher rate in Madras, and a near-zero rate in north India.[28] It is unlikely that the eighteenth-century population growth rate would significantly exceed zero anywhere in India; any prospect of a rise would be negated by the two major famines that occurred in the last quarter of the century. The use of population to infer levels of living in the long run depends on how the relationship between the two variables is conceived. This is a controversial task and best abandoned, even if it has seen a revival of late.[29]

One approach to the measurement of the scale of regional income makes use of government tax receipts. Based on the premise that government income was a significant source of aggregate demand, an exercise in this class suggests that the Bengal economy possibly experienced some growth in the first half of the eighteenth century.[30] Such measures must necessarily assume that the tax-income ratio did not change. Furthermore, the scale of real tax collection can be shown to be sensitive to the price series used to deflate the nominal collection. It has been shown in a more recent study that the most widely used grain prices should lead to the conclusion that tax collection in real terms did not change in Bengal between 1720 and 1763.[31]

A steady rise after that owed to successful manipulation of the East India Company regime's tax-income ratio.

Finally, an innovative exercise in estimating GDP per head based on a production function approach has found enough bases to suggest that 'Indian per capita GDP declined steadily between 1600 and 1871.'[32] The decline holds true for the eighteenth century and is confirmed by the evidence of silver wages deflated by major consumption articles' prices.[33] The advantage of an exercise like this one, compared with the before–after kind of exercises, is that it allows us to observe a trend rather better and, therefore, corresponds to a more realistic sense of time. In this case, the period did see a decline in inferred GDP per head. But the order of the decline was not large, nor was there a sharp reversal in the trend at any time. Stories that explain economic trends with reference to political shifts lead us to expect otherwise.

The pessimistic reading of wages, yields, and GDP does not necessarily dispute another set of findings suggesting commercialization and 'proto-industrialization' in the deltaic-coastal zones.

Agriculture: expansion of trade and cultivation

Bengal is often seen as a prosperous area before colonial rule. The truth is that it was much too diverse to sustain any general statement. Still, in some parts of Bengal, relatively high agricultural yield and access to transportation by navigable waters created strong domestic demand for manufactures and enabled wealthier states. This was true of parts of the Bengal delta, the eastern Gangetic Basin, and the Kaveri delta studied by Parthasarathi.

In these zones, or near them, there was a growth of long-distance trade in wheat, rice, and cotton in the second half of the eighteenth century. It could not have been a revolution. After all, much of the new trade depended on the few roads that existed in the interior, highly labour-intensive caravan trade, and coastal shipping that served only a limited hinterland. Nevertheless, commercialization of grain and cotton is at least compatible with the pattern of regional specialization in the manufacturing industry. In the second half of the eighteenth century, Gujarat cotton found an outlet in China. Berar cotton was traded overland to Bengal, and a flourishing eastern coastal trade in rice continued. In studies on the middle-Gangetic plains, considerable inter-regional trade in grain is noticed too. By the end of the eighteenth century, opium and indigo had joined rice and cotton as articles of long-distance trade. Was this commercialization sufficiently general and present in most regions of the subcontinent? Did it contribute to agricultural growth?

Ghulam Nadri sees 'expansion in agricultural production in the second half of the eighteenth century' in Gujarat, based on the evidence of the increased sale of cotton.[34] Recent historical research without exception notes agricultural growth in many other regions in the eighteenth century. Nearly always, the growth involved the settlement of migrant peasants and labourers in new lands, and in some cases, resettlement in regions deserted due to famine or war. In arid regions like Punjab or the Deccan Plateau, scarcity of water imposed limits upon what expansion was possible. On the other hand, in areas with a plentiful supply of water, such as Bengal, resettlement of forested zones was proceeding apace. Both demographic expansion and the offer of economic incentives by zamindars to induce reclamation of forest lands played visible roles. Richard Eaton shows that there were many land grants to religious institutions in the eastern Bengal delta, where there was also extensive forest clearance.[35] In western Bengal, the evidence on area expansion and forest clearance was much weaker, and the famine of 1770 placed a check on such developments that possibly lasted for more than a generation. The localized growth experiences could partly be an effect of a shift of resources from famine-ravaged and war-torn zones to safer areas.

The story of agricultural expansion allows us to speculate upon income and wealth inequality in the rural economy. The scholarship on the countryside in the eighteenth century suggests that in some regions where land was more fertile and water more abundant, political fragmentation saw a consolidation of rural magnates, who eventually exercised considerable control over property rights in the colonial period (see also Chapter 4). If this seems to indicate increasing inequality, we need to remember that land was still available in plenty, the peasants willing to spare the effort to cultivate these lands were still relatively few, and the states and the magnates were dependent on the peasantry to meet their own needs. Furthermore, magnate formation, or 'gentrification,' was not a universal phenomenon, being distinctly weaker in the arid areas where land was harder to cultivate, produced too little to sustain a magnate group, and willing hands were harder to find. Overall, it is possible to discount a trend towards consolidation of hierarchy, class, and inequality in the eighteenth-century rural world, even as institutional control passed on from the top layers of the governing elite to bottom layers located near the village.

Two final points in the story of change in the quality of life need only a brief reference. One of these is the falling capacity of the regional governments to create public goods, but this issue has been discussed in Chapter 3. The second one is the rising consumption of cotton cloth. The nineteenth century saw a large fall in the price of cloth thanks to the Industrial Revolution in England. India, a textile producer, not only lost a part of its domestic industry from the competition but also imported British cloth in large quantities. For the average buyer, the effect depended on substitution and net rise in consumption. Until 1840, the substitution effect prevailed, that is, buyers reduced their purchases of domestic cloth and bought the same quantity of imported cloth. After 1840, the income effect kicked in, that is, buyers (thinking they were better-off overall) bought more cloth on average. Per capita consumption of cotton cloth rose by 40–45% between 1840 and 1860.[36] Since this change happened so late in the time covered in the book, a detailed discussion is not needed.

Conclusion

We do not know enough to say that ordinary people were better-off in the Mughal times or in the successor states and they became poor under Company rule. None of the statistical data currently used to make some judgement of the trend is rich enough or direct enough to sustain any big claim.

Regional inequality would surely have changed. Trading conditions worsened in areas suffering from frequent warfare and disruption to trade. These declines were balanced by commercial expansion in the deltas, the ports, and the eastern Gangetic plains. The political transition between 1707 and 1857 induced a redistribution of capital and skill between geographical regions. If the recent reworking of GDP per capita is to be believed, the average may have changed due to the uneven commercialization. From the conditions of production, there is little indication that peasants, artisans, and workers were either better off or worse off in the timespan of the book.

A core characteristic of the redistribution process was the decline of landed power and the rise of capitalistic power. In 1857, these two worlds clashed.

Notes

1 T. Raychaudhuri, 'A Reinterpretation of Indian Economic History?,' *Indian Economic and Social History Review*, 5(1), 1968, 77–100.
2 'The most common rate of wages for ordinary unskilled work at the time of Jehangir was about Rs. 3 per month.' *Indian Economic Life: Past and Present*, Lahore: Uttar Chand Kapur & Sons, 1929, 13. With wheat selling at 185 lbs per rupee (*Ain-i-Akbari*, Brij Narain defended the use of the *Ain* prices for 1637), if even 70% of this income was spent on food, these wages meant a daily access to wheat as high as 7 kilograms per earner per day, or in a family of four, 1.75 kilograms per capita. Spring millets sold at nearly half the price.
3 *From Akbar to Aurangzeb: A Study in Indian Economic History*, London: Macmillan, 1923. See also W.H. Moreland, 'The *Ain-i-Akbari* – A Base-Line for the Economic History of India,' *Indian Journal of Economics*, 1(1), 1917–8, 44–53.
4 Francisco Pelsaert, *Jahangir's India: The Remonstrantie of Francisco Pelsaert* (W.H. Moreland and P. Geyl, tr.), Cambridge: W. Heffer, 1925, 64.
5 Shireen Moosvi, 'The World of Labour in Mughal India (c.1500–1750),' *Proceedings of the Indian History Congress*, 71, 2010–2011, 343–357. All citations in this paragraph come from this paper.
6 Kent Deng and Patrick O'Brien, 'Establishing Statistical Foundations of a Chronology for the Great Divergence: A Survey and Critique of the Primary Sources for the Construction of Relative Wage Levels for Ming-Qing China,' *Economic History Review*, 69(4), 2016, 1057–1082.
7 Prasannan Parthasarathi, 'Rethinking Wages and Competitiveness in the Eighteenth Century: Britain and South India,' *Past and Present*, 158, 1998, 79–109.
8 Sashi Sivramkrishna, 'Ascertaining Living Standards in Erstwhile Mysore, Southern India, from Francis Buchanan's Journey of 1800–01: An Empirical Contribution to the Great Divergence Debate,' *Journal of the Economic and Social History of the Orient*, 52(4), 2009, 695–733.

9 R.C. Allen, 'Real Wages in Europe and Asia: A First Look at the Long-term Patterns,' in R.C. Allen, T. Bengtsen, M. Dribe, *Living Standards in the Past: New Perspectives on Well-being in Asia and Europe*, Oxford University Press, Oxford, 2005, 111–30; and S. Broadberry and B. Gupta, 'The Early Modern Great Divergence: Wages, Prices and Economic Development in Europe and Asia, 1500–1800,' *Economic History Review*, 59(1), 2006, 2–31.

10 Stephen Broadberry, Johann Custodis and Bishnupriya Gupta, 'India and the Great Divergence: An Anglo-Indian Comparison of GDP Per Capita, 1600–1871,' *Explorations in Economic History*, 55(1), 2015, 58–75.

11 P.B. Mayer, 'Trends of Real Income in Tiruchirapalli and the Upper Kaveri Delta, 1819–1980: A footnote in honour of Dharma Kumar,' *Indian Economic and Social History Review*, 43(3), 2006, 349–364.

12 A.V. Desai, 'Population and Standards of Living in Akbar's Time,' *Indian Economic and Social History Review*, 9(1), 1972, 43–62. See Satish Chandra, 'Standard of Living I: Mughal India,' in Tapan Raychaudhuri and Irfan Habib, eds., *The Cambridge Economic History of India vol. 1: c. 1200–c. 1750*, Cambridge: Cambridge University Press, 1983, 458–71, for a somewhat different result based on wages.

13 Cited by Desai, 'Population and Standards of Living.'

14 'The Mid-eighteenth-century Background,' in Dharma Kumar, ed., *The Cambridge Economic History of India, vol. 2: c. 1757–1970*, Cambridge: Cambridge University Press, 1983, 3–35, 17.

15 Prasannan Parthasarathi, 'Rethinking Wages and Competitiveness in the Eighteenth Century: Britain and South India,' *Past and Present*, 158, 1998, 79–109.

16 Tapan Raychaudhuri and Irfan Habib, eds., *The Cambridge Economic History of India vol. 1: c. 1200–c. 1750*, Cambridge: Cambridge University Press, 1983, 218, 232. Madras, *Season and Crop Report of the Madras State*, Madras: Department of Statistics, 1905–6, 15. The average paddy yield for Tanjore was 1600 lbs/acre, which translates to 436 kgs of rice per acre. The average for Madras Presidency was less than 300 kgs per acre.

17 D. Clingingsmith and J.G. Williamson, 'Deindustrialization in 18th and 19th Century India: Mughal Decline, Climate Shocks and British Industrial Ascent,' *Explorations in Economic History*, 45(3), 2008, 209–234.

18 Binay Chaudhuri, *Peasant History of Late-precolonial and Colonial India*, New Delhi: Pearson Longman, 2008, 12.

19 Chaudhuri, *Peasant History*, 49–107.

20 Satpal Sangwan, 'Level of Agricultural Technology in India (1757–1857),' *Asian Agri-History*, 11(1), 2007, 5–25.

21 Neeraj Hatekar, 'Economic History as an Endangered Discipline: Issues in Pre-Colonial Studies,' *Economic and Political Weekly*, 39(12), 2004, 1075 6.

22 J.A. Voelcker, *Report on the Improvement of Indian Agriculture*. London: Eyre and Spottiswoode, 1893, 40–41.

23 In 1900, by official metrology, one maund was divided into 40 seers, and 1 seer was divided into 80 tolas, each tola being 180 grains Troy. Each seer was then equivalent to 2.057 lbs, and one maund 37 kgs. In the seventeenth century, the man-i-Akbari of northern India was again divided into 40 seers, but the seer of Akbar was of 30 dams, dam being the copper coin, and weighed less. In eighteenth-century eastern India, both the Akbari maund (25 kgs.) and the colonial maund (37 kgs.) were in usage. Bigha, the common unit of measurement of land area in northern India came in two versions, the bigha-ilahi of 0.6 acres, and the raiyati bigha of 0.33 acres. In parts of northern India, the same term applied to different measures. For example in Bengal, the raiyati bigha was in

common usage in the late eighteenth century in rice cultivation, but the bigha-ilahi was the common unit in indigo cultivation.

24 W. W. Hunter, *Famine Aspects of Bengal Districts*, London: Trübner, 1874, 17, 36, 64, 94, 100, 105, *passim*; and Bengal, *Season and Crop Report of Bengal*, Calcutta: Government Press, 1901–2.

25 'Five quarters of rice per acre are reckoned a large produce' in Bengal, Walter Hamilton, *The East India Gazetteer*, London: John Murray, 1815, 122. The measure of a quarter elsewhere in the same report is stated as follows: 15 maunds to 7 quarters, 20. H. T. Colebrooke in two different measures took 7 maunds and 10 maunds per bigha of unhusked rice the standard for one crop, *Remarks*, 101, 107. Another contemporary writer on standard of living, Robert Kyd, reported a large rice yield to consist of '13 maunds per beegah.' The bigha measure was specified at 3600 square 'guz,' or the *ilahiguz*, see the India Office Record manuscript number IOR Mss Eur F95, 21.

26 Rajat Datta, *Society, Economy, and the Market: Commercialization in Rural Bengal 1760–1800*, New Delhi: Manohar, 2000, 41.

27 John F. Richards, 'Early Modern India and World History,' *Journal of World History*, 8(2), 1997, 197–209.

28 Sumit Guha, 'The Population History of South Asia from the Seventeenth to the Twentieth Centuries: An Exploration,' in Ts'ui-jung Liu, James Lee, David Sven Reher, Osamu Saito and Wang Feng, eds. *Asian Population History*, Oxford: Oxford University Press, 2001, 63–78.

29 André Gunder Frank, *ReOrient: Global Economy in the Asian Age*, Berkeley and Los Angeles: University of California Press, 1998. See also, Tirthankar Roy, 'An Asian World Economy?,' *Economic and Political Weekly*, 36(31), 2001, 2937–42, for a discussion of Frank's use of demographic data in relation to economic growth and levels of living.

30 Satish Chandra, *Parties and Politics at the Mughal Court*, Delhi: People's Publishing House, 1979.

31 Tirthankar Roy, 'Economic Conditions in Early Modern Bengal: A Contribution to the Divergence Debate,' *Journal of Economic History*, 70(1), 2010, 179–94.

32 S. Broadberry and B. Gupta, 'Indian GDP before 1870: Some Preliminary Estimates and a Comparison with Britain,' CEPR Working Paper, London, 2010.

33 S. Broadberry and B. Gupta, 'Indian Economic Performance and Living Standards: 1600–2000,' in Latika Chaudhury, Bishnupriya Gupta, Tirthankar Roy and Anand Swamy, eds., *India under Colonial Rule: An Economic Analysis*.

34 *Eighteenth Century Gujarat: The Dynamics of its Political Economy*, Leiden: Brill, 2010, 141.

35 *The Rise of Islam and the Bengal Frontier, 1204–1760*, Berkeley and Los Angeles: University of California Press, 1993.

36 Tirthankar Roy, *The Crafts and Capitalism: Handloom Weaving Industry in Colonial India*, Abingdon: Routledge, 2020.

8

THE REBELLION OF 1857–58

'All classes of people in India,' the historian R.C. Majumdar wrote in 1957, 'were thoroughly discontented and disaffected against the British' just before the outbreak of the sipahi mutiny in May 1857.[1] This chapter will show that not only did 'all classes' not join the rebellion but that the divided response followed a definite pattern and was a crucial reason for its failure. The chapter illustrates a key thesis of this book: the inequality in north Indian society between landholders and capitalists had deepened during the Company rule. One set had lost, and another gained, by the operation of what I called earlier, a new political economy. Most large-scale businesses made common cause with the Company regime.

The mutiny broke out in May 1857 in isolated military camps. Before ending in the monsoon months of 1858, it had developed into a civilian resistance to the British East India Company rule over Indian territories.[2] Infantry soldiers had their reasons to be disaffected by the attitudes of their commanders and employers. Until 1818, the distance between the Indian soldiers and the European commanders in the Company army had been relatively close. In the 30 years of peace that followed, the hierarchy hardened. The regime might still have handled the mutiny as it had done mutinies before. But as private landlord armies joined the rebel soldiers, and they jointly set up governments in the rebel-held territories, the crisis became unmanageable using conventional means. This was by far the most serious and large-scale conflict to have engaged the British Indian state, then nearly a century old, and the only one staged (mainly) in the Gangetic plains, the heart of the subcontinent.

By March or April 1858, the course of the rebellion was clear enough. It was failing, because the Indian population even in the core areas of the rebellion were deeply divided in their sympathies towards the rebel cause. Even if that point was obvious to many contemporaries, historians in the present days have not explored it far enough.

The rebel military campaign was led by professional soldiers, whereas the civilian rebellion engaged the landlords, princely states, peasants, sometimes urban artisans. Many infantry soldiers joined the mutiny. And many did not. 'British victory,' wrote C.A. Bayly, 'partly resulted from the failure of the Bombay and Madras armies to follow the lead of the north Indian sepoys.'[3] If this statement points at divided sympathy within the army, similar divisions existed among the civilian population too. The kingdoms and the aristocrats were divided, and some larger ones close to the action acted as 'breakwaters to the storm which would otherwise have swept over us.'[4] That was sometimes from a sense of loyalty to the Company regime, but not always. The infantry soldiers came mainly from the middle-Gangetic Basin, where a broad coalition between former warlords, landholders, and the soldiers was possible. In the rest of India, princes and landlords could not take a chance. Peasants were in a similar situation. It mattered little what the peasants thought or did about the cause; they lacked the capacity to influence the outcome in most places.

Townsmen, by contrast, had a significant role to play. Since the main stages where the battles were fought were a few towns, the sympathies of the urban capitalists did matter to the result. The capitalists, by and large, did not join the rebels. On the outbreak of the mutiny, wealthy and literate residents of Bombay, Madras, Calcutta, Malabar, and other places sent a series of declarations of support for the Company rule. If they were inside the rebel-held towns or near these, merchants and bankers secretly helped the British Indian campaign. Not all did so. But most did. If their support had gone to the rebels, British colonialism would have ended in India in 1857 (see Map 8.1 on the areas most affected).

How do we understand this undercurrent of capitalist acceptance of British rule? Why did the town merchants and bankers turn their backs against the rebel cause? In specific sites, who took which side depended on many factors. Still, since the capitalist resistance was near-universal, we need a universal story. My thesis is that the Company was trusted more to sponsor trade and finance, and that its government represented an economic system that suited the Indian businesses better than what the indigenous regimes joining the rebels could offer.

Much of the historiography stays too focused on the small sites of conflict and contestation to see how deep the divisions were in Indian society.

An uneven historiography

Rebellion study has developed along four themes, military strategy, representations (in colonial historiography, Indian and Victorian literary imagination), rebel actions and intentions, and the aftermath.[5] More recently, innovations in sources have introduced further divisions. These analyses have, in turn, led to arguments about overt or inchoate nationalistic and anti-colonial discourses. My reading of the rebellion connects to a fifth set of writings, and corresponding sources, which are about the economic factors that caused it and contributed to its failure. This is much smaller literature. But some of the contributors to it are illustrious figures.

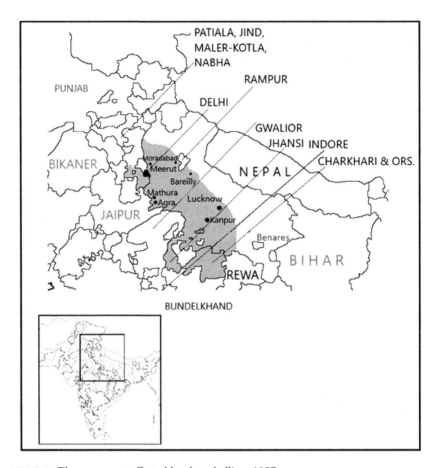

MAP 8.1 The area most affected by the rebellion, 1857.

For example, Karl Marx was fascinated by the episode as much as he was in India's British rule and suggested that the mutiny reflected a class struggle induced by British attempts at institutional reform.[6] Marx had little interest in Indian capitalists. Friedrich Engels, who endorsed the class struggle view, was mainly interested in the countryside. So were later Marxist readings by M.N. Roy and R. Palme Dutt. Both observed that the rebellion entailed a conflict between mercantile and landed interests, but followed Marx to situate the capitalist within a narrative of the village. In a polemic against the then-prevailing view that the mutiny was a feudal backlash and a religious reactionary one, a Marxist-nationalist work of the 1960s argued that it was an uprising against 'the commercial and industrial classes, the bankers and the mahajans.'[7] The work did not sufficiently elaborate who these people were and their reasons to go to either side. Still later, Eric Stokes showed that some of the soldiers shared beliefs and attitudes with the peasantry because they came from the same world.[8] A recent contribution reiterates that the soldier–peasant order, joined in some cases by the urban artisans, had suffered 'growing economic distress and pauperisation.'[9]

It is true that in the early stages, moneylenders and indigo planters were attacked.[10] After British takeover of Awadh (1856), some of the auction purchasers of large landlord (talukdar) estates were mercantile in background. And the peasants disliked them, though not necessarily because of the new economic relationships that had emerged.[11] Studies of Awadh and Bundelkhand also show that rural merchants and moneylenders were often targets of attack by peasants.[12] Some of these later works have been influenced by the subaltern studies reinterpretation of Indian nationalism.

There are two problems with this broadly Marxist approach to understanding class alliances and class conflicts. First, it is too focused on the village, where the actions were sporadic and often irrelevant to the rebellion's outcome. The implicit thesis that peasants joined the rebels and the capitalists joined the British because peasants resented economic exploitation is nothing more than a Marxist motif and begs the question of merchant calculations. The short-lived rebel governments did not think that capitalistic exploitation was a matter of concern. None of their proclamations, as far as we know, mentioned exploitation of the poor by the rich, and at least one backed the merchants.[13] The class conflict thesis lives uneasily with the diversity in peasant response.

Second, in this narrative of how the society responded to the mutiny, the urban merchants and bankers, 'capitalists' for short, remain shadowy if not missing altogether (I will soon give this word a concrete meaning). For example, the words 'merchant,' 'banker,' 'trade,' or 'market' do not appear either as index entries or as important topics in a selection of major works, old and new, on the subject.[14] In recent writings on Delhi under rebel administration, the banker has received some attention, only tangentially in discussions of court politics and city administration.[15] The 'moneylender' receives attention too, but almost always as a part of the peasant world. This is a curious oversight since the most critical military actions happened not in open battlefields, but in and around towns. The most consequential economic actors were the urban firms who had little direct contact with cultivation but who did have a potential role in strengthening the fiscal enterprise on either side.

The oversight is also curious because military intelligence revealed many cases of opportunistic attacks on merchant property by soldiers and urban gangs, as would happen in any episode of the state's temporary breakdown. There was an undercurrent of capitalist resistance to the rebel military enterprise within the rebel-held territories and an expression of support to the British Indian army outside this zone. Why these patterns arose is unexplained. The nature of the capitalist contribution to the war is not fully analysed either. As in any war, the supply of materiel and finance was of great importance to the armies. Business interests could either help the campaign by maintaining supplies or damage it by blocking them. The mutiny disrupted grain trade and trade financing over a large area between May and September 1857. Provisioning of the 'field armies,' therefore, was a challenge for both parties. The rebels who held key cities needed to build partnerships with the city merchants and bankers. The British needed the Indian merchants even more, because the expatriate merchants in the Gangetic plains were either dead or under siege. The historical scholarship provides some snapshots on how the enterprise of building a partnership developed but does not offer useful generalizations on the process.

I will show that capitalistic sympathies did take a definite form and that this fact was of crucial significance. Was this, however, merely a case of sympathy? Some merchants and bankers might have foreseen that British rule would serve their economic interests better. But that is an incomplete story. In a battle zone, taking any side carried risks and threats, merchants and bankers had a lot to lose, and economic history of the mutiny needs to consider these short-term risks as well as the expected long-term returns. Immediate threats to property played a larger role in capitalistic calculations than did imperialist loyalties. Their decisions need to be understood as a reaction to the insecurity of private property. Their response did contribute to the outcome of the war. In the material discussed here, we cannot directly correlate specific battles and capitalist agency therein. There is still a case that merchant disaffection and passive resistance damaged the rebel cause and that merchants and bankers were a party to the British war effort, which focused on keeping long-distance trade routes open, safe, and well supplied.

Who were the capitalists? I refer to people who conducted and financed long-distance trade and were usually based in the towns. In mutiny scholarship, the trading group that figures most prominently consisted of people financing cultivation and dealing with the peasants. There were some overlaps between these groups, but they were also distinct in institutional and social terms. The former group operated on a larger scale, issued bills (hundi), whereas the latter did not. Its clients were other substantial traders and officers of the courts, and they belonged in well-known trading castes and communities. In contrast, the rural lenders were a more mixed set and included peasants. The urban bankers operated is a less seasonal money market than the rural groups, operated on a larger scale, and they accepted deposits, whereas the rural moneylenders rarely did so.[16]

The former segment is of particular interest for the urban actor operated on a sufficiently large scale, had long taken part in fiscal administration, and was reputed enough to be seen as an ally during a war. Since this group financed trade, the alliance would matter to securing supplies and raising loans. The documents I use contain debt contract agreements between some bankers who figure in the chapter and members of the Mughal court dating back to the decades before the mutiny. Both the rebels and the British understood the strategic importance of the urban capitalist. In this time, the prominent urban groups came from a few castes and communities. They were mainly Hindu Khatris in Delhi and Jain and Hindu trading castes from Rajasthan or elsewhere. Some of them, especially Gujarati Brahmins, either operated from or had a base in the temple towns. Thus, Mathura became a base for Gokuldas Parikh, former Treasurer of Gwalior state, which played a significant role in the counteraction against the rebels. The inheritors of the firm were Jain Oswals.

How vital was this section of the population in society? How large and how robust was urban trade in the decades leading up to 1857? The western and central parts of the Gangetic plains had been relatively urbanized. Despite some decline in the urban population in the western regions, the population of the major towns in the eastern areas increased.[17] The cities' traders and bankers were not a depressed group. As Chapter 5 showed, even as some of their traditional businesses connected to tax collection had declined, commodity trade in sugar, cotton, indigo, and grain grew. Directly or indirectly, these trades had created scope for collaboration between overseas trade and overland trade, and in turn, between Europeans and Indians. Despite the end of the textile export trade, Calcutta and Bombay ports' shipping tonnage increased threefold between 1840 and 1857, and exports exceeded imports. A significant part of the trade occurred in the Gangetic plains and travelled by the Ganges towards the port cities.

Unlike the previous chapters in the book, which build on existing scholarship, this one is based on source analysis. A fuller discussion of the sources can be found in a paper published in 2016. There is some novelty in the material; a detailed description, therefore, is necessary.

Source analysis

What are the sources on this event? A substantial part of the official documents on the event is available in the British Parliamentary Papers. Some compilations of printed documents were also published around 1900 and are available as digital books.[18] These volumes contain reports sent by officers of the civil administration to the Governor General's office on the state of their jurisdiction; correspondence of Military, Railway, Home, and Political departments; and reports of battles contributed by military officers.[19] Contemporary accounts, such as John Kaye's work extended by G.B. Malleson, used mainly these sources supplementing these with memoirs and eyewitness accounts.[20] This corpus runs into several thousand printed pages, but economic history material on trade, markets, supplies, and transport is scattered through these in a few isolated statements. I supplement these materials with a few obscure printed sources, such as biographical dictionaries.

Nonofficial English-language documents like memoirs of former soldiers and contemporary accounts form a larger body of material. These are mainly descriptions of battles, sometimes written by those who took part in the action, and sometimes, as with George Forrest, archivists.[21] Meant to be 'tributes to the glory of our arms,' military memoirs were often reserved on Indian roles.[22] This oversight meant that the nonofficials overlooked subjects like feeding, clothing, and servicing the armies, primarily done with indigenous resources. Indian-language materials are crucial to understanding the conditions within rebel-held towns. These resources include folklore, newspapers, private accounts, pamphlets, and proclamations issued by the rebel governments.[23] However, whereas the translation project has shed more light on cultural history, it has not yet shown much promise in building knowledge of economic, business, or military history.

There is one exception to that rule. British Indian military intelligence and the testimony of people living in the rebel-held towns converge in an extensive collection of more than a thousand documents in Persian and Urdu produced between

May and September 1857. Some of these were official messages and orders, others reports by spies, a few were deeds between merchants and court officers, and a few others were extracts from newspapers. They were preserved and catalogued for use in the trial of the last Mughal emperor Bahadur Shah Zafar. In the words of John Lawrence, the Chief Commissioner of Punjab and a major player in the war effort, these documents formed evidence of 'the system in which the general Government was conducted' including '*the raising of loans*.'[24] In detail, for the first time, this resource has been used in Mahmood Farooqui's work on Delhi.[25] Another piece on Delhi uses English sources that covered some of the same subjects.[26] I draw on a printed volume in English describing the messages' subject, rather than the full contents.[27] This 400-page 'press-list' has a lot of value for economic history, the purpose it serves in this chapter.

I start with reports on merchant disaffection with the rebel enterprise.

Disaffection

In the middle-Gangetic plains, the most significant battles were for control of Delhi, Lucknow, and Kanpur. The battles occurred between stationary armies and had elements of siege warfare. These were densely populated, large, and prosperous urban centres, containing many markets within them and large settlements of merchants and bankers. The surrounding countryside was heavily cultivated and produced much of north India's grain output. The country was flat, with many good roads and a good prospect of river-borne trade. Overland trade, therefore, was large. For these reasons, supplies were initially a small problem for the several hundred-thousand rebel soldiers who moved into the cities. At least, military intelligence in May rarely mentions the issue of provision for the towns. The new government seized hold of the government treasury. On most occasions, convicts were released from prison. One report suggests that the freed convicts were seen as more loyal transporters of goods than the population at large.[28] In most parts of the Ganges–Jumna Doab, the Company's civil authority had crumbled away, and the landlords were, even when not welcoming to the rebels, not strong enough to stop or refuse supplies to soldiers. In the eastern districts of Awadh, the Baiswara landlords supported rebels reportedly because a large number of the Bengal army soldiers were Baiswara Rajputs.

And yet, managing the resources in an organized way and sustaining the flow of revenues both posed challenges to the new governments. Little information is available directly on the fiscal and monetary administration of the rebel-governed cities. We know that from the start, money was raised from the bankers and merchants of the cities by the rebels, and the British, as we see later. Although such evidence is cited in the literature, from the usually brief citations, it is not clear what the bankers themselves thought of these arrangements. The documents show that in early May, as soon as an administrative structure was established in Delhi, upon an order from the Commander-in-Chief Mirza Mughal, the *Kotwal* or police chief prepared lists of merchants and bankers and estimated the 'subscriptions' to be raised from them.[29] In May and June, there were complaints from grain traders of harassment and extortion by bands of soldiers.[30] Bankers did not complain, but they were in the spotlight throughout. On June 11, an officer of the court again raised the matter of subscriptions from bankers.[31] On July 1, two bankers petitioned that although they paid money to the King, 'they are subjected to the oppression of the Princes and the plunder of their houses and property by the sepoys.'[32] On July 11, 'the Mutineers demand money from the money-lenders of Delhi.'[33] Bakht Khan, commander of an army from Bareilly, arrived in Delhi in the same month to find that '[m]any ruffians were committing atrocities in the guise of sepoys' and that '[s]ome of the Princes notably Mirza Khizr Sultan were active in exacting money from the bankers.'[34]

A fortnight later, the King directed the Commander-in-Chief 'to borrow money from the Punjabis and other wealthy people to meet war expenses.'[35] On several occasions in August, the court summoned the city's bankers to discuss how to raise more money.[36] One witness recalled a near-death experience in the court early in August.[37] The court also tried to pacify the bankers, who had by then been subjected to many unauthorized demands for money by the Kotwal, by individual officers, and by soldiers. At least four orders were passed in August to state that only the court could deal with the bankers.[38] Little heed, it seems, was paid to these orders. Mirza Khizr was believed to have forced the bankers to lend him money for the soldiers' pay and kept the money for himself. So annoyed were the merchants and bankers at the bullying that Bakht Khan advised the firms to stay armed.[39]

In September, some soldiers 'decided to plunder the town of Delhi to realize their pay,' and a few others declared their intention not to fight until paid.[40] Mutineers who had not been paid did loot several shopkeepers.[41] Saltpetre stocks were running out. The dealer Debi Das' shop was raided by the soldiers to recover more of the article.[42] 'Respectable persons at Delhi have been imprisoned as they failed to pay money to the Mutineers.'[43] Shops closed for fear of raids.[44]

How do we read these reports? In one interpretation, these reports suggested that the police made sure that the merchants and bankers did pay up.[45] That leaves open the questions of why forced extraction was necessary and whether it hurt or helped the war. Reports on extortion confirm the general and well-founded point that the rebels' administrative setup was 'loose and precarious,' even 'chaotic and incompetent.'[46] They suggest two further points explaining why the setup was precarious. First, the court turned towards the city's bankers and merchants for accommodation because it had failed to secure a stable source of revenue from land. In turn, the court's weakness exposed the capitalists to soldiers' opportunistic attacks that the court could not stop. The weakness stemmed from the state's shaky finances and the fact that the rebel soldiers divided into groups that followed their commanders more than they did the writs issued by the court.

The second point is that the merchants and bankers responded to these risks by various acts of passive resistance and covert spying for the British. Of course, bankers were frequently mentioned in the capacity of agents or court officers. The most prominent example is Lala Jawalanath, who is often ordered to pay for an item of expenditure by the court or by a band of soldiers. Such orders meant either that

Jawalanath had taxation powers, perhaps he undertook to raise money from fellow merchants and bankers, or that he managed a part of the revenues. On the other side, there was Kanhaiyya Lal Saligram, who had an ambiguous relationship with the court. He worked for it, but on one occasion, was ordered to be arrested by the court. He was not alone, but one of several bankers who hid or refused to pay for the war. Saligram went further. Unknown to the rebels, he kept the British informed of the situation inside the city. In June, communiqués from Lala Saligram (along with Mathra Das, Jainal, and Rup Kishor of Moradabad) reached the British Agent in Delhi on the conditions of people (presumably merchants and bankers) loyal to the Company and imprisoned by the court.[47] We would not be surprised if there were many more figures like Saligram. Indeed, another Delhi merchant Jat Mall, a witness in the trial of Bahadur Shah, stated that 'the merchants and respectable tradesmen among the Hindus regretted [the overthrow of the British government].'[48]

Likewise, several prominent merchants and bankers inside and outside Lucknow were willing to help the rebel government. We know about these networks from British intelligence from after they consolidated their positions in Benares, Mathura, Patna, Meerut, and Lucknow's outskirts. It is not known from the same source in how many of these cases the rebel landlords or generals were the bankers' clients who wanted to secure their interest. In June 1857, when the British had established authority in Meerut, efforts to raise a public loan failed because local bankers did not respond.[49] Until the winter of 1857, Lucknow traders refused to serve the British. Bairo Pershad and Esree (Ishwar) Pershad, Benares bankers, maintained a secret correspondence with the rebel government in Lucknow.[50] They were said to be close to Madho Singh, the landlord of Amethi. The Patna banker Lootf Ali Khan was arrested on suspicion of sheltering rebel soldiers but released for lack of proof.[51] As a matter of strategy, the rebels knew the value of befriending the merchants and bankers. The governments of the occupied cities held meetings with them. Nana Saheb's war council in Kanpur did not include the wealthy merchants and bankers but was willing to listen to them.[52]

Suspicions of collaboration disturbed these efforts to create a common platform. Nowhere was this more obvious than in Kanpur. In Kanpur, potential suspects included a large segment of the middle class. Far more than Delhi or Lucknow, Kanpur was an Indo-European city. Its prominence had owed to a military camp, administrative offices, and long-distance trade in sugar and indigo. Few indigenous bankers, merchants, and Bengali 'writers' or clerks settled in the city felt compelled to join the Europeans sheltered in an entrenchment. But many 'received much annoyance from the mutineers,' were imprisoned, and '[hid] themselves to save their lives.'[53] Proven cases of a transaction with the European entrenchment were dealt with death.[54]

By June 1857, military intelligence was rife with reports of tensions inside Kanpur. A large part of the seized government treasure had leaked out. These acquisitions did not strengthen the fiscal enterprise. For example, a vast quantity of stamp paper taken in Allahabad turned up in underground markets in Bengal and Bihar months later, on one occasion sold by sailors employed by river steamers.[55] The governance of Kanpur effectively passed on from Nana Saheb to the soldiers. 'The mutineers, being in want of saltpetre confined Juggunnath, seller of that article, in order to extort the requisite supply.'[56] The soldiers operating the batteries outside the besieged European entrenchment plundered 'supplies brought in, ... helping themselves to large quantities of sugar...'[57] When reports of an imminent British attack reached the city in July, it proved difficult for the war council to procure carriage and supplies.[58]

In or near Kanpur, merchants secretly supplied intelligence and protection to the Company and its allies. In July, in Kalpi, a cloth merchant Ganesh was caught trying to protect a party of Europeans.[59] In June, Kanpur's merchants sent out intelligence to the British garrisons about conditions of the besieged European population. 'A Native merchant's letter from Cawnpore' brought to light, very usefully for the British, the discord between Nana Saheb and the soldiers, which at one point threatened his life.[60] That many rebel soldiers saw themselves as mercenaries made these disputes difficult to resolve.[61]

If Kanpur, Delhi, and Lucknow had rebel governments, and therefore a prospect of negotiation between the state and business interests, in other towns of the Gangetic plains, any party's authority was weak.[62] From these places, numerous reports of attacks on merchant property began to come in. On the night of May 10, urban gangs raided merchant homes in Meerut.[63] These raids turned into small-scale battles because the merchants had private armies. In Banda town in June, the merchant armies succeeded in driving off the raiders.[64] In Azamgarh town in June 1857, 'large sums of money were extorted by violence or threats of it from the merchants and bankers of the city.'[65] On the news of the outbreak in Meerut, 'black-mail ... was freely levied by the rioters from all the bunniyahs and muhajans in their neighbourhood.'[66] In May 1857, rebel soldiers attacked in Moradabad, the home of a 'wealthy bunneah,' and tortured one family member.[67] In September 1857, when British troops entered Hazaribagh, they found the bazaar plundered.[68] 'The little band of rebels traversing Mirzapoor' took supplies by force.[69] As late as March 1858, attacks on merchants were reported from villages in the Doab, but the attackers were not known.[70]

Some of these attacks on merchant property took the form of attempts at taxation, authorized or not, and some were attempts to punish collaborators. In August 1857, a minister (nazim) of the King of Lucknow occupied Gorakhpur town and 'forcibly exacted large sums of money from the merchants of the city.'[71] In October 1857, a rebel general Niaz Mahomed Khan 'levied fines' from merchants in Sahaswan.[72] In Tirhoot, the army of Kooar Singh of Jagdishpur caused great anxiety to the town merchants. Letters intercepted south of the Jumna in November 1857 revealed evidence of enquiries made by the rebels on which merchants traded with the English.[73] In Moradabad, a tense moment occurred in April 1858 when a commander of Rohilkhand rebels arrived and 'demanded money and supplies.' The course of the war was already decided, and it was not surprising that 'the towns-people refused ... whereupon the prince, after some negotiation, endeavoured to help himself by force.'[74]

In the early days of the outbreak in Punjab, there were episodes of seizure of mercantile property. Grain was taken by force from shops in Ludhiana, and 'wherever a horse or mule could be found, the rebel hand was laid instantly upon it.'[75] The bankers were reported to have quietly transferred their money chests, and the merchants locked up shops. In Jullunder, the mutineers caused little damage except for 'an occasional ... demand for money, [and] carrying off flour and grain from the bunniahs' shops.'[76]

In Rajputana and Mewat, 'the air was infected with panic.'[77] Containing important overland trade routes and settlements of merchants and bankers, and yet, poorly defended, Rajputana was particularly exposed to attacks, on these occasions, not by rebel generals but semi-nomadic groups. In July 1857, armed Gujar troops moved about Mewat. The most notorious in British records was Deohans, who attacked Dholepur town. Among his casualties were three town merchants. The merchants sought protection from one Buham, killed in an encounter with Deohans in July.[78] In 'the great centres' of trade in Rajputana, bankers sent away their families in June 1857 and sent petitions to the Governor-General seeking 'advice and protection.' In Mewat itself, the Gujar attackers were in some cases inspired by the prospect of targeting their creditors and destroying account books.[79]

Some of the raids conducted in September–October were related to the high price of food in that season.[80] The kharif (autumn) harvest of 1857 was good, but grain prices were higher than usual on account of disruption of supplies.[81] In the Rohilkhand plains, the stationary battles had been over by December with Lucknow's fall, giving way, in winter and spring of 1858, to small-scale encounters between mobile armies. These episodes were frequent enough to exhaust the countryside of supplies, and both parties faced difficulties in procuring food. When food ran scarce in the bazaars, traders' choices mattered more crucially. Months before, in the market towns of Rajputana, British troops failed to procure any supplies in June until the news of the battle at Badli-ki-Sarai (June 8) reached the towns, and the supply situation reversed dramatically.[82] The same thing happened in Awadh in winter. Victory in Lucknow and against the Gwalior Contingent changed merchant attitudes dramatically in the heart of the war zone.[83] On the British side, punitive raids on minor landlords suspected of helping the rebels targeted food. 'We took all the grain we could find, and burnt the village' was a refrain that was to be repeated again and again in the autumn of 1857.[84] By then, the Awadh landlords had turned against the British out of desperation.[85]

If these reports illustrate the fraught relationship between the rebel governments and the capitalists, attempts to build links with private trade were relatively trouble-free on the British side.

War supplies

This section gathers evidence on two things that mattered to the British war effort, protection and financial help extended by merchants in conflict zones and keeping long-distance trade routes safe, well stocked, and running. The second strategy could not possibly succeed without Indian traders choosing to help the Commissariat

Department. This was so because the Company state neither had the administrative means nor intended to follow what modern states often did in periods of conflict, directly regulate markets.

'An army in India,' wrote one veteran of the Anglo-Punjab wars, 'is followed by another army whose general or commander-in-chief is the bazaar kotwal.'[86] Shortly after the fall of Delhi on May 11 1857, the troops that moved from Punjab to the outskirts of the city functioned in a two-tiered setup of this kind. Many members of the rear were artisans and service workers, 'barbers, cooks, shoeblacks, and so forth,' and a large number of bheesties or water carriers. The elderly members of the group recalled the Afghan wars of 1840–2.[87] The bazaar kotwal supervised the procurement of food. In the eighteenth century, supplies were managed mainly by dealing with the bullock convoys that transported grain and camp followers who supplied artisanal services and sometimes managed the procurement of grain on the way.

Early in the crisis, as the downfall of the Company regime seemed a certainty, 'the camp followers, so necessary to the efficiency of an army in India, deserted like rats from a sinking ship.'[88] Indeed, camp followers subsequently received scant mention in mutiny sources. In one rare instance, the ancient system revived. In February 1858, Major (later Major-General) John Coke stationed near Moradabad enlisted the mobile caravan-runners or Banjara headmen who had been grazing their cattle in the Terai.[89] But contracting with caravan-runners was not the norm.

This is not surprising. In 1857, the Company army fought a different form of warfare than those it had engaged in before. It had never fought battles on such a large scale in the Ganges–Jumna plains before. Its forces were larger on average than in the eighteenth century. And it was trying to retake cities under enemy occupation, which operation took time. These circumstances made supplies a crucial problem and made it necessary to procure supplies by bureaucratic means, relying on revenue and trade.

The Company regime received many declarations of loyalty from the nonofficial European and Eurasians during the campaign. But if the nonofficial Europeans were useful as military volunteers, they rarely could help as traders, artisans, and planters. Except in Kanpur, their knowledge of overland and domestic trade was not valuable. Few had the experience of trading in grain and saltpetre, the two vital resources. Most had conducted businesses within the European quarters, were small in number, and with few exceptions, fugitives, killed or besieged.

The British authorities believed that the Indian merchants owed their wealth to the Raj and would naturally come to its aid. 'If there was any body of men in India who ought to have come forward to help us in difficulty it was "the monied interest".'[90] There was an element of truth in this assertion. Some merchants and bankers were mobile and had more information about the course of events on a larger scale. For example, in Assam and Rangpur, the Marwari merchants made statements in public that 'as every one must know … who, like us, has travelled,' the scale of reinforcement from Calcutta was too large for the rebellion to withstand.[91] In Meerut and Peshawar, the British acted on their belief and called upon the merchants in May and June to subscribe to war loans. The response was lukewarm in Meerut, as we have seen. It was generous in Punjab, but not before arm-twisting had been resorted to.[92] A show of neutrality was the politically safer option for the merchants and made economic sense since government paper was rapidly losing value. In Awadh and Rohilkhand, the confidence that merchants would voluntarily risk their lives for the British disappeared quickly.

Still, collaborations were present on a noticeable scale. In the early months of the mutiny, taking the British side anywhere in the middle Gangetic plains would have carried grave risks. Many firms, however, did so. The banking firms Lakshmi Chand Jain of Mathura and Manik Chand of Allahabad are prominent examples.[93] Mathura was an important centre of finance in north India. With his brothers Radha Krishan and Gobind Das, Lakshmi Chand sent the first pieces of intelligence to Agra's revenue officer of restlessness in the army, which led to a disarming of the infantry troops in Agra. Upon the Nimach brigade's approach in August 1857, the brothers provided shelter to fugitive European families, transported them safely to Agra, kept the flow of intelligence intact, and during the months when the banking system in northern India had collapsed completely, made loans to the administration.[94] They could offer some of these services because the bankers commanded armies and believed that they could meet small-scale threats independently. There were similar stories from Rajputana and Punjab. The Marwari banker of Bikaner, Bansi Lal Daga, started buying up Company government security that sold at one-quarter of the face value in May 1857, ending up exceedingly rich seven months later. To defend his investment, he 'identified himself so thoroughly with the cause of the Government as to undertake large contracts for the supply of food for the troops in the field, and freely advanced money on supply lines drawn on other parts of the country, disorganized as it was.'[95]

The control of Agra Fort in July 1857 led to the establishment of a market inside the garrison compound. Artisans and shopkeepers came inside the fort. The same thing happened inside Saugor Fort later. On supply of food to the Agra Fort, 'the cares of the Commissariat Department … were greatly lightened by the influence exerted by … Lala Joti Parshad, a contractor whose successful provisionment of the army during the Afghan, the Sikh, and the Gwaliar wars had gained him a great and deserved reputation.'[96] In Dehra Dun, 'food was procured through local merchants.'[97] In August, the government urged Jyoti Prasad to supervise regular horse vans from Agra southwards for the carriage of supplies.[98]

Colonel R. Baird Smith's report from Roorkee on the Ganges Canal stated that the first intelligence on the prospect of a mutiny came from the merchants engaged in grain trade for the military bazaar at Fatehgarh.[99] They were also grain millers and were implicitly accused of mixing bone-dust with the flour. The scale in which the rumour circulated alarmed them. However, the merchants continued making investments, which led Baird Smith to suspect that 'although, conscious of the general feeling of … alienation, the actual outburst of the mutiny took their class almost as much by surprise as it did ourselves.'[100]

Despite these instances, specific firms, individuals, or groups of traders remained rare in military intelligence. Far more space is devoted to reviving trade on the western and eastern sides of the war zone. The British could hope to hold on to the two strategic supply routes: the Punjab segment of the Grand Trunk Road, between

Jumna and Sutlej, connecting via the Sutlej–Indus river-borne trade with Bombay and Aden, and the Ganges river traffic linking north India with Calcutta. After Punjab came back into British control, the collaboration between the merchants and the small army that laid siege in Delhi without immediate hope of a re-conquest proved to be of crucial help. After Delhi fell on September 14, the commanding officer's report in the battles for Delhi acknowledged two initiatives on keeping the Company army well stocked. One of these was the Commissariat General. The other was the contribution of the Punjab states, Patiala, Kapurthala, Nabha, Maler Kotla, and Jind, in protecting trade routes and supplying carriages and cargo (see Figure 8.1).[101] The states did not procure the goods, the merchants did, but they

FIGURE 8.1   Three Sikh officers who fought during the mutiny. Felice Beato (c.1832–1909) was a British-Italian photographer based in the Mediterranean in 1857. He went to Calcutta on hearing the news of the mutiny. But he reached too late to witness action, as he had hoped. His mutiny album contains photographs of several significant sites and buildings, and a few group photos of soldiers like this one. © Album / Alamy Stock Photo.

protected property. 'The great thoroughfare [Punjab-Delhi] was soon alive with carts and carriages and beasts of burden conveying downwards all that was most needed by the Army.'[102] On the western side, cargo boats came up to Ferozepur on the Sutlej from Karachi, and they carried freight from Aden and Bombay. These were crucial services and explained why the Delhi campaign managers, such as the Military Secretary General Archibald Alison, never had to worry about food or other necessities of life seriously.

With the trade routes and commercial intelligence in their hands, the British in Punjab could restrict the sale of sulphur, saltpetre, and lead, and starve Delhi of these materials.[103] Hundreds of artisans were gathered in Ferozepur, well away from the reach of the rebels. The town turned into a major manufacturing centre for tent cloth.[104] How much of a difference the hold on sulphur and saltpetre made had been demonstrated on August 7. Several hundred artisans in Delhi had been pressed to manufacture gunpowder in Begum Samroo's house.[105] On August 7, a shell destroyed this factory and storage, along with the lives of five hundred or more artisans.[106] It is not surprising then that this one attack was celebrated as a substantial strategic victory by the British camp.

If the Cis-Sutlej rulers protected trade routes in Punjab, in the Ganges between Calcutta and Allahabad, the Company picketed the river. Despite an uprising in Danapur (July 25), there never was a decisive attempt by the rebel commanders to stop supplies up the river. River steamers were used to move commanders and reconnaissance missions by the British, bring wounded soldiers and their families to Calcutta, and for cargo. In August 1857, baggage boats organized by merchants travelled along the Jumna to reach supplies to units operating in the strategic grounds of the Doab.[107] These boats were targeted from the land and were often stranded for fear of attacks.[108] But the rivers continued to be used by the troops and the traders.

Newly started offices coordinated the procurement effort. In August, an office called Superintendent of carriage and supplies was established. The Commissariat in Bengal was issuing numerous indents and contracts for the procurement of food, coal, sulphur and saltpetre, and cloth.[109] These departments' correspondence suggests that market purchase and transportation of supplies worked better after the August reorganization. At any rate, procuring materiel from the market turned into a big subject of discussion.[110]

Although neither Bombay nor Calcutta was a battlefront, both played a critical role in supplies. In June 1857, the new commander of the Bengal Army, Patrick Grant, transferred the field's command to Henry Havelock, citing the necessity to stay back and manage supplies from Calcutta.[111] In later months, 'Calcutta deserves notice as the … depot of stores and supplies.'[112] Bombay, likewise, was far from the action but served Punjab. Jabalpur and Saugor, two large market towns, similarly served the central Indian front in 1858. The overland route between Bombay and Jabalpur played a role similar in importance to that of the Grant Trunk Road up north.[113]

In Bombay and Calcutta merchants and bankers needed no pressure to back the Company regime. In Calcutta, when the first stirrings of mutiny occurred among the 19th and 34th 'native infantry' in March-June 1857, and especially after Delhi's fall, sections of the Bengali press expressed sympathies for the rebels. The authorities quietly overlooked the matter. The divergence in tone between the Bengali and the English press soon disappeared. After all, 'as traders, the interests of the European and of the native merchants were identical.'[114]

In September 1857, led by the Maharaja of Burdwan and leading members of the Sovabajar estate, Radhakanta Deb and Kalikrishna Deb, more than 2,500 prominent Indian citizens of Calcutta signed on an address congratulating the Viceroy on the recapture of Delhi.[115] The signatories, in their testimony, included 'merchants and tradesmen.' Another followed this message submitted a few months later and signed by more than 5,000 individuals; again many of the signatories were merchants. The addresses were not just expressions of loyalty; they also expressed anxiety over private property and lives of expatriate Bengalis. The Bengali press of the time lamented 'the disorganization caused by [the] mutiny.'[116]

In Bombay and Surat, the mutiny brought in its wake a panic among the mercantile community. Order was restored when the only potentially serious episode among an infantry regiment was crushed brutally by the police chief Charles Forjett. When Forjett retired from service, he was honoured by 'the native cotton merchants' with a purse of fifteen hundred pounds and shares in a cotton mill worth thirteen thousand more.[117] Christopher Birdwood was also honoured by Bombay merchants; his contribution was to organize, as the commissariat's chief officer, bullock trains between Bombay, Vasind, and Mhow.[118] In Surat, a trading town, a panic broke out in the middle of 1858, when Tatya Tope planned an attack on the city. The merchant-landlord Syad Hossan-Al Edrus offered to join the campaign against Tope.[119] Similar declarations came from several towns in Malabar.[120]

With the trade infrastructure in place, markets revived during winter. In the relatively peaceful Champaran, European indigo planters had carried on their business as usual, if inconvenienced by indigenous bankers' refusal of cash advances. Money was scarce between May and August because of the collapse of the remittance and bills business. In Monghyr, bankers refused to issue drafts.[121] But by September, in Bihar, 'trade was reviving … and money-orders were procurable.'[122] As the British consolidated command over the two river-borne transportation and trade channels, it was only rebel-held Awadh in the middle that remained cut off from trade and the normal flow of funds.

Re-conquest caused a backlash against merchants who had remained in rebel-held cities, or they were simply targets of a further round of looting. An October 1857 dispatch from Muzaffarpur reported that the Company's Indian soldiers were intimidating the shopkeepers into selling food at lower than market prices.[123] There were similar complaints from Patna. In Delhi, there was extensive looting that targeted the merchants. A captain of the 61st Regiment that recaptured Delhi delightedly recalled how he and a colleague, after several days of unsuccessful raids, came upon a vast store of gold brocade in a secret vault of a merchant home seemingly abandoned.[124]

But there was also growing anxiety about merchant disaffection, fed by the feeling that private trade had been a crucial ally. Thus, even when soldiers went out of control, the administration went the other way. Upon regaining full control of Awadh cities in January 1858, the administration issued proclamations to reassure merchants that procurements would be paid for.[125] The pacification process turned out to be more tortuous in Lucknow. The merchants' loyalty being more in question in Lucknow, the oppression and extortion of the marauding Company army were especially severe here. 'They were pacified by the personal interest displayed by the new Chief Commissioner in their welfare and by the practical measures he took to put a stop to the seizures and demolition of houses in the city, which had formed one staple of their grievances.'[126]

After November 1857, the mutiny axis shifted towards central India, where Tatya Tope commanded an alliance. It is sufficient here to add only a short note on central India. The important distinction of the region was its economic geography. Bundelkhand and Malwa consisted mainly of forested uplands that did not have densely cultivated tracts outside the Narmada river valley. There were few towns comparable in size with those of northern India. Transportation arteries were smaller in capacity. The engagements involved mobile armies, which made supplies on the roads of critical importance. The British Indian army and the rebels both needed to enlist the support of the princely states.

As things turned out, except Jhansi, most states in central India remained loyal to the British, though often paralysed by divided loyalty within the court.[127] The uncertainty was intense with Rewa, which faced a revolt in October. Several Bundelkhand chiefs had announced that if Rewa joined the rebels, they would do too. This buffer's great value was that 'daily at least 200 bullocks laden with grain pass through' this area (see Figure 8.2).[128] Elsewhere, alliances between local troops and rebels induced the rulers to open up supply lines to the latter. This was the situation with the Holkar when the residency in Indore was attacked on July 1.[129] It happened again after Tope captured Charkhari in December and Gwalior in May 1858. The Gwalior finance minister handed over the treasury to the combined rebel army. After that, the central Indian campaign effectively ended. The depleted Tope army moved in territories south of the Narmada, occasionally raiding merchant caravans and facing resistance from merchants and peasants elsewhere.[130] Several reports of opportunistic raids on merchant convoys came to light in 1860 when Bombay's opium merchants petitioned for compensation. It transpired that for some time in 1858 and 1859, opium trains had also received protection from armed escorts supplied by the state.[131]

Conclusion

At a narrow level, the chapter's message is that merchants shaped the course of the rebellion of 1857. Political decisions by merchants and bankers did not just reflect loyalty or fear. Merchants in the war zone were at risk and took a risk in making political decisions. Capitalist attitudes were shaped by attacks on private property

FIGURE 8.2 The King of Rewa in court, c. 1880. Several central Indian states lost control over their soldiers during the mutiny. Rewa, a large state and crucial for the safety of north–south trade routes, wobbled for a time, but eventually stayed loyal to the Company raj, to the great relief of the latter. © Antiqua Print Gallery / Alamy Stock Photo.

and the fraught relationship between the rebel soldiers, rebel governments, and wealthy townsmen. The rebels' fiscal basis was limited to the economies of a few cities. Increasingly cut off from trade and revenue flows, the war effort within the cities turned extortionate on the resident merchants, some among whom secretly helped the Company's military action. Outside the war zone, military control of the riparian trade highways gave the British access to the ports and food, saltpetre, and carriages from friendlier traders located in the interior. Their war effort succeeded because trade and procurement joined forces.

At a broader level, the chapter confirms a key thesis in this book: urban classes saw the empire differently from the peasants and landlords. The urban classes not only contained traders and bankers but also the service elite working in schools, colleges, hospitals, and offices, and artists and intellectuals. Many among them had embraced English education and the cosmopolitanism of the Company town and rejected the tropes of the old regime that found a brief revival during the rebellion.

An example of the service elite was the poet Mirza Ghalib (Asadullah Baig Khan 1797-1869), who lived in Delhi during the rebellion. He did not think much of the myth that the British were usurpers of a power that rightfully belonged to the Mughal kings. He was no Anglophile, however. He observed with horror the atrocities committed by the British on recapturing the city and lost his savings to the looting British Indian troops. He escaped death because he lived in an area where hakims or doctors lived, and the Patiala king wanted them protected. Some of his friends were not so lucky Ghalib emerged from the old world, his creativity had roots there, and found appreciation there. He was just well-travelled enough to compare the old world and the cosmopolitanism of the new and chose the latter. An illustrious intellectual and social reformer of his times, Syed Ahmad Khan (1817-98) made a similar choice (V.N. Datta, 'Ghalib's Delhi,' *Proceedings of the Indian History Congress*, 64, 2003, 1103-1109).

Notes

1 *The Sepoy Mutiny and the Revolt of 1857*, Calcutta, Firma K.L. Mukhopadhyay, 1963, 99. Sipahi or sepoy referred to the Indian (mainly infantry) soldiers in the East India Company army. Most mutineers belonged in 'native infantry' and irregular regiments. See the next section for a fuller discussion of the historiography.

2 Because the mutiny turned into a civil rebellion, the appropriateness of the term 'mutiny' to describe the episode is disputed. Alternative terms include uprising, rebellion, mutiny-rebellion, revolt, and the first war of independence. In this chapter, 'mutiny' is retained. The reasons for continuing with the term are that it is handy and conventional, and that none of the alternatives is completely satisfactory either. As Clare Anderson writes, no matter what we call it, 'it is impossible to capture the essence or meaning of the revolt in … simplistic, singular ways,' *The Indian Uprising of 1857–8. Prisons, Prisoners and Rebellion*, London: Anthem, 2007. Furthermore, in this essay, the character of the revolt is not the main issue under investigation.

3 C.A. Bayly, *Indian Society and the Making of the British Empire*, Cambridge: Cambridge University Press, 1988, 179. For a similar view, Burton Stein, *A History of India*, Chichester: Wiley, 2010, 222.

4 Charles John Canning, Governor-General in India. Canning mentioned Gwalior, Hyderabad, Patiala, Rampur and Rewa. Cited in S.K. Pachauri, 'British Relations with Princely States in the 19th Century - Case Study of Relation of Trust and Fealty with the Ruler of Patiala,' *Proceedings of the Indian History Congress*, 56, 1995, 532–544, cited text on p. 540.

5 See Michael Barthorpe and Douglas Anderson, *The British Troops in the Indian Mutiny 1857–59*, Oxford: Osprey, 1994; Kaushik Roy, 'The Beginning of 'People's War' in India,' *Economic and Political Weekly*, 42(19), 2007, 1720–8; Sabyasachi Dasgupta, 'The Rebel Army in 1857: At the Vanguard of the War of Independence or a Tyranny of Arms?,' *Economic and Political Weekly*, 42(19), 2007, 1729–33 on military history; Christopher Herbert, *War of No Pity: The Indian Mutiny and Victorian Trauma*, Princeton: Princeton University Press, 2007, on representations; E.I. Brodkin, 'The Struggle for Succession: Rebels and Loyalists in the Indian Mutiny of 1857,' *Modern Asian Studies*, 6, 1972, 277–290; Eric Stokes, *The Peasant Armed: Indian Revolt of 1857*, Oxford: Oxford University Press, 1986; Bayly, *Indian Society*; Rudrangshu Mukherjee, *Awadh in Revolt, 1857–1858: A Study in Popular Resistance*, New York: Oxford University Press, 1984; Tapti Roy, *The Politics of a Popular Uprising: Bundelkhand 1857*, Delhi: Oxford University Press, 1994, on rebel action and intentions. A recent collection of essays, Biswamoy Pati, ed., *The Great Rebellion of 1857 in India: Exploring Transgressions, Contests and Diversities*, London: Routledge, 2010, contains new research on marginal groups and women. On institutional effects, see Ira Klein, 'Materialism, Mutiny and Modernization in British India,' *Modern Asian Studies*, 34(3), 2000, 545–80; Thomas Metcalf, *The Aftermath of Revolt: India 1857–1870*, Princeton: Princeton University Press, 1964; Jagdish Raj, *The Mutiny and British Land Policy in North India, 1856–1868*, New York: Asia, 1965.

 6 Shlomo Avineri, ed., *Karl Marx on Colonialism and Modernisation*, New York: Doubleday, 1969.
 7 Sashi Bhushan Chaudhuri, *Theories of the Indian Mutiny, 1857–59*, Calcutta: The World Press, 1965, 144.
 8 Stokes, *The Peasant Armed*.
 9 Iqtidar Alam Khan, 'The Gwalior Contingent in 1857–58: A Study of the Organisation and Ideology of the Sepoy Rebels,' *Social Scientist*, 26(1/4), 1998, 53–75. See also Irfan Habib, 'The Coming of 1857,' *Social Scientist*, 26(1/4), 1998, 6–15.
10 Majumdar, *Sepoy Mutiny*, 101.
11 Ibid.
12 Roy, *Politics*, Mukherjee, *Awadh in Revolt 1857–8*.
13 For one example, see Habib, 'The Coming of 1857,' 13.
14 Metcalf, *Aftermath of Revolt*; Stokes, *Peasant Armed*; Mukherjee, *Awadh in Revolt*; Biswamoy Pati, ed., *The 1857 Rebellion*, Delhi: Oxford University Press, 2007; and Crispin Bates, ed., *Mutiny at the Margins: New Perspectives on the Indian Uprising of 1857*, vol. 1 of 6, New Delhi and Thousand Oaks: Sage, 2013.
15 William Dalrymple, *The Last Mughal*, London: Bloomsbury, 2007, contains an index entry on 'moneylenders,' and a brief discussion on bankers of Delhi, 319–20; M. Farooqui, 'The Police in Delhi in 1857,' in Bates, ed., *Mutiny at the Margins*, 98–128, has a longer discussion on bankers.
16 'One important line of distinction was between those who were broadly urban and those who were broadly rural bankers,' C.A. Bayly, 'Patrons and Politics in Northern India,' *Modern Asian Studies*, 7(3), 1973, 349–88.
17 Chapter 6; Tom Kessinger, 'Regional Economy: North India,' in Dharma Kumar, ed., *Cambridge Economic History of India, vol. 2, 1757–1970*, Cambridge: Cambridge University Press, 1983, 242–270; India, *Statistical Abstract relating to British India*, London, various years.
18 British Parliamentary Papers (B.P.P. from now on), *Further Papers, No. 5 relative to the Mutinies in the East Indies*, Paper No. 2295, London: HMSO, 1857; B.P.P., *Further Papers (No. 7, in continuation of No. 5) relative to the Mutinies in the East Indies*, Paper No. 2363, London: HMSO, 1857; India, *Narratives of Events regarding the Mutiny in India of 1857–58 and the Restoration of Authority*, Vol. I, Calcutta: Foreign Department Press, 1881; B.P.P., *Papers relating to the Mutiny in the Punjab, in 1857*, Paper No. 75, London: HMSO, 1858; B.P.P., *Further Papers (No. 6 in continuation of no. 4) in relation to the Mutinies in the East Indies*, Paper No. 2330 (London, 1857); B.P.P., *Appendix (A) to Further Papers (No. 5) relative to the Mutinies in the East Indies*, Paper No. 2302, London: HMSO, 1857. Two further compilations – B.P.P., *Further Papers (No. 8, in Continuation of No.. 6) relating to the Insurrection in the East Indies*, Paper No. 2448, London: HMSO, 1858, and B.P.P., *Further Papers (No. 9, in continuation or No. 7) relating to the Insurrection in the East Indies*, Paper No. 2449, London: HMSO, 1858 – consisted of dispatches to the Board of Control in London, and have been used sparingly in this essay.
19 See Rosemary Seton, *The Indian 'Mutiny' 1857–58: A Guide to Source Material in the India Office Library and Records*, London: The British Library, 1986, for description of the departmental resources.
20 G.B. Malleson, *Kaye and Malleson's History of the Indian Mutiny of 1857–8*, London: Longmans Green, 1914, vols. 1–6. This consolidated edition consists of three volumes produced by John Kaye in 1864, and three follow-up volumes by Malleson prepared in 1888. John Kaye (1814–1876) was soldier, journalist, military historian; and George Malleson (1825–1898) was an army officer (during the mutiny), journalist, and military historian.

21 *Selections from the Letters Despatches and other State Papers of the Military-Department, the Government of India, 1857–58*, vols. 1–3, Calcutta: Government Press, 1898–1902.

22 A.R.D. Mackenzie, *Mutiny Memoirs*, Allahabad: Pioneer Press, 1892, 93.

23 Badri Narayan, 'Popular Culture and 1857: A Memory against Forgetting,' *Social Scientist*, 26(1/4), 1998, 86–94; and Syed Najmul Raza Rizvi and Saiyid Zaheer Husain Jafri, eds., *The Great Uprising of 1857: Commentaries, Studies and Documents*, New Delhi: Anamika, 2009, Section C.

24 India, *Press-list of 'Mutiny Papers' 1857, being a collection of the correspondence of the mutineers at Delhi, reports of spies to English officials and other miscellaneous papers*, Calcutta: Imperial Records Office, 1921, ii. Emphasis added.

25 Farooqui, 'The Police in Delhi in 1857.'

26 Dalrymple, *The Last Mughal*, 319–20.

27 India, *Press-list*.

28 B.P.P., *Further Papers, No.5*, 55.

29 India, *Press-list*, 100–01.

30 Ibid., 106, 311.

31 Ibid., 384.

32 Jugal Kishor and Sheo Parshad, bankers, Ibid., 373.

33 Ibid., 3.

34 Iqbal Husain, 'Bakht Khan–A Leading Sepoy General of 1857,' *Proceedings of the Indian History Congress*, 46, 1985, 373–386. Mirza Khizr was one of the sons of Bahadur Shah Zafar.

35 Ibid., 406.

36 Ibid., 102.

37 Dalrymple, *The Last Mughal*, 320.

38 India, *Press-list*, 272–4.

39 Husain, 'Bakht Khan.'

40 Ibid., 4.

41 Majumdar, *Sepoy Mutiny*, 81, 110, 158.

42 India, *Press-list*, 4,8.

43 Ibid., 5.

44 Ibid., 8, 98, 117, 278.

45 Farooqui, 'Police in Delhi,' 104–5 on 'bankers.'

46 Mukherjee, *Awadh in Revolt*, 140; W. Dalrymple, 'Logistic Failure on the Part of the Rebels in 1857,' in G. Rand and C. Bates, eds., *Mutiny at the Margins: New Perspectives on the Indian Uprising of 1857*, vol. 4 of 6, New Delhi and Thousand Oaks: Sage, 2013, 61–75.

47 India, *Press-list*, 11.

48 Malleson, *Kaye and Malleson's History*, 5, 335.

49 Kaye, *Kaye and Malleson's History*, 6, 127.

50 B.P.P., *Appendix (A) to Further Papers (No. 5)*, 299.

51 Ibid., 35, 38–9, 53.

52 For example, on June 10, 1857, 'the city mohajuns … and influential men, such as Shew Pershaud, the present treasurer; Gunga Pershaud, tent-maker; Jogul Kishore, Jeweller; and Biddee, Pawn seller' could have their favourite city police chief Hoolas Singh reappointed to his post after he had been initially suspended. N.A. Chick, *Annals of the Indian Rebellion*, Calcutta, 1859, 677. More on the role of merchants in Nana Saheb's government can be found in a source discussed in Pankaj Nag, '1857: Need for Alternative Sources,' *Social Scientist*, 26(1/4), 1998, 113–147, see 123. Nana Saheb or Dhondu Pant (1824 - c. 1859) was a Peshwa who briefly captured Kanpur from the British.

53 Forrest, *Selections*, vol. 2, 126.

54 Chick, *Annals*, 679

55 B.P.P., *Further Papers, No. 5*, 102.

56 Chick, *Annals*, 678.

57 Ibid., 679.

58 Ibid., 688.

59 India, *Narrative of Events*, 583.

60 Forrest, *Selections*, vol. 2, 82.

61 Saul David, *The Indian Mutiny: 1857*, London: Penguin, 2002, explores the soldiers' motivations.

62 Kanpur was retaken by the British in July, and was briefly re-occupied by the rebels after a victory by the Gwalior Contingent on 25 November 1857.

63 Meerut, India, *Narrative of Events*, 306, 335. Deposition of Babu Coylash Chandra Ghose, Sundar Dass, merchants of Meerut, 336–7, 342. See also, 345.

64 India, *Narrative of Events*, 521.

65 Ibid., 56

66 Ibid., 461.

67 Ibid., 406.

68 B.P.P., *Further Papers (No. 7, in continuation of No. 5)*, 7.

69 India, *Narrative of Events*, 47.

70 Ibid., 249.

71 Petition of Khodabuksh Khan, B.P.P., *Further Papers (No. 7, in continuation of No. 5)*, 223.

72 India, *Narrative of Events*, 464.

73 B.P.P., *Further Papers (No. 8)*, 714–6.

74 Malleson, *Kaye and Malleson's History*, vol. 4, 364.

75 Ibid., 2, 381

76 B.P.P., *Papers relating to the Mutiny in the Punjab, in 1857*, 116.

77 Malleson, *Kaye and Malleson's History*, vol. 4, 386.

78 Chick, *Annals*, 770.

79 India, *Narrative of Events*, 487.

80 B.P.P., *Further Papers (No. 7, in continuation of No. 5)*, 15.

81 B.P.P., *Further Papers, No. 5*, 86–7.

82 Lionel Showers, *A Missing Chapter of the Indian Mutiny*, London: Kessinger, 1888, 40.

83 The Gwalior Contingent was the forces under the Sindhias that joined the rebels, defying the Sindhia's orders.

84 B.P.P., *Further Papers (No. 7, in continuation of No. 5)*, 275.

85 John Pemble, *The Raj, the Indian Mutiny and the Kingdom of Oudh 1801–1859* (Delhi: Oxford University Press, 1960, 203–4

86 William Forbes-Mitchell, *Reminiscences of the Great Mutiny 1857–59*, London: Macmillan, 1897, 29–30. Bazaar kotwal would roughly translate into supplies inspector.

87 Forbes-Mitchell, *Reminiscences*, 29 30

88 Punjab, *Mutiny Records* (Lahore, 1911), 6.

89 Malleson, *Kaye and Malleson's History*, vol. 4, 359–60.

90 India, *Narrative of Events*, 74.

91 B.P.P., *Appendix (A) to Further Papers N. 5*, 244.

92 B.P.P., *Papers relating to the Mutiny in the Punjab, in 1857*, 75.

93 Bayly, 'Eric Stokes and the Uprising,' 232–3.

94 The brigade was a rebel force sent from Delhi to attack the rear of the British forces besieging Delhi. Bakht Khan, mentioned above, stayed with the brigade but did not join the battle. Husain, 'Bakht Khan;' F.S. Growse, *Mathura: A District Memoir*, Lucknow: Government Press, 1883, 14–5; C.E. Buckland, *A Dictionary of Indian Biography*, London: Swan Sonnenschein, 1905, 242.

95 Loke Nath Ghose, *The Modern History of the Indian Chiefs, Rajas, Zamindars*, Calcutta: Presidency Press, 1881, 477.

96   Malleson, *Kaye and Malleson's History*, vol. 3, 190–1.

97   Ibid., vol. 6, 120.

98   B.P.P., *Further Papers (No. 6, in continuation of No. 4)*, 158.

99   India, *Narrative of Events*, 488.

100   Ibid., 488.

101   Forrest, Selections, vol. 1, 36, 382–3.

102   Malleson, *Kaye and Malleson's History*, vol. 2, 384.

103   Punjab, *Mutiny Records*, 17.

104   Ibid., 88–9.

105   Begum Samroo or Samru (c. 1753 - c. 1836), the Indian wife of a European mercenary, who inherited the army on his death. The Begum died wealthy, and in possession of several palaces and estates, one of which was in Chandni Chowk in Delhi.

106   Forrest, *Selections*, vol. 1, 333, Telegram from Brigadier-General, J.G.S. Neill.

107   India, *Narrative of Events*, 176. A rare Indian eyewitness account of the cargo boats was left by the Bengali litterateur and religious reformer Debendranath Tagore, who travelled from Allahabad to Calcutta by a military cargo-cum-passenger boat in October 1857, *Jiban Charit*, Calcutta, 1911, 159–65.

108   India, *Narrative of Events*, 202.

109   B.P.P., *Further Papers (No. 7, in continuation of No. 5)*, 88.

110   B.P.P., *Further Papers (No. 6, in continuation of No. 4)*, 31.

111   Malleson, *Kaye and Malleson's History*, vol. 3, 19.

112   Ibid., vol. 4, 291.

113   Ibid., vol. 5, 101.

114   Ibid., vol. 3, 11.

115   A Hindu, 'The Mutinies and the People or Statements of Native Fidelity, Exhibited during the Outbreak of 1857–58' (Pamphlet), Calcutta, 1858, 139–40.

116   Ram Gopal Sanyal, *The Life of the Hon'ble Rai Kristo Das Pal Bahadur*, Calcutta: The Bengalee Press, 1886, 189.

117   Malleson, *Kaye and Malleson's History*, vol. 5, 35.

118   Buckland, *Dictionary of Indian Biography*, 42.

119   Ghose, *Modern History*, 514. Tatya or Tantia Tope was a rebel commander, and an associate of Nana Saheb.

120   Shumais U, 'Impact Of The Revolt Of 1857 In South India,' *Proceedings of the Indian History Congress*, 77, 2016, 410–417.

121   B.P.P., *Appendix (A) to Further Papers (No. 5)*, 92, 97.

122   B.P.P., *Further Papers, No. 5*, 50.

123   B.P.P., *Further Papers (No. 7, in continuation of No. 5)*, 3.

124   Charles John Griffiths, *A Narrative of the Siege of Delhi with an Account of the Mutiny at Ferozepore in 1857*, London: John Murray, 1910.

125   B.P.P., *Further Papers (No. 8)*, 109.

126   Malleson, *Kaye and Malleson's History*, vol. 3, 238.

127   Jhansi, a sufferer on account of the doctrine of lapse (Chapter 2), was loyal to start with, but in the end joined the rebels, and lost a series of closely fought battles under the charismatic leadership of the deposed queen.

128   B.P.P., *Further Papers (No. 7, in continuation of No. 5)*, 84.

129   Malleson, *Kaye and Malleson's History*, vol. 3, 152–3, 159.

130   Ibid., vol. 5, 240, 304–10; India, *Narrative of Events*, 620–21.

131   B.P.P., 1862 (53), *East India (Native Merchant Claims). Papers relating to the Claims of Tarrachand Seetaram and other Native Merchants of Bombay.*

9

CONCLUSION

According to all general readings of the time, the period 1707–1857 saw significant changes in economic conditions in India. What were these changes? Why were they significant? This book answers the questions.

The period mattered in Indian economic history, I show, for two reasons: the emergence of a merchant-friendly regime; and innovation in the state structure, from a decentred political system towards the consolidation of taxes and military capacity in one centre. A strong form of political integration also integrated markets – that was good news for merchants and bad news for the older regime's landed elite. However, the transition had little direct effect upon production conditions in the countryside, leaving many livelihoods practically untouched. The book uses these ideas as the building blocks in a story that starts with the Mughal Empire's collapse and ends with the great rebellion of 1857.

Jointly, they explain why the process of state consolidation delivered greater changes in institutions like commercial law, property law, and the fiscal system than in building rural infrastructure (Chapter 3). Or why the older military-cum-land-holding elite sometimes lost authority, but that did not necessarily affect the land-lords close to the village or the peasants (Chapter 4). Some of the most dynamic shifts occurred in mercantile enterprise in the port cities where a cosmopolitan business world was in the making and towns in the eastern Gangetic Basin that came into British control earlier. This business world's mainstay was agricultural trades, with strong links maintained with the ports and overseas trade. This form of integration of agriculture and overseas trade, or integration of the land and the sea, had no precedence in Indian economic history (Chapter 5).

Exposure to long-distance trade was greater mainly in the ocean littoral, the deltaic regions, and along the Ganges. Trading hubs from a long time past tended to be situated on the mouths of four river systems – the Ganges, the Godavari-Krishna, the Kaveri, and the Narmada-Tapti. As in periods before, in this period, too, these clusters saw flourishing textile production and export trade in the eighteenth century. The establishment of a merchant-friendly regime over these clusters helped market integration and offered capitalists the scope to move money and people around them.

The development of these clusters, in turn, stimulated long-distance domestic trade in cotton and grain. The scope of a more broad-based trade expansion away from these hubs was limited by the high cost of bulk transportation. Whatever interregional reshuffle there was, and there was quite a lot of reshuffle, it was confined to trade, banking, and services. The providers of these services became more mobile than they were before and more interconnected thanks to a common and growing interest in grain and cotton.

Population growth in towns reflected these shifts in the axis of capitalist enterprise away from the core regions under the Mughals, and the successor states towards those sites where migrant merchants gathered (Chapter 6). The Company towns and towns allied to the dynamic business world grew in scale. They represented a new model of urbanization, one wherein business attracted business, and agglomeration economies kicked in, as opposed to the old imperial and interior towns where the concentration of military-political-religious power attracted business. Although still small in absolute and relative scale, the urban littoral space drew in enterprise.

We should not overstress the dynamism. Levels of living did not display almost any trend at all. Famines affected the agricultural classes in all areas from time to time. Wages, yields, and income statistics appears to suggest the conditions deteriorated in the long run, but none of these datasets are robust enough to sustain such a strong claim. The Company served its aim to curb potential troublemakers, was somewhat successful in reviving trade, but did not have the capacity to develop production conditions in agriculture.

Why would the state be needed in agriculture? Geographical constraints upon agricultural technology made a significant rise in yield without outside help almost impossible. The evidence of either an increase or a decrease in average yield remains weak because documentation of any change in agricultural technology, cultivation practices, and access to natural resources cannot be found anywhere. If there was any effect of a political shift upon agriculture, the effect, good or bad, was confined to commercial possibilities alone. There were emerging commercial zones, where industry flourished too, and there were de-commercialized areas. These two worlds were neither deeply connected nor interdependent.

As this political-economic world unfolded, the class structure changed. The military-political layer, consisting of generals, ministers, and soldiers, occasionally secondary and primary landlords, took the most chances and experienced the most changes during the state formation process in the eighteenth century. Numerous groups had seen a fall in wealth and power, and the perception of the Company as a usurper of power was entrenched among a section of them. There was considerable reshuffle among merchants and bankers too. Like the shipowning merchants of Surat, some groups had seen their fortunes fall with the fall of the Asian empires. Hordes of Europeans had entered the scene. But overall, political power had been good for trade, as it had reduced transaction costs in moving bulk goods over a larger area and linked up maritime trade and the countryside more closely than before.

The real change, then, was the start of a process that would see a firmer integration of the littoral with the interior, of maritime trade with overland trade, of trade with production, of land with the sea, and between markets for commodity, capital, knowledge, enterprise, and labour. If an integrated market is a marker of modern capitalism, the eighteenth century initiated that process in India. The move did have something to do with the rise of the Company as a political power. From decades before colonialism began, the three East India Company ports, Bombay, Madras, and Calcutta, were acquiring strengths that would eventually make them sites of agricultural export, industrialization, and Indo-European joint ventures. Merchant migration had already started creating new hubs of cosmopolitan enterprise in these sites.

Although established by the Company, livelihoods in these towns did not rely on the military-political elite's power and consumption as they did in the interior cities. These were cities where businesses had developed considerable synergy among themselves and with overseas trade. The factor markets –capital and skilled labour – were significantly more outward-looking in these cities. The Company's presence and later a new state run by merchants had already set in motion processes that made for an institutional environment more conducive to unorthodox partnerships. Migration of both European and Indian capital and labour rapidly enriched these Indo-European port towns' resource base. This urbanism, which began with the Company cities on the coasts, became more general in the nineteenth century and changed the character of some of the regional political capitals.

The rebellion of 1857–58 was a backlash caused by these shifts. The construction of a new state that took away warlord-power and empowered the merchant came to a head. Interpretations of this episode tell us that a mutiny of infantry soldiers turned into a civil rebellion. However, the rebellion failed because not all parts of society joined the rebels, and some parts resisted them. There is no clear explanation of why these divisions arose. An older Marxist view that the enemies of the rebels were exploiters is crude and unworkable. The book's central thesis that the eighteenth century saw the emergence of a state that had uneven impact upon wealth holders can supply a better explanation (Chapter 8).

At the end of the rebellion, India became a colony of the British Crown. The Government announced a halt to further territorial acquisition. An uneasy peace prevailed, disturbed by episodes of mass protest and violence, like the Blue Mutiny of 1859 or the Deccan Riots of 1875. But these episodes did not challenge the state's authority. Some historians say that the Government turned more conservative, especially in the matter of changing institutions. That claim is not valid. After 1858, the state passed more not less laws dealing with business and property. It reformed the judicial infrastructure and passed laws protecting commercial and peasant property, including major tenancy and debt laws. A correct assessment would be that the new laws reflected caution about avoiding property transfer in the countryside while encouraging contractual exchange in commerce and industry.

Directly or indirectly, the market integration process, building on the political integration process earlier, continued after 1858, now drawing strength from railway building. The shifts in business dynamics that had begun presaged more significant changes to come. Without the eighteenth-century transformation of Bombay, Calcutta, and Madras, without the emerging trades in cotton and grain, without the extension of Company power inland, without Indian businesses migrating to the port cities, without the enterprise of the private traders in indigo or opium, and without the institutional consequences of Indo-European trade, it would be hard to explain the emergence of a nineteenth-century economic system in India that was modern in two senses, in enabling the prospect of one of the most impressive episodes of industrialization outside Europe, and in establishing India as a trading power in a globalizing world.

REFERENCES

A Hindu (1858), '*The Mutinies and the People or Statements of Native Fidelity, Exhibited during the Outbreak of 1857–58*', Calcutta: Pamphlet.

Ahmad, Ehtesham Uddin (2008), 'Agricultural Production and Prices in Late Nawabi Awadh (1801–1856),' *Proceedings of the Indian History Congress*, 69(2008), 603–611.

Ahmed, Feroz (1984), 'Agrarian Change and Class Formation in Sindh,' *Economic and Political Weekly*, 19(39), A149–A164.

Ahuja, Ravi (2001), 'Expropriating the Poor: Urban Land Control and Colonial Administration in Late Eighteenth Century Madras City,' *Studies in History*, 17(1), 81–99.

Ahuja, Ravi (2004), "Opening up the Country'? Patterns of Circulation and Politics of Communication in Early Colonial Orissa,' *Studies in History*, 20(1), 73–130.

Alam, Muzaffar (1986), *The Crisis of Empire in Mughal North India: Awadh and the Punjab, 1707–48*, New York: Oxford University Press.

Alam, Muzaffar and Sanjay Subrahmanyam (1998), 'Introduction,' in Alam and Subrahmanyam, eds., *The Mughal State 1526–1750*, New Delhi: Oxford University Press, 1–71.

Alavi, Seema, ed. (2002), *The Eighteenth Century in India*, New Delhi: Oxford University Press.

Ali, Athar M. (2003), 'Recent Theories of Eighteenth Century India,' in P.J. Marshall, ed., *The Eighteenth Century in Indian History: Evolution or Revolution?*, Delhi: Oxford University Press.

Allen, R.C. (2005), 'Real Wages in Europe and Asia: A First Look at the Long-term Patterns,' in R.C. Allen, T. Bengtsen and M. Dribe, *Living Standards in the Past: New Perspectives on well-being in Asia and Europe*, Oxford: Oxford University Press, 111–130.

Allen, Robert C., Jean-Pascal Bassino, Debin Ma, Christine Mollmurata and Jan Luiten Van Zanden (2011), 'Wages, Prices, and Living Standards in China, 1738–1925: In Comparison with Europe, Japan, and India,' *Economic History Review*, 64(S1), 8–38.

Anderson, Clare (2007), *The Indian Uprising of 1857–8. Prisons, Prisoners and Rebellion*, London: Anthem.

Anon. (1793), *British India Analyzed: The Provincial and Revenue Establishments of Tipu Sultan*, London: E. Jeffrey, vol. 1.

Anon. (1799), 'An Account of the Battle of Panipat,' *Asiatic Researches*, 3, 91–140.

Anon. (1801), 'Account of the Present State of Carrachee in Sind,' *Asiatic Annual Register*, London: J. Debrett, 69–70.

Arasaratnam, Sinnapah (1980), 'Weavers, Merchants and Company: The Handloom Industry in Southeastern India 1750–1790,' *Indian Economic and Social History Review*, 17(3), 257–281.

———. (1986), *Merchants, Companies and Commerce on the Coromandel Coast, 1650–1740*, New Delhi: Oxford University Press.

Arshi, Nida (2011), 'The East India Company, Rajput Chieftaincies and Pindaris: Changing Dynamics of a Triangular Relationship,' *Proceedings of the Indian History Congress*, 72(I), 650–662.

Avineri, Shlomo, ed. (1969), *Karl Marx on Colonialism and Modernisation*, New York: Doubleday.

Axelrod, Paul (2008), 'Living on the Edge: The Village and the State on the Goa-Maratha Frontier,' *Indian Economic and Social History Review*, 45(4), 553–580.

Bagchi, Amiya Kumar (1982), *The Political Economy of Underdevelopment*, Cambridge: Cambridge University Press.

Bagchi, Amiya Kumar. (1985), 'Transition from Indian to British Indian Systems of Money and Banking 1800–1850,' *Modern Asian Studies*, 19(3), 501–519.

Bajekal, Madhavi (1988), 'The State and the Rural Grain Market in Eighteenth Century Eastern Rajasthan,' *Indian Economic and Social History Review*, 25(4), 443–473.

Banerjee, Kumkum (1986), 'Grain Traders and the East India Company: Patna and its Hinterland in the Late Eighteenth and Early Nineteenth Centuries,' *Indian Economic and Social History Review*, 23(4), 403–429.

Barnett, Richard (1980), *North India between Empires: Awadh, the Mughals, and the British, 1720–1801*, Berkeley: University of California Press.

Barthorpe, Michael and Douglas Anderson (1994), *The British Troops in the Indian Mutiny 1857–59*, Oxford: Osprey.

Basu, Purnendu (1943), *Oudh and the East India Company 1785–1801*, Lucknow: Maxwell.

Bates, Crispin (1981), 'The Nature of Social Change in Rural Gujarat: The Kheda District, 1818–1918,' *Modern Asian Studies*, 15(4), 771–821.

Bates, Crispin, ed. (2013), *Mutiny at the Margins: New Perspectives on the Indian Uprising of 1857*, vol. 1 of 6, New Delhi and Thousand Oaks: Sage.

Bayly, C.A. (1973), 'Patrons and Politics in Northern India,' *Modern Asian Studies*, 7(3), 349–388.

Bayly, C.A. (1983), *Rulers, Townsmen and Bazaars: North Indian Society in the Age of British Expansion 1770–1870*, Cambridge: Cambridge University Press.

Bayly, C.A. (1985), 'State and Economy in India over Seven Hundred Years,' *Economic History Review*, 38(4), 583–596.

Bayly, C.A. (1988), *Indian Society and the Making of the British Empire*, Cambridge: Cambridge University Press.

Bayly, C.A. (1989) *Imperial Meridian: The British Empire and the World 1780–1830*, London: Routledge.

Bayly, C.A. (2002), 'Epilogue to the Indian Edition,' in Seema Alavi, ed., *The Eighteenth Century in India*, New Delhi: Oxford University Press, 165–198.

Bayly, C.A. (n.d.), 'Das Family,' Oxford Dictionary of National Biography, https://doi.org/10.1093/ref:odnb/75041 (accessed on January 20 2021).

Bengal (1901–2), *Season and Crop Report of Bengal*, Calcutta: Government Press.

Benjamin, N. (1978), 'The Trade of the Central Provinces of India (1861–1880),' *Indian Economic and Social History Review*, 15(4), 505–514.

Bhadani, B.L. (1992), 'Land Tax and Trade in Agricultural Produce in Seventeenth Century Western Rajasthan,' *Indian Economic and Social History Review*, 29(2), 215–225.

Bhambi, Rita P. (2012), 'Great Indian Peninsula Railway Company and its Contractors (1853–1871),' *Proceedings of the Indian History Congress*, 73, 880–887.

Bhargava, Meena (1996), 'Landed Property Rights in Transition: A Note on Cultivators and Agricultural Labourers in Gorakhpur in the Late Eighteenth and Nineteenth Centuries,' *Studies in History*, 12(2), 243–253.

Bhattacharjee, J.B. (2000–2001), 'Lord Dalhousie on Naga And Garo Policy: The Non-Interventionist Face of an Expansionist Governor General,' *Proceedings of the Indian History Congress*, 61(I), 612–616.

Bhattacharya, Ananda (2012), 'Reconsidering the Sannyasi Rebellion,' *Social Scientist*, 40(3/4), 81–100.

Bhukya, Bhangiya (2007), '"Delinquent Subjects": Dacoity and the Creation of a Surveillance Society in Hyderabad State,' *Indian Economic and Social History Review*, 44(2), 179–212.

Bhukya, Bhangiya (2010), *Subjugated Nomads: The Lambadas under the Rule of the Nizams*, Hyderabad: Orient Blackswan.

Bissell, William C. (2011), 'Between Fixity and Fantasy: Assessing the Spatial Impact of Colonial Urban Dualism' *Journal of Urban History*, 37(2), 208–229.

Black, Jeremy (1998), *War and the World*, New Haven and London: Yale University Press.

Blake, Stephen P. (1987), 'The Urban Economy in Pre-modern Muslim India: Shahjahanabad, 1639–1739,' *Modern Asian Studies*, 21(3), 447–471.

Blunt, J.T. (1801), 'Narrative of a Route from Chunargarh to Rajahmundry,' *Asiatic Annual Register*, London: J. Debrett, 128–200.

Bowen, H.V. (2010), 'Bullion for Trade, War, and Debt-Relief: British Movements of Silver to, around, and from Asia, 1760–1833,' *Modern Asian Studies*, 44(3), 445–475.

Boxer, Charles R. (1969), *The Portuguese Seaborne Empire, 1415–1825*, London: Hutchinson.

Brennig, Joseph (1986), 'Textile Producers and Production in Late Seventeenth Century Coromandel,' *Indian Economic and Social History Review*, 23(4), 333–355.

Briggs, John (1819), 'Account of the Origin, History, and Manners of the Race of Men called Bunjaras,' *Transactions of the Literary Society of Bombay*, vol. I, London: John Murray, 170–197.

British Parliamentary Papers (1857a), *Appendix (A) to Further Papers (No. 5) relative to the Mutinies in the East Indies*, Paper No. 2302, London: HMSO.

British Parliamentary Papers. (1857b), *Further Papers (No. 6 in continuation of no. 4) in relation to the Mutinies in the East Indies*, Paper No. 2330, London: HMSO.

British Parliamentary Papers. (1857c), *Further Papers (No. 7, in continuation of No. 5) relative to the Mutinies in the East Indies*, Paper No. 2363, London: HMSO.

British Parliamentary Papers. (1857d), *Further Papers, No. 5 relative to the Mutinies in the East Indies*, Paper No. 2295, London: HMSO.

British Parliamentary Papers. (1858a), *Further Papers (No. 8, in Continuation of No. 6) relating to the Insurrection in the East Indies*, Paper No. 2448, London: HMSO.

British Parliamentary Papers. (1858b), *Further Papers (No. 9, in continuation or No. 7) relating to the Insurrection in the East Indies*, Paper No. 2449, London: HMSO.

British Parliamentary Papers. (1858c), *Papers relating to the Mutiny in the Punjab, in 1857*, Paper No. 75, London: HMSO.

British Parliamentary Papers (1862) (53), *East India (Native Merchant Claims). Papers relating to the Claims of Tarrachand Seetaram and other Native Merchants of Bombay*, London: HMSO.

Broadberry, S. and B. Gupta (2006), 'The Early Modern Great Divergence: Wages, Prices and Economic Development in Europe and Asia, 1500–1800,' *Economic History Review*, 59(1), 2–31.

Broadberry, S. and B. Gupta (2010), '*Indian GDP before 1870: Some Preliminary Estimates and a Comparison with Britain*,' London: CEPR Working Paper.

Broadberry, S. and B. Gupta (2013), 'Indian Economic Performance and Living Standards: 1600–2000,' in Latika Chaudhury, Bishnupriya Gupta, Tirthankar Roy and Anand Swamy, eds., *India under Colonial Rule: An Economic Analysis*, 15–32.

Broadberry, Stephen, Johann Custodis and Bishnupriya Gupta (2015), 'India and the Great Divergence: An Anglo-Indian Comparison of GDP Per Capita, 1600–1871,' *Explorations in Economic History*, 55(1), 58–75.

Brodkin, E.I. (1972), 'The Struggle for Succession: Rebels and Loyalists in the Indian Mutiny of 1857,' *Modern Asian Studies*, 6, 277–290.

Brown, Rebecca M. (2003), 'The Cemeteries and the Suburbs: Patna's Challenges to the Colonial City in South Asia,' *Journal of Urban History*, 29(2), 151–172.

Bryant, G.J. (2004), 'Asymmetric Warfare: The British Experience in Eighteenth-Century India,' *The Journal of Military History*, 68(2), 431–469.

Bryant, G.J. (n.d.-a), 'Munro, Sir Hector (1725/6–1805/6),' *Oxford Dictionary of National Biography*, https://doi.org/10.1093/ref:odnb/19546 (accessed on December 3 2020).

Bryant, G.J. (n.d.-b), 'Adams, Thomas (1730?–1764),' *Oxford Dictionary of National Biography*, https://doi.org/10.1093/ref:odnb/134 (accessed on December 3 2020).

Buckland, C.E. (1905), *A Dictionary of Indian Biography*, London: Swan Sonnenschein.

Buckler, F.W. (1922), 'The Political Theory of the Indian Mutiny,' *Transactions of the Royal Historical Society*, 5, 71–100.

Calangutcar, Archana (2012), 'Marwaris in the Cotton Trade of Mumbai: Collaboration and Conflict (Circa: 1850–1950),' *Proceedings of the Indian History Congress*, 73, 658–667.

Calkins, Philip (1970), 'The Formation of a Regionally Oriented Ruling Group in Bengal, 1700–1740,' *The Journal of Asian Studies*, 29(4), 799–806.

Carlos, A.M. and S. Nicholas (1988), '"Giants of an Earlier Capitalism": The Chartered Trading Companies as Modern Multinationals,' *Business History Review*, 62(3), 398–419.

Chaiklin, Martha (2018), 'Surat and Bombay: Ivory and Commercial Networks in Western India,' in Adam Clulow and Tristan Mostert, eds., *The Dutch and English East India Companies: Diplomacy, trade and violence in early modern Asia*, Amsterdam: Amsterdam University Press, 101–124.

Chandra, Satish (1973), 'Social Background to the Rise of the Maratha Movement during the 17th Century in India,' *Indian Economic and Social History Review*, 10(3), 209–217.

Chandra, Satish. (1979), *Parties and Politics at the Mughal Court*, Delhi: People's Publishing House.

Chandra, Satish. (1983), 'Standard of Living I: Mughal India' in Tapan Raychaudhuri and Irfan Habib, eds., *The Cambridge Economic History of India vol. 1: c. 1200–c. 1750*, Cambridge: Cambridge University Press, 458–471.

Chatterjee, Kumkum (1996), *Merchants, Politics and Society in Early Modern India. Bihar, 1733–1820*, Leiden: E.J. Brill.

Chattopadhyay, Swati (2000), 'Blurring Boundaries: The Limits of 'White Town' in Colonial Calcutta,' *Journal of the Society of Architectural Historians*, 59(2), 154–179.

Chaudhuri, Binay Bhushan (2008), *Peasant History of Late-precolonial and Colonial India*, New Delhi: Pearson Longman.

Chaudhuri, K.N. (1985), *Trade and Civilisation in the Indian Ocean: An Economic History from the Rise of Islam to 1750*, Cambridge: Cambridge University Press.

Chaudhuri, K.N. (1991), *Asia before Europe: Economy and Civilisation of the Indian Ocean from the Rise of Islam to 1750*, Cambridge: Cambridge University Press.

Chaudhuri, K.N. (1978), 'Some Reflections on the Town and Country in Mughal India,' *Modern Asian Studies*, 12(1), 77–96.

Chaudhuri, Sashi Bhushan (1965), *Theories of the Indian Mutiny, 1857–59*, Calcutta: The World Press.

Chaudhury, Sushil (1993), 'European Companies and the Bengal Textile Industry in the Eighteenth Century: The Pitfalls of Applying Quantitative Techniques,' *Modern Asian Studies*, 27(2), 321–340.

Chaudhury, Sushil. (1995), *From Prosperity to Decline: Eighteenth Century Bengal*, New Delhi: Manohar.

Chaudhury, Sushil and Michel Morineau, eds. (1999), *Merchants, Companies and Trade: Europe and Asia in the Early Modern Era*, Cambridge: Cambridge University Press.

Choksey, R.D. (1969), *Economic Life in the Bombay Gujarat (1800–1939)*, London: Asia Publishing House.

Clingingsmith, D. and J.G. Williamson (2008), 'Deindustrialization in 18th and 19th Century India: Mughal Decline, Climate Shocks and British Industrial Ascent,' *Explorations in Economic History*, 45(3), 209–234.

Cohn, Bernard (1962), 'Political Systems in Eighteenth Century India: The Banaras Region,' *Journal of the American Oriental Society*, 82(3), 312–320.

Colebrooke, H.T. (1804), *Remarks on the Husbandry and Internal Commerce of Bengal*, Calcutta.

Dale, Stephen F. (2008), 'Middle Towns to Middle Cities in South Asia, 1800–2007,' *Journal of Urban History*, 35(1), 15–38.

Dale, Stephen F. (2010), 'Empires and Emporia: Palace, Mosque, Market, and Tomb in Istanbul, Isfahan, Agra, and Delhi,' *Journal of the Economic and Social History of the Orient*, 53 (1–2), 212–229.

Dalrymple, William (2007), *The Last Mughal*, London: Bloomsbury.

Dalrymple, William. (2013), 'Logistic Failure on the Part of the Rebels in 1857,' in G. Rand and C. Bates, eds., *Mutiny at the Margins: New Perspectives on the Indian Uprising of 1857*, vol. 4 of 6, New Delhi and Thousand Oaks: Sage, 61–75.

Dalrymple, William. (2019), *The Anarchy: The Relentless Rise of the East India Company*, London: Bloomsbury Publishing.

Das Gupta, Ashin (1967), *Malabar in Asian Trade 1740–1800*, Cambridge: Cambridge University Press.

Das Gupta, Ashin (1979), *Indian Merchants and the Decline of Surat c. 1700–1750*, Wiesbaden: Franz Steiner Verlag.

Das Gupta, Ashin (2001), *The World of the Indian Ocean Merchant 1500–1800*, New New Delhi: Oxford University Press.

Das Gupta, Ashin and Michael N. Pearson, eds. (1987), *India and the Indian Ocean*, Calcutta: Oxford University Press.

Dasgupta, Sabyasachi (2007), 'The Rebel Army in 1857: At the Vanguard of the War of Independence or a Tyranny of Arms?,' *Economic and Political Weekly*, 42(19), 1729–1733.

Datta, K.K. (1959), 'India's Trade with Europe and America in the Eighteenth Century,' *Journal of the Economic and Social History of the Orient*, 2(3), 313–323.

Datta, Rajat (2000), *Society, Economy, and the Market: Commercialization in Rural Bengal, c. 1760–1800*, New Delhi: Manohar.

Datta, V.N. (2003), 'Ghalib's Delhi,' *Proceedings of the Indian History Congress*, 64, 1103–1109.

David, Saul (2002), *The Indian Mutiny: 1857*, London: Penguin.

Deng, Kent and Patrick O'Brien (2016), 'Establishing Statistical Foundations of a Chronology for the Great Divergence: A Survey and Critique of the Primary Sources for the Construction of Relative Wage Levels for Ming-Qing China,' *Economic History Review*, 69(4), 1057–1082.

Derbyshire, Ian (1987), 'Economic Change and the Railways in North India, 1860–1914,' *Modern Asian Studies*, 21(3), 521–545.

Desai, A.V. (1972), 'Population and Standards of Living in Akbar's Time,' *Indian Economic and Social History Review*, 9(1), 43–62.

Divekar, V.D. (1982), 'The Emergence of an Indigenous Business Class in Maharashtra in the Eighteenth Century,' *Modern Asian Studies*, 16(3), 427–443.

Downing, Brian (1991), *The Military Revolution and Political Change in Early Modern Europe*, Princeton: Princeton University Press.

Duff, James Grant (1826), *A History of the Mahrattas*, London: Longman, Rees, Orme, Brown and Green, vols. I and II.

Eaton, Richard (1993), *The Rise of Islam and the Bengal frontier, 1204–1760*, Berkeley and Los Angeles: University of California Press.

Elphinstone, Mountstuart (1821), *Report on the Territories Conquered from the Paishwa*, Calcutta.

Embree, Ainslie T. (n.d.), 'Napier, Sir Charles James (1782–1853),' *Oxford Dictionary of National Biography*, available at https://doi.org/10.1093/ref:odnb/19748 (accessed on December 16 2020).

Farooqui, M. (2013), 'The Police in Delhi in 1857,' in Crispin Bates, ed., *Mutiny at the Margins: New Perspectives on the Indian Uprising of 1857*, vol. 1 of 6, New Delhi and Thousand Oaks: Sage, 98–128.

Forbes-Mitchell, William (1897), *Reminiscences of the Great Mutiny 1857–59*, London: Macmillan.

Frank, André Gunder (1998), *ReOrient: Global Economy in the Asian Age*, Berkeley and Los Angeles: University of California Press.

Furber, Holden (1940), 'Review of A. Mervyn Davies, Clive of Plassey: A Biography,' New York: Charles Scribner's Sons, 1939, *American Historical Review*, 45(3), 635–637.

Furber, Holden. (1948), *John Company at Work*, Cambridge, MA: Harvard University Press.

Geller, Jay Howard (2000), 'Towards a New Imperialism in Eighteenth-Century India: Dupleix, La Bourdonnais and the French Compagnie des Indes,' *Portuguese Studies*, 16(2000), 240–255.

Ghose, Loke Nath (1881), *The Modern History of the Indian Chiefs, Rajas, Zamindars*, Calcutta: Presidency Press.

Ghulam Husain Khan (1832), *The Siyar-ul-Mutakherin* (trans. John Briggs), London: John Murray.

Gokhale, B.G. (1969), 'Ahmadabad in the XVIIth Century,' *Journal of the Economic and Social History of the Orient*, 12(2), 187–197.

Gokhale, B.G. (1985), 'The Religious Complex in Eighteenth-Century Poona,' *Journal of the American Oriental Society*, 105(4), 719–724.

Gommans, Jos (1995), 'Indian Warfare and Afghan Innovation during the Eighteenth Century,' *Studies in History*, 11(3), 261–280.

Gopal, Surendra (1975), *Commerce and Crafts in Gujarat, 16th and 17th Centuries: A Study in the Impact of European Expansion on a Pre-capitalist Economy*, New Delhi: People's Publishing House.

Gordon, Stewart (1977), 'The Slow Conquest. Administrative Integration of Malwa into the Maratha Empire, 1720–1760,' *Modern Asian Studies*, 11(1), 1–40.

Gordon, Stewart. (1986), *Marathas, Marauders, and State Formation*, Delhi: Oxford University Press, 1994.

Gordon, Stewart. (1993), *The Marathas 1600–1818*, Cambridge: Cambridge University Press.

Goswami, Chhaya (2016), *Globalization before its Time. The Gujarati Merchants from Kachchh*, New Delhi: Penguin.

Griffiths, Charles John (1910), *A Narrative of the Siege of Delhi with an Account of the Mutiny at Ferozepore In 1857*, London: John Murray.

Growse, F.S. (1883), *Mathura: A District Memoir*, Lucknow: Government Press.

Guha, Nikhiles (1985), *Pre-British State System in South India: Mysore 1761–1799*, Calcutta: Ratna Prakashan.

Guha, Sumit (2001), 'The Population History of South Asia from the Seventeenth to the Twentieth Centuries: An Exploration,' in Ts'ui-jung Liu, James Lee, David Sven Reher, Osamu Saito and Wang Feng, eds. *Asian Population History*, Oxford: Oxford University Press, 63–78.

Guha, Sumit. (2015), 'Rethinking the Economy of Mughal India: Lateral Perspectives,' *Journal of the Economic and Social History of the Orient*, 58(4), 532–575.

Habib, Irfan (1964), 'Usury in Medieval India,' *Comparative Studies in Society and History*, 6(4), 393–419.

Habib, Irfan. (1969), 'Potentialities of Capitalistic Development in the Economy of Mughal India,' *Journal of Economic History*, 29(1), 32–78.

Habib, Irfan. (1985), 'Studying a Colonial Economy – Without Perceiving Colonialism,' *Modern Asian Studies*, 19(3), 355–381.

Habib, Irfan. (1998), 'The Coming of 1857,' *Social Scientist*, 26(1/4), 6–15.

Habib, Irfan. (2003), 'The Eighteenth Century in Indian Economic History,' in Marshall, ed., *The Eighteenth Century in Indian History: Evolution or Revolution?*, Delhi: Oxford University Press.

Habib, Irfan and Faiz Habib (2014), 'Mapping the Dismemberment of Awadh 1775–1801,' *Proceedings of the Indian History Congress*, 75, 455–460.

Hamilton, Walter (1815), *The East India Gazetteer*, London: John Murray.

Hardgrave, Jr., R.L. (2004), *A Portrait of the Hindus: Balthazar Solvyns and the European Image of India 1760–1824*, New York: Oxford University Press.

Hatekar, Neeraj (2003), 'Farmers and Markets in the Pre-Colonial Deccan: The Plausibility of Economic Growth in Traditional Society,' *Past and Present*, 178(1), 116–147.

Hatekar, Neeraj. (2004), 'Economic History as an Endangered Discipline: Issues in Pre-Colonial Studies,' *Economic and Political Weekly*, 39(42), 4675–4676.

Heathcote, T.A. (1995), *The Military in British India: The Development of British Land Forces in South Asia, 1600–1947*, Manchester: Manchester University Press.

Hejeebu, Santhi (2005), 'Contract Enforcement in the English East India Company,' *Journal of Economic History*, 65(2), 496–523.

Herbert, Christopher (2007), *War of No Pity: The Indian Mutiny and Victorian Trauma*, Princeton: Princeton University Press.

Hossain, Hameeda (1988), *The Company Weavers of Bengal: The East India Company and the Organization of Textile Production in Bengal, 1750–1813*, Delhi: Oxford University Press.

Hunter, W.W. (1874), *Famine Aspects of Bengal Districts*, London: Trübner.

Hunter, W.W. (1868), *The Annals of Rural Bengal*, vol. 1, New York: Leypoldt and Holt.

Husain, Iqbal (1985), 'Bakht Khan–A Leading Sepoy General of 1857,' *Proceedings of the Indian History Congress*, 46, 373–386.

Ibrahim Kunju, A.P. (1960), 'Relations between Travancore and Mysore in the 18th Century,' *Proceedings of the Indian History Congress*, 23(II), 56–61.

India (1881), *Narratives of Events regarding the Mutiny in India of 1857–58 and the Restoration of Authority*, Vol. I, Calcutta: Foreign Department Press.

India (1898–1902), *Selections from the Letters Despatches and other State Papers of the Military-Department, the Government of India, 1857–58*, vols. 1–3, Calcutta: Government Press.

India (1908), *The Imperial Gazetteer of India*, Oxford: Clarendon Press.

India. (1921), *Press-list of 'Mutiny Papers' 1857, being a collection of the correspondence of the mutineers at Delhi, reports of spies to English officials and other miscellaneous papers*, Calcutta, Imperial Records Office.

India. (annual publication), *Statistical Abstract relating to British India*, London: HMSO.

Innes, A.D. (1919), *A Short History of British in India*, London: Macmillan.

Jain, Shalin (2001), 'East India Company's Trading Interests in Awadh, 1764–1787,' *Proceedings of the Indian History Congress*, 62, 390–399.

Kanakarathnam, N. (2014), 'Maritime Trade and Growth of Urban Infrastructure in Port Cities of Colonial Andhra: A Study of Masulipatnam,' *Proceedings of the Indian History Congress*, 75, 690–696.

Kazmi, Sabina (2013), 'Colonial Intervention in Awadh: Indigenous Political Structures and Indirect Rule in Eighteenth Century,' *Proceedings of the Indian History Congress*, 74, 447–457.

Keene, H.G. (1894), *An Oriental Biographical Dictionary founded on materials collected by the late Thomas William Beale*, London: W.H. Allen.

Kemme, Clara (2014), 'The History of European International Law from a Global Perspective: Entanglements in Eighteenth and Nineteenth Century India,' in Thomas Duve, ed., *Entanglements in Legal History: Conceptual Approaches*, Frankfurt am Main: Max Planck Institute for European Legal History, 489–542.

Kessinger, Tom (1983), 'Regional Economy (1757–1857): North India,' in Dharma Kumar, ed., *Cambridge Economic History of India*, vol. 2, Cambridge: Cambridge University Press, 242–270.

Khan, Iqtidar Alam (1976), 'The Middle Classes in the Mughal Empire,' *Social Scientist*, 5(1), 28–49.

Khan, Iqtidar Alam. (1998), 'The Gwalior Contingent in 1857–58: A Study of the Organisation and Ideology of the Sepoy Rebels,' *Social Scientist*, 26(1/4), 53–75.

Klein, Ira (2000), 'Materialism, Mutiny and Modernization in British India,' *Modern Asian Studies*, 34(3), 545–580.

Kling, Blair B. (1977), *Partner in Empire: Dwarkanath Tagore and the Age of Enterprise in Eastern India*, Berkeley and Los Angeles, University of California Press.

Kochhar, Rajesh (2011), 'Hindoo College Calcutta Revisited: Its Pre-History and the Role of Rammohun Roy,' *Proceedings of the Indian History Congress*, 72(I), 841–862.

Kolff, Dirk H.A. (1998), *Naukar, Rajput, Sepoy: An Ethno-History of the Military Labour Market in North India*, Cambridge: Cambridge University Press.

Kolff, Dirk H.A. (2013), 'Peasants Fighting for a Living in Early Modern North India,' in Erik-Jan Zürcher, ed., *Fighting for a Living: A Comparative Study of Military Labour 1500–2000*, Amsterdam: Amsterdam University Press, 243–265.

Kosambi, Meera and John E. Brush (1988), 'Three Colonial Port Cities in India,' *Geographical Review*, 78(1), 32–47.

Kranton, R.E. and A.V. Swamy (2008), 'Contracts, Hold-up, and Exports: Textiles and Opium in Colonial India,' *American Economic Review*, 98(5), 967–989.

Kulkarni, A.R. (1996), *The Marathas*, New Delhi: Books and Books.

Kumar, Dharma (1965), *Land and Caste in South India*, Cambridge: Cambridge University Press.

Kumar, Dharma, ed. (1983), *The Cambridge Economic History of India, vol. 2, 1750–1970*, Cambridge: Cambridge University Press.

Kumar, Vinod and Shiv Narayan (2012), 'Colonial Policy and the Culture of Immigration: Citing the Social History of Varanasi in the Nineteenth Century,' *Proceedings of the Indian History Congress*, 73, 888–897.

Lal, Deepak (2003), 'Asia and Western Dominance,' *Journal of the Asia Pacific Economy*, 8(3), 283–299.

Lal, Neha (2015), 'Mirzapur: Did the Railways Change its Commercial Narrative?,' *Proceedings of the Indian History Congress*, 76, 408–425.

Leonard, Karen (1971), 'The Hyderabad Political System and its Participants,' *Journal of Asian Studies*, 30(3), 569–582.

Leonard, Karen. (1979), 'The "Great Firm" Theory of the Decline of the Mughal Empire,' *Comparative Studies in Society and History*, 21(2), 151–167.

Leonard, Karen. (1981), 'Indigenous Banking Firms in Mughal India: A Reply,' *Comparative Studies in Society and History*, 23(2), 309–313.

Levi, Scott C. (1999), 'India, Russia and the Eighteenth-century Transformation of the Central Asian Caravan Trade,' *Journal of the Economic and Social History of the Orient*, 42(4), 519–548.

Levi, Scott C. (2002), *The Indian Diaspora in Central Asia and Its Trade, 1550–1900*, Leiden: Brill.

Lewandowski, Susan J. (1975), 'Urban Growth and Municipal Development in the Colonial City of Madras, 1860–1900,' *Journal of Asian Studies*, 34(2), 341–360.

Lindert, Peter (2017), 'European and Asian incomes in 1914: New take on the Great Divergence,' available at https://voxeu.org/article/european-and-asian-incomes-1914-new-take-great-divergence (accessed December 15 2020).

Lombard, Denys and Jean Aubin, eds. (2000), *Asian Merchants and Businessmen in the Indian Ocean and the China Sea*, New Delhi: Oxford University Press.

Lucassen, Jan (2006), 'The Brickmakers' Strikes on the Ganges Canal in 1848–1849,' *International Review of Social History*, 51(Supplement 14), 47–83.

Ludden, David (1985), *Peasant History in South India*, Princeton: Princeton University Press.

Ludden, David. (1994), 'Introduction,' in Ludden, ed., *Agricultural Production and Indian History*, Delhi: Oxford University Press, 1–23.

Ludden, David. (1999), *An Agrarian History of South Asia*, Cambridge: Cambridge University Press.

Ludden, David. (2002), 'Spectres of Agrarian Territory in Southern India,' *Indian Economic and Social History Review*, 39(2–3), 233–257.

Machado, Pedro (2009), 'A Regional Market in a Globalised Economy: East Central and South Eastern Africans, Gujarati Merchants and the Indian Textile Industry in the Eighteenth and Nineteenth Centuries,' in Giorgio Riello and Tirthankar Roy, eds., *How India Clothed the World: the World of South Asian Textiles 1500–1850*, Leiden: Brill, 53–84.

Mackenzie, A.R.D. (1892), *Mutiny Memoirs*, Allahabad: Pioneer Press.

Madras (1905–6), *Season and Crop Report of the Madras State*, Madras: Department of Statistics.

Major, Andrew (1996), *Return to Empire: Punjab under the Sikhs and British in the Mid-Nineteenth Century*, New Delhi: Sterling.

Majumdar, R.C. (1963), *The Sepoy Mutiny and the Revolt of 1857*, Calcutta: Firma K. L. Mukhopadhyay.

Malik, Z.U. (1990), 'The Core and the Periphery: A Contribution to the Debate on the Eighteenth Century,' *Social Scientist*, 18(11/12), 3 35.

Malleson, G.B. (1914), *Kaye and Malleson's History of the Indian Mutiny of 1857–8*, London: Longmans Green, vols. 1–6.

Marshall, P.J. (1975), 'Economic and Political Expansion: The Case of Oudh,' *Modern Asian Studies*, 9(4), 465–482.

Marshall, P.J. (1988), *Bengal – The British Bridgehead: Eastern India 1740–1828*, Cambridge: Cambridge University Press.

Marshall, P.J. (2000a), 'The White Town of Calcutta under the Rule of the East India Company,' *Modern Asian Studies*, 34(3), 307–331.

Marshall, P.J. (2000b), 'Presidential Address: Britain and the World in the Eighteenth Century: III, Britain and India,' *Transactions of the Royal Historical Society*, 10, 1–16.

Mayer, P.B. (1980), 'The Penetration of Capitalism in a South Indian District,' *South Asia*, 3(2), 1–24.

Mayer, Peter B. (2006), 'Trends of Real Income in Tiruchirapalli and the Upper Kaveri Delta, 1819–1980: A Footnote in Honour of Dharma Kumar,' *Indian Economic and Social History Review*, 43(3), 349–364.

McLane, John R. (1993), *Land and Local Kingship in Eighteenth-Century Bengal*, Cambridge: Cambridge University Press.

McPherson, Kenneth (1998), *The Indian Ocean: A History of People and the Sea*, Delhi and Oxford: Oxford University Press.

Metcalf, Thomas (1964), *The Aftermath of Revolt: India 1857–1870*, Princeton: Princeton University Press.

Metcalf, Thomas (1988), *An Imperial Vision: Indian Architecture and Britain's Raj*, Berkeley: University of California Press.

Mill, James (1858), *The History of British India from 1805 to 1835* in H.H. Wilson ed., 3 vols., London: James Madden.

Mishra, Kamala Prasad (1973), 'The Role of the Banaras Bankers in the Economy of Eighteenth Century Upper India,' *Proceedings of the Indian History Congress*, 34(II), 63–76.

Mizushima, Tsukasa (2013), 'The Mirasi System and Local Society in Pre-colonial South India,' in Peter Robb, Kaoru Sugihara, Haruka Yanagisawa, eds., *Local Agrarian Societies in Colonial India: Japanese Perspectives*, Abingdon: Routledge, [1996], 77–146.

Moosvi, Shireen (2010–2011), 'The World of Labour in Mughal India (c.1500–1750),' *Proceedings of the Indian History Congress*, 71, 343–357.

Moreland, W.H. (1917–8), 'The *Ain-i-Akbari* – A Base-Line for the Economic History of India,' *Indian Journal of Economics*, 1(1), 44–53.

Moreland, W.H. (1923), *From Akbar to Aurangzeb: A Study in Indian Economic History*, London: Macmillan.

Mosse, David (1999), 'Colonial and Contemporary Ideologies of "Community Management": The Case of Tank Irrigation Development in South India,' *Modern Asian Studies*, 33(2), 303–338.

Mukherjee, Nilmani (1962), *The Ryotwari System in Madras: 1792–1827*. Calcutta: Firma K.L. Mukhopadhyay.

Mukherjee, Rila (1994), 'The Story of Kasimbazar: Silk Merchants and Commerce in Eighteenth-Century India,' *Review*, 17(4), 499–554.

Mukherjee, Rudrangshu (1982), 'Trade and Empire in Awadh 1765–1804,' *Past and Present*, 94, 85–102.

Mukherjee, Rudrangshu. (1984), *Awadh in Revolt, 1857–1858: A Study in Popular Resistance*, New York: Oxford University Press.

Mukherjee, Tilottama (2009), 'The Co-Ordinating State and the Economy: The Nizamat in Eighteenth-Century Bengal,' *Modern Asian Studies*, 43(2), 389–436.

Mukhia, Harbans (1977), 'Illegal Extortions from Peasants, Artisans and Menials in Eighteenth Century Eastern Rajasthan,' *Indian Economic and Social History Review*, 11(2), 231 245.

Murton, Brian J. (1973), 'Key People in the Countryside: Decision-makers in Interior Tamilnadu in the Late Eighteenth Century,' *Indian Economic and Social History Review*, 10(2), 157–180.

Nadkarni, R.V. (1966), *The Rise and Fall of the Maratha Domain*, Bombay: Popular Prakashan.

Nadri, Ghulam A. (2010), *Eighteenth Century Gujarat: The Dynamics of its Political Economy*, Leiden: Brill.

Nadri, Ghulam A. (2018), 'The English and Dutch East India Companies and Indian Merchants in Surat in the Seventeenth and Eighteenth centuries: Interdependence, competition and contestation,' in Adam Clulow and Tristan Mostert, eds., *The Dutch and English East India Companies: Diplomacy, trade and violence in early modern Asia*, Amsterdam: Amsterdam University Press, 125–149.

Nag, Pankaj (1998), '1857: Need for Alternative Sources,' *Social Scientist*, 26(1/4), 113–147.

Naqvi, H.K. (1967), 'Progress of Urbanization in United Provinces, 1550–1800,' *Journal of the Economic and Social History of the Orient*, 10(1), 81–101.

Narain, Brij (1929), *Indian Economic Life: Past and Present*, Lahore: Uttar Chand Kapur and Sons.

Narayan, Badri (1998), 'Popular Culture and 1857: A Memory against Forgetting,' *Social Scientist*, 26(1/4), 86–94.

Neild, Susan M. (1979), 'Colonial Urbanism: The Development of Madras City in the 18th and 19th Centuries,' *Modern Asian Studies*, 13(2), 217–246.

Oak, Mandar and Anand Swamy (2012), 'Myopia or Strategic Behavior? Indian Regimes and the East India Company in Late Eighteenth Century India,' *Explorations in Economic History*, 49(3), 352–366.

O'Brien, Patrick Karl (2012), 'Fiscal and Financial Preconditions for the Formation of Developmental States in the West and the East from the Conquest of Ceuta (1415) to the Opium War (1839),' *Journal of World History*, 23(3), 513–553.

O'Neill, Daniel I. (2009), 'Rethinking Burke and India,' *History of Political Thought*, 30(3), 492–523.

Ogawa, Michihiro (2012), 'Socio-economic Study of Indapur Pargana (1761–1828),' PhD Dissertation of Pune University.

Pachauri, S.K. (1995), 'British Relations with Princely States in the 19th Century - Case Study of Relation of Trust and Fealty with the Ruler of Patiala,' *Proceedings of the Indian History Congress*, 56, 532–544.

Parker, Geoffrey (1998), *The Military Revolution: Military Innovation and the Rise of the West 1500–1800*, Cambridge: Cambridge University Press.

Parthasarathi, Prasannan (1998), 'Rethinking Wages and Competitiveness in the Eighteenth Century: Britain and South India,' *Past and Present*, 158, 79–109.

Parthasarathi, Prasannan. (2001), *The Transition to a Colonial Economy: Weavers, Merchants, and Kings in South India, 1720–1800*, Cambridge: Cambridge University Press.

Parthasarathi, Prasannan. (2011), *Why Europe Grew Rich and Asia Did Not: Global Economic Divergence 1600–1850*, Cambridge: Cambridge University Press.

Parthasarathi, Prasannan. (2017), 'Water and Agriculture in Nineteenth-century Tamilnad,' *Modern Asian Studies*, 51(2), 485–510.

Patel, M.A. (1979), 'Indigenous Banking into the Baroda State during the Closing years of the 18th Century and the Beginning of the 19th Century,' *Proceedings of the Indian History Congress*, 40, 768–773.

Pati, Biswamoy, ed. (2007), *The 1857 Rebellion*, Delhi: Oxford University Press.

Pati, Biswamoy, ed. (2010), *The Great Rebellion of 1857 in India: Exploring Transgressions, Contests and Diversities*, London: Routledge.

Peers, Douglas M. (1989), 'War and Public Finance in Early Nineteenth Century British India: The First Burma War,' *International History Review*, 11(4), 628–647.

Pelsaert, Francisco (1925), *Jahangir's India: The Remonstrantie of Francisco Pelsaert* (W.H. Moreland and P. Geyl, tr.), Cambridge: W. Heffer.

Pemble, John (1960), *The Raj, the Indian Mutiny and the Kingdom of Oudh 1801–1859*, Delhi: Oxford University Press.

Pemble, John. (1976), 'Resources and Techniques in the Second Maratha War,' *The Historical Journal*, 19(2), 375–404.

Perlin, Frank (1978), 'Of White Whale and Countrymen in the Eighteenth Century Maratha Deccan: Extended Class Relations, Rights and the Problem of Rural Autonomy under the Old Regime,' *Journal of Peasant Studies*, 5(1), 172–237.

Perlin, Frank. (1983), 'Proto-industrialisation in Precolonial South Asia, *Past and Present*, 98, 30–95.

Perlin, Frank. (2003), 'The Problem of the Eighteenth Century,' in P.J. Marshall, ed., *The Eighteenth Century in Indian History: Evolution or Revolution?*, Delhi: Oxford University Press, 53–61.

Prakash, Anita (2009–2010), 'Indigenous Knowledge System and Colonial Intervention in Central Doab in Early Nineteenth Century - Some Observations,' *Proceedings of the Indian History Congress*, 70, 413–420.

Prakash, Om (1976), 'Bullion for Goods: International Trade and the Economy of Early Eighteenth Century Bengal,' *Indian Economic and Social History Review*, 13(2), 159–186.

Prakash, Om. (1985), *The Dutch East India Company and the Economy of Bengal, 1630–1720*, Princeton: Princeton University Press.

Prakash, Om. (1998), *The New Cambridge History of India; Vol. II.5. European Commercial Enterprise in Pre-colonial India*, Cambridge: Cambridge University Press.

Prakash, Om. (2002), 'Trade and Politics in Eighteenth Century Bengal, in P.J. Marshall, ed. *The Eighteenth Century in India*, New New Delhi: Oxford University Press, 136–164.

Prakash, Om. (2005), '*The Great Divergence: Evidence from Eighteenth Century India*,' paper presented at the *Seventh Global Economic History Network Conference* at Istanbul.

Prakash, Om. (2007), 'From Negotiation to Coercion: Textile Manufacturing in India in the Eighteenth Century,' *Modern Asian Studies*, 41(5), 1331–1368.

Prior, D.L. (n.d.) 'Carnac, John (1721–1800),' in *Oxford Dictionary of National Biography*, https://doi.org/10.1093/ref:odnb/4711 (accessed December 3 2020).

Raj, Jagdish (1965), *The Mutiny and British Land Policy in North India, 1856–1868*, New York: Asia.

Raj, Kapil (2011), 'The Historical Anatomy of a Contact Zone: Calcutta in the Eighteenth Century,' *Indian Economic and Social History Review*, 48(1), 55–82.

Rana, R.P. (1981), 'Agrarian Revolts in Northern India during the Late 17th and Early 18th Century,' *Indian Economic and Social History Review*, 18(3–4), 287–325.

Rao, G.N. (1977), 'Agrarian Relations in Coastal Andhra under Early British Rule,' *Social Scientist*, 6(1), 19–29.

Rao, Narayan Singh (2002), *Rural Economy and Society: Study of South-eastern Rajasthan during the Eighteenth Century*, Jaipur and New Delhi: Rawat, 61–62.

Ray, Ratnalekha (1979), *Change in Bengal Agrarian Society c. 1760–1850*, Delhi: Manohar.

Raychaudhuri, Tapan (1962), *Jan Company in Coromandel, 1600–1690: A Study in the Interrelations of European Commerce and Traditional Economies*, The Hague, Martunus Nijhoff.

Raychaudhuri, Tapan. (1968), 'A Reinterpretation of Indian Economic History?,' *Indian Economic and Social History Review*, 5(1), 77–100.

———. (1983a), 'Inland Trade,' in Tapan Raychaudhuri and Irfan Habib, eds., *The Cambridge Economic History of India, vol. 1: c.1200-c.1750*, Cambridge: Cambridge University Press, 325 359.

———. (. (1983b), 'The Mid-eighteenth-century Background,' in Dharma Kumar, ed., *The Cambridge Economic History of India, vol. 2: c. 1757–1970*, Cambridge: Cambridge University Press, 3–35.

Richards, John F. (1975), 'The Hyderabad Karnatik, 1687–1707,' *Modern Asian Studies*, 9(2), 241–260.

Richards, John F. (1981), 'Mughal State Finance and the Premodern World Economy,' *Comparative Studies in Society and History*, 23(2), 285–308.

Richards, John F. (1995), *The Mughal Empire*, Cambridge: Cambridge University Press.

Richards, John F. (1997), 'Early Modern India and World History,' *Journal of World History*, 8(2), 197–209.

Richards, John F. (2004), 'Warriors and the State in Early Modern India,' *Journal of the Economic and Social History of the Orient*, 47(3), 390–400.

Riello, Giorgio and Tirthankar Roy, eds. (2009), *How India Clothed the World: the World of South Asian Textiles 1500–1850*, Leiden: Brill.

Rizvi, Syed Najmul Raza and Saiyid Zaheer Husain Jafri, eds. (2009), *The Great Uprising of 1857: Commentaries, Studies and Documents*, New Delhi: Anamika.

Robb, Peter (2000), 'Credit, Work and Race in 1790s Calcutta: Early Colonialism through a Contemporary European View,' *Indian Economic and Social History Review*, 37(1), 1–25.

Rothermund, Dietmar (2014), *Violent Traders: Europeans in Asia in the Age of Mercantilism*, Delhi: Manohar.

Roy, Kaushik (2005), 'Military Synthesis in South Asia: Armies, Warfare, and Indian Society, c. 1740–1849,' *Journal of Military History*, 69(3), 651–690.

Roy, Kaushik. (2007), 'The Beginning of 'People's War' in India,' *Economic and Political Weekly*, 42(19), 1720–1728.

Roy, Tapti (1994), *The Politics of a Popular Uprising: Bundelkhand 1857*, Delhi: Oxford University Press.

Roy, Tirthankar (2001), 'An Asian World Economy?,' *Economic and Political Weekly*, 36(31), 2937–2942.

Roy, Tirthankar. (2010a), 'Economic Conditions in Early Modern Bengal: A Contribution to the Divergence Debate,' *Journal of Economic History*, 70(1), 179–194.

Roy, Tirthankar. (2010b), 'Indigo and Law in Colonial India,' *Economic History Review*, 64(S1), 60–75.

Roy, Tirthankar. (2010c), *Company of Kinsmen: Enterprise and Community in South Asian History 1700–1940*, New Delhi: Oxford University Press.

Roy, Tirthankar. (2011a), 'Law and the Economy of Early Modern India,' in Debin Ma and Jan Luiten van Zanden, eds., *Law and Long-term Economic Change: A Eurasian Perspective*, Stanford: Stanford University Press, 115–137.

Roy, Tirthankar. (2011b), 'Where is Bengal? Situating an Indian Region in the Early Modern World Economy,' *Past and Present*, 213, 115–146.

Roy, Tirthankar. (2011c), *East India Company: The World's Most Powerful Corporation*, Delhi: Allen Lane.

Roy, Tirthankar. (2012a), 'Consumption of Cotton Cloth in India, 1795–1940,' *Australian Economic History Review*, 52(1), 61–84.

Roy, Tirthankar. (2012b), 'Empire, Law and Economic Growth,' *Economic and Political Weekly*, 47(8), 98–104.

Roy, Tirthankar. (2012c), *India in the World Economy from Antiquity to the Present*, Cambridge: Cambridge University Press.

Roy, Tirthankar. (2012d), *Natural Disasters and Indian History*, New Delhi: Oxford University Press.

Roy, Tirthankar. (2013), 'Rethinking the Origins of British India: State Formation and Military-fiscal Undertakings in an Eighteenth Century World Region,' *Modern Asian Studies*, 47(4), 1125–1156

Roy, Tirthankar. (2020a), *The Economic History of India 1857–2010*, Delhi: Oxford University Press, 4th Edition.

Roy, Tirthankar. (2020b), *The Crafts and Capitalism: Handloom Weaving Industry in Colonial India*, Abingdon: Routledge.

Roy, Tirthankar and Anand V. Swamy (2016), *Law and the Economy in Colonial India*, Chicago: University of Chicago Press.

Sachdeva, V. (1993), *Polity and Economy of the Punjab during the Late-Eighteenth Century*, Delhi: Manohar.

Sahai, Nandita Prasad (2005), 'Artisans, the State, and the Politics of Wajabi in Eighteenth-Century Jodhpur,' *Indian Economic and Social History Review*, 42(1), 41–68.

Sahai, Nandita Prasad. (2006), *Politics of Patronage and Protest: The State, Society, and Artisans in Early Modern Rajasthan*, New Delhi: Oxford University Press.

Sangwan, Satpal (2007), 'Level of Agricultural Technology in India (1757–1857),' *Asian Agri-History*, 11(1), 5–25.

Sanyal, Ram Gopal (1886), *The Life of the Hon'ble Rai Kristo Das Pal Bahadur*, Calcutta: The Bengalee Press.

Sarada Raju, A. (1941), *Economic Conditions in the Madras Presidency, 1800–1850*, Madras: Madras University Press.

Sarkar, Jadunath (1932–50), *Fall of the Mughal Empire 1789–1803*, 4 vols., Calcutta: M.C. Sarkar.

Seshan, Radhika (2009–2010), 'From Chief Merchant to Joint Stock Merchant: A Comparative Study of Kasivirana and Pedda Venkatadri, Chief Merchants of Madras,' *Proceedings of the Indian History Congress*, 70, 347–353.

Seton, Rosemary (1986), *The Indian 'Mutiny' 1857–58: A Guide to Source Material in the India Office Library and Records*, London: The British Library.

Sharma, G.D. (1985), 'Business and Accounting in Western India during the Eighteenth Century,' *Proceedings of the Indian History Congress*, 46, 308–315.

Showers, Lionel (1888), *A Missing Chapter of the Indian Mutiny*, London: Kessinger.

Shrivastava, Nripendra Kumar (2010–2011), 'Contribution of Trade and Commerce in the Trend and Pattern of Urban Growth of Patna (1657–1765),' *Proceedings of the Indian History Congress*, 71, 327–334.

Shumais U (2016), 'Impact of The Revolt Of 1857 in South India,' *Proceedings of the Indian History Congress*, 77, 410–417.

Siddiqi, Asiya (1981), 'Money and Prices in the Earlier Stages of Empire: India and Britain 1760–1840,' *Indian Economic and Social History Review*, 18(3–4), 231–262.

Singh, Dilbagh (1974), 'The Role of the Mahajans in the Rural Economy in Eastern Rajasthan during the 18th Century,' *Social Scientist*, 2(10), 20–31.

Singh, Dilbagh. (1990), *The State, Landlords and Peasants: Rajasthan in the 18th Century*, Delhi: Manohar.

Singh, Khushwant (1963), *A History of the Sikhs. Volume I. 1469–1839*, Princeton: Princeton University Press.

Sinha, N.K. (1962), *Economic History of Bengal - from Plassey to the Permanent Settlement*, vol. II, Calcutta: Firma KLM.

Sivakumar, S.S. (1978), 'Transformation of the Agrarian Economy in Tondaimandalam: 1760–1900,' *Social Scientist*, 6(10), 18–39.

Sivramkrishna, Sashi (2009), 'Ascertaining Living Standards in Erstwhile Mysore, Southern India, from Francis Buchanan's Journey of 1800–01: An Empirical Contribution to the Great Divergence Debate,' *Journal of the Economic and Social History of the Orient*, 52(1), 695–733.

Spodek, Howard (1974), 'Rulers, Merchants and Other Groups in the City-States of Saurashtra, Around 1800,' *Comparative Studies in Society and History*, 16, 448–470.

Spodek, Howard. (1980), 'Studying the History of Urbanization in India,' *Journal of Urban History*, 6(3), 251–295.

Sreemani, Soumitra (1998), 'Problems of Writing a History of Calcutta of the Late 18th Century,' *Proceedings of the Indian History Congress*, 59, 579–586.

Stein, Burton (1990), 'A Decade of Historical Efflorescence,' *South Asia Research*, 10, 125–138.

Stein, Burton. (2010), *A History of India*, Chichester: Wiley.

Stein, Burton, ed. (1992), *The Making of Agrarian Policy in British India 1770–1900*, New Delhi: Oxford University Press.

Stern, Philip J. (2011), *The Company-State: Corporate Sovereignty and the Early Modern Foundations of the British Empire in India*, Oxford: Oxford University Press.

Stokes, Eric (1983), 'Agrarian Relations: Northern and Central India,' *The Cambridge Economic History of India, vol. 2, 1750–1970*, Cambridge: Cambridge University Press, 36–85.

Stokes, Eric. (1986), *The Peasant Armed: Indian Revolt of 1857*, Oxford: Oxford University Press.

Strachey, John (1902), *India: Its Administration and progress*, London: Macmillan.

Studer, Roman (2008), 'India and the Great Divergence: Assessing the Efficiency of Grain Markets in Eighteenth- and Nineteenth-Century India,' *Journal of Economic History*, 68(4), 393–437.

Subrahmanyam, Sanjay (1989), 'Warfare and State Finance in Wodeyar Mysore, 1724–25: A Missionary Perspective,' *Indian Economic and Social History Review*, 26(2), 203–233.

Subrahmanyam, Sanjay. (1990), *The Political Economy of Commerce: Southern India, 1500–1650*, Cambridge: Cambridge University Press.

Subrahmanyam, Sanjay. (1992), 'The Mughal State - Structure or Process? Reflections on Recent Western Historiography,' *Indian Economic Social History Review*, 29(3), 291–321.

Subrahmanyam, Sanjay (2001), *Penumbral Visions: Making Politics in Early Modern South India*, Ann Arbor: University of Michigan Press.

Subrahmanyam, Sanjay and C.A. Bayly (1988), 'Portfolio Capitalists and the Political Economy of Early Modern India,' *Indian Economic & Social History Review*, 25(4), 401–424.

Subramanian, Lakshmi (1991), 'The Eighteenth-Century Social Order in Surat: A Reply and an Excursus on the Riots of 1788 and 1795,' *Modern Asian Studies*, 25(2), 321–365.

Subramanian, Lakshmi. (1996), *Indigenous Capital and Imperial Expansion: Bombay, Surat and the West Coast*, New Delhi: Oxford University Press.

Subramanian, Lakshmi. (2010), *History of India 1707–1857*, New Delhi: Orient Blackswan.

Sur, Nikhil (1977), 'The Bihar Famine of 1770,' *Indian Economic and Social History Review*, 13(4), 525–531.

Swarnalatha, P. (2001), 'Revolt, Testimony, Petition: Artisanal Protests in Colonial Andhra,' *International Review of Social History*, 46(1), 107–129.

Tagore, Debendranath (1911), *Jiban Charit*, Calcutta.

Tharoor, Shashi (2017), *Inglorious Empire: What the British did to India*, London: Hurst.

Thomas, P.J. and B. Natarajan (1936), 'Economic Depression in the Madras Presidency (1825–54),' *Economic History Review*, 7(1), 67–75.

Thomson, J.P. (1923), 'An Autobiographical Memoir of Louis Bourquien,' *Journal of the Punjab Historical Society*, 9(1), 36–71.

Thornton, Edward (1854), *A Gazetteer of the Territories under the Government of the East India Company, and of the Native States on the Continent of India*, London: W.H. Allen.

Tilly, Charles (1989), 'Cities and States in Europe, 1000 1800,' *Theory and Society*, 18(5), 563–584.

Timberg, Thomas (1973), 'Three Types of the Marwari Firm,' *Indian Economic and Social History Review*, 10(1), 3–36.

Tod, James (1920), *Annals and Antiquities of Rajasthan*, 3 vols London: Humphrey Milford.

Torri, Michelguglielmo (1987), 'Surat during the Second Half of the Eighteenth Century: What Kind of Social Order? A Rejoinder to Lakshmi Subramanian,' *Modern Asian Studies*, 21(4), 679–710.

Tripathi, Dwijendra (1981), 'Occupational Mobility and Industrial Entrepreneurship in India: A Historical Analysis,' *Developing Economies*, 19(1), 52–68.

Varady, R.G. (1979), 'North Indian Banjaras: Their Evolution as Transporters,' *South Asia*, 2(1), 1–18.

Vartavarian, Mesob (2014), 'An Open Military Economy: The British Conquest of South India Reconsidered, 1780–1799,' *Journal of the Economic and Social History of the Orient*, 57(4), 486–510.

Verma, Tripta (1994), *Karkhanas under the Mughals, from Akbar to Aurangzeb: A Study in Economic Development*, Delhi: Pragati.

Voelcker, J.A. (1893), *Report on the Improvement of Indian Agriculture*. London: Eyre and Spottiswoode.

Wallerstein, Immanuel (1986), 'Incorporation of Indian Subcontinent into Capitalist World-Economy,' *Economic and Political Weekly*, 21(4), PE28–PE39.

Waring, E.S. (1810), *A History of the Mahrattas*, London: J.F. Richardson.

Washbrook, David (2007), 'India in the Early Modern World Economy: Modes of Production, Reproduction and Exchange,' *Journal of Global History*, 2(1), 87–111.

Webster, Anthony (2009), *The Twilight of the East India Company: The Evolution of Anglo-Asian Commerce and Politics, 1790–1860*, Rochester: Boydell and Brewer.

White, David L. (1979), 'Parsis as Entrepreneurs in Eighteenth Cnetury Western India: The Rustum Manock Family and the Parsi Community of Surat and Bombay,' University of Virginia PhD Dissertation.

Wilson, Jon (2003), 'False and Dangerous,' available at https://www.theguardian.com/education/2003/feb/08/highereducation.britishidentity (accessed September 20 2020).

Wink, André (1986), *Land and Sovereignty in India*, Cambridge: Cambridge University Press.

Yang, Anand A. (1998), *Bazaar India: Markets, Society and the Colonial State in Bihar*, Berkeley: University of California Press.

INDEX

Note: Page numbers in *italics* refer to figures; page numbers in *bold* refer to tables; and page numbers followed by 'n' refer to notes

Printed in the United States
by Baker & Taylor Publisher Services